Statue of Angel Moroni is hoisted onto the top of the Manhattan New York Temple, October 9, 2004.

**NEW YORK NEW YORK STAKE LDS HISTORY COMMITTEE**
RICHARD L. BUSHMAN, CHAIR

| | | |
|---|---|---|
| SARA ANDERSON | RAQUEL COOK | JOANNA LEGERSKI |
| SARAH ARCHER-BECK | AMÉRICA CRUZ | JAMES LUCAS |
| MATTHEW ARCHER-BECK | TODD FLYR | GLEN NELSON |
| DARRELL BABIDGE | AL GÁMEZ | TAYLOR PETREY |
| BRENT J. BELNAP | MARIA HUNTER | JENNIFER REEDER |
| AMBER BLAKESLEY | DELIA JOHNSON | JOANNE ROWLAND |
| CLAUDIA L. BUSHMAN | ANNE KNIGHT | SCOTT TIFFANY |
| ALLISON CLARK | KENT LARSEN | SARIAH TORONTO |

# CITY SAINTS
## *Mormons* in the NEW YORK metropolis

BY THE NEW YORK NEW YORK STAKE LDS HISTORY COMMITTEE
SCOTT TIFFANY, EDITOR

CITY SAINTS: MORMONS IN THE NEW YORK METROPOLIS

City Saints: Mormons in the New York Metropolis was published
November 13, 2004 to commemorate the 70th anniversary of the founding
of the New York New York Stake of The Church of Jesus Christ of Latter-day Saints.
1st edition, 2004.

copyright 2004 New York Stake History Group
No part of this book may be reproduced, stored in a retrieval system,
or transmitted in any form or by any means-electronic, mechanical,
digital, photocopy, recording, or any other-except for brief
quotations in printed reviews, without prior permission in writing
from the New York Stake History Group.

Distributed by:
Nauvoo Books
560 West 180th St, Suite 304
New York, NY 10033

Order toll-free: 800-796-9721
Website: www.mormonpavillion.com
Internet: info@mormonpavillion.com

ISBN+10: 0-85051-303-0
ISBN+13: 978-0-85051-303-5

Library of Congress Control Number: 2004111260

The New York New York Stake LDS History Group is a volunteer group of professional
and amateur historians researching the history of the Church of Jesus
Christ of Latter-day Saints and its members in the New York City area.

Further information about this book and about the New York Stake
History Group can be found at:
www.nycldshistory.com

Text and cover design by Amber Blakesley

First Edition
1 3 5 7 9 8 6 4 2

## ACKNOWLEDGEMENTS

**THE NEW YORK NEW YORK STAKE LDS HISTORY COMMITTEE** began researching and writing the story of Mormons in Manhattan and the greater metro region nearly a seven years ago. Perhaps a hundred local Church members have assisted in the effort.

Grateful acknowledgement is made to those metro-region members who provided archival photographs for CITY SAINTS Among them, América Cruz, Lisa Anderson, Kent Christensen, Natasha Brien and Maria Hunter were particularly helpful. The presidency of the New York New York Stake has been supportive of writing this history since the outset. The committee expresses its gratitude to Stake President Brent J. Belnap and his counselors, including David Santamaría, Scott Baxter, James C. Green, Josh Yamada and Stephen M. Hodson, for their support. At the end, President Belnap became in effect a working editor of the book.

Among the committee itself, nearly every member has contributed material to this book. Richard and Claudia Bushman, both history professors at Columbia University, acted as the source of motivation, organization and support behind the work. In addition to the Bushmans, committee members Scott Tiffany and Sariah Toronto guided the editorial and production process. Sara Anderson and Darrell Babidge collected hundreds of photographs and created related captions. James Lucas and Glen Nelson offered valuable legal, technical and creative input to shape the book. Elizabeth Anne Knight studied and captured highlights of the stake's 70-year archives in an unprecedented manner. Joanne Rowland, Allison Clark and Joanna Legerski were each responsible for researching and writing many articles and essays among these pages. Jenny Reeder offered valuable proofing and writing in the book's critical stages. Kent Larsen, besides writing for the book, arranged the printing and assisted in arranging the book's format. Amber Blakesley designed the layout and book cover and performed the hard labor of fitting the copy into the format.

These contributors only represent some of the many, many people and hours dedicated to this project. For more information about the New York New York Stake LDS History Committee and all of the contributors for CITY SAINTS, please see the complete list at the end of the appendix.

CITY SAINTS: MORMONS IN THE NEW YORK METROPOLIS
**TABLE OF CONTENTS**

**9 INTRODUCTION**

**11 PART 1 CITY SAINTS STORY**

**12** MORMONITES IN MANHATTAN: 1828-1858 Early Days, Mission City, Miracles in Manhattan, *Mormon Mummies in Manhattan,* International Reach, Exodus, *New York City's Ocean Pioneers,* Parley Pratt's Last Visit

**28** A RISING OR SETTING SUN? 1858-1900 Civil War Years, The City as Gateway, The City as Destination

**31** SAINTS IN THE CITY: 1900-1934 Missionary Scandals, *A Building in Brooklyn,* The Roaring 20s, *B.H. Roberts: Father of Modern Missionary Work,* A New Stake

**41** A STAKE IN BABYLON: 1934-1964 The Depression, World War II, Post-War, Renewal, Gradual Growth, The World's Fair, *Visiting the Mormon Pavilion*

**50** WELCOME TO THE WORLD: 1964-1997 Impact of the Mormon Pavilion, A Stake Center, The "Subway" Stake, *Conversations: Frank Miller, Stake President 1978-1985,* Growth and Challenges, *Reflections: Michael Young, Stake President 1985-1989, Reflections: Eliot Brinton, Stake President 1989-1991,* The Evolving Church at the End of a Century, *Reflections: John Stone, Stake President 1991-1997*

**71 PART 2 NEW STAKE, NEW CENTURY: 1997-2004**

**72** BUILDING FAITH: MANHATTAN REACHES NEW HEIGHTS A Prophet in the Garden, A Church Uptown, *Next-Door Neighbors,* A Church in Harlem, A Church Downtown, *Selfless Service at Union Square,* A Church on the East Side

**87** THE CITY MOURNS September 11, 2001: Reflections of the Stake President, Neighborhood Resident: Susan Robison, *In Memoriam: Ivhan Carpio,* Working at the Hospital: Debbie Bingham, Downtown Trader: Kristopher Woolley

**96** A TEMPLE IN THE CITY The Coming of a Temple, *The Temple Site, A Prophet's Promise,* A People Prepare, Family History Work, Hottest Ticket in Town: The Temple Open House, Encapsulating the Present: The Temple Cornerstone, Service Project on the "Big Stage," Manhattan Temple Dedication, The First Manhattan Temple President and Matron: John and Helen Stone

**121 PART 3 IT'S A WONDERFUL TOWN: NEW YORK CITY LIVES**

122 GROWING UP IN THE CITY Strollers on the Island, Jordan Gunther, Kamla Fennimore

127 SINGLE IN THE CITY On Moving to New York, On Singles Wards, On Dating, On Service

130 MARRYING IN THE CITY Stories of couples who met in the city

134 A WOMAN'S VIEW A Student Wife and Mother, A Mother and a Career, Conversations: Single Women on Church, School and Work

141 VARIATIONS IN THE CITY Reflections: Joseph Smith's Letter to Emma Reflections: Early Spanish-speaking Church Members, Conversations: Harlem Pioneers, The Harlem Garden, Visiting the Deaf Branch Primary Program, From the Far Corners of the Earth: The Canal Street (Chinese) Branch, NYC in Utah: Stake Young Women Share Their City, Waiting at the Bar: The Conversion Story of Jessica Lopez, Washing and Drying in the City: Pat and Steve Hodson, Soul (and Virtual-Office) Mates: Ben and Julie McAdams, The Juggling Act: John and Amy Warner, Living in the Church: Tom and Megumi Vogelmann

161 ARTISTS IN THE CITY A Portrait of Latter-day Saint Art, 1890-1964, Manhattan LDS Artists in the 21st Century, Conversations: Mormon Artists Speak Their Minds, An Ecumenical Song Fest— The Mormons and Martin Luther King, Only in New York

**173 PART 4 THE CHURCH IN MANHATTAN AND THE METRO AREA**

174 1997-2004: NEW YORK NEW YORK STAKE AUXILIARIES Relief Society, Youth Activities, Young Women, Young Men, Sunday School, Primary

184 UNIT HISTORICAL OVERVIEWS Manhattan First Ward, Manhattan Second Ward, Manhattan Third Ward, Manhattan Fourth Ward, Inwood Second Ward, Inwood First Ward, Union Square Second Branch, Manhattan Eighth Ward, Harlem First Branch, Union Square First Ward, Union Square Third Ward, Canal Street Branch

225 NEW YORK STAKE'S ORIGINAL REGION SEVENTY YEARS LATER Brooklyn, Long Island, New Jersey, Queens/Westchester

243 APPENDIX
244 NEW YORK NEW YORK STAKE TIMELINE: 1997 - 2004
247 PRIESTHOOD AND AUXILIARY LEADERS: 1934 - 2004
252 MEETING LOCATIONS: 1837 - 2004
253 CHART: NEW YORK STAKE AND ITS DESCENDANTS
255 THE EARLY CHURCH IN NEW YORK CITY: A WALKING TOUR
271 NOTES
280 CONTRIBUTORS

# INTRODUCTION

New York City probably has a longer continuous involvement with The Church of Jesus Christ of Latter-day Saints than any large city in the world. Utah cities and towns are latecomers compared to a history that begins in 1828 with Martin Harris' visit to Charles Anthon of Columbia College on Park Row. Joseph Smith visited in 1832; Parley Pratt wrote *A Voice of Warning* in 1837; European migrants flowed through the port of New York on their way to Utah; and the Church organized the first stake east of Colorado in New York City in 1934.

This book celebrates the 70th anniversary of the birth of the New York New York Stake. It begins in the 19th century and brings the story up to the dedication of the Manhattan New York Temple on June 13, 2004. Over that century and three quarters, Latter-day Saints have kept up a longstanding love affair with New York City–even if at times it seems like Babylon.

Although this is the history of a single stake, at one time the stake encompassed large portions of New Jersey and extended to the tip of Long Island, virtually the same area as the 14-stake and district Manhattan New York Temple district. We begin with this larger story and gradually narrow the focus to the current stake on the island of Manhattan.

The history was commissioned by President Brent Belnap soon after his call to be stake president in 1997. I was asked to head up an effort that came to involve scores of willing volunteers laboring under the heading of the stake history committee. These volunteers were a cross-section of the stake: students, teachers, arts people, married and single, old-time members and recent converts, businessmen and lawyers, and a variety of ethnicities. (You can read about them in the short bios at the back.) For years now we have been meeting in the Bushman apartment on the first Sunday of the month to produce *The New York LDS Historian,* a newsletter on aspects of Church life in the city.

Our first number appropriately described the voyage of the ship *Brooklyn* around Cape Horn to Yerba Buena in 1846, in the same months Nauvoo pioneers were trekking to Winter Quarters. The *Brooklyn* pioneers were the first

Mormons to settle in the West. The issue announced that New York City played an important role in Church history and has a story of its own to tell.

In subsequent issues of the newsletter, the committee compiled much of the information needed to produce this book. Scott Tiffany, who has served as editor from the beginning, cut, pasted, spliced and remolded copy from our previous work to create Parts 1 and 2 of City Saints. This is the history of Church development from the beginning until the temple dedication.

In addition, the committee wanted to record the lives of Latter-day Saints in New York. What does it mean to be a "City Saint?" The information we gathered appears in Part 3–"It's a Wonderful Town"—where the book departs from the standard history format to offer a collage of people, stories, and events that depict the lives of modern, urban Latter-day Saints.

Part 4 tells how the Church organization has worked, especially since 1997 when the stake with its current boundaries was formed. Who were the leaders, what were the activities? What was happening in our common life?

We are happy with the story we tell, but regret the absences. We know hundreds of significant people put their hearts into scores of important activities that uplifted thousands of people, and yet receive no mention in these pages. They all deserve to be here. We hope this book will provoke all LDS New Yorkers to write their stories and send them to the committee. They will add to the growing stake archive and perhaps find their way into a later edition of the history. Every one of these stories helps us understand how Mormons have made a place for themselves in this gargantuan, terrifying, splendid world capital of finance, arts, and migration.

We have dedicated the book to Latter-day Saint New Yorkers everywhere and express our appreciation for having been, along with them, part of Church life in this wonderful place.

Richard Lyman Bushman

October 2004

# PART 1: THE CITY SAINTS STORY

1828-1858
# MORMONITES IN MANHATTAN
SCOTT D. TIFFANY

### EARLY DAYS

The Church of Jesus Christ of Latter-day Saints connected with New York City two years before the official organization of the Church in Fayette, New York, April 6, 1830.

In February 1828, Martin Harris traveled to Manhattan to seek the opinions of two distinguished linguists, Charles Anthon and Samuel Mitchill, about characters taken from the Book of Mormon plates. Anthon, a Classics professor at Columbia College (now Columbia University) met with Harris, probably at the college then in Lower Manhattan on Park Row just west of City Hall.

According to Harris' version of the story, Anthon first endorsed and then rejected the translation. The story has been memorialized in Latter-day Saint history because the encounter in Manhattan appeared to fulfill a prophecy in Isaiah about the translation of a sealed book.

The subsequent publication of the Book of Mormon attracted attention throughout the country. Early in his career, one of nineteenth-century America's most important journalists, James Gordon Bennett, spent two months in Western New York in summer 1831. He wrote a two-part "view of the rise and progress of the Mormon Religion" for New York City's *Morning Courier and Enquirer.*[1]

He described the "Mormonites" as a strange piece of fanaticism and called it "the latest device of roguery, ingenuity, ignorance and religious excitement combined."[2] Just four years later, Bennett established the New York Herald, a four-page daily that became one of the East Coast's most prominent newspapers and featured dozens of articles on the Church.[3]

Joseph Smith first visited New York City in October 1832. He and Bishop Newel K. Whitney came to purchase goods for Whitney's store. While here, Joseph Smith took temporary lodgings at the Pearl Street House at Pearl Street in lower Manhattan where he wrote to his wife, Emma "this day I have been walking through the most splendid part of the city of New York. The buildings are truly great and wonderful, to the astonishing of every beholder."

He was less impressed with the crowds on the street. "The inequity of the people is printed in every countinance and nothing but the dress of the people makes them look fair and beautiful." Joseph's heart went out to the inhabitants: "My bowels are filled with compassion towards them and I am determined to lift up my voice in this city." He also noted the diversity of residents in the boarding house, "from all parts of the world."[4]

## MISSION CITY

On Sunday, June 4, 1837, Joseph Smith called Heber C. Kimball on the first overseas mission to England. He was to be accompanied by several elders of the Church including Orson Hyde, Willard Richards, Joseph Fielding, Isaac Russell, John Goodson and John Snyder.[5] These pioneering elders met in New York City in June 1837. There, they found only one member in the city, Elijah Fordham, a diligent elder who helped form the first Manhattan branch. Two days before leaving for England, the missionaries mailed out an early Mormon tract, Orson Hyde's *Timely Warnings,* to every minister in the city. Then they engaged passage on the merchant ship *Garrick,* and set sail on June 30.

In late July, Parley P. Pratt came to New York to escape the contention in Kirtland over the collapse of the Kirtland bank.[6] He and Elijah Fordham preached together and began writing a book, entitled *A Voice of Warning,* which eventually became a Church standard. They wrote 216 pages in just two months and the book went to press in New York in late September 1837. *A Voice of Warning* frankly set forth Mormonism's distinctive cornucopia of beliefs. New Yorkers shunned the book and the local press attacked Mormons for their claims.

Despite six months of work, Parley and Elijah met with little success. Parley described his frustration: "Of all the places in which the English language is spoken, I found the City of New York to be the most difficult as to access to the minds or attention of the people. From July to January we preached, advertised, printed, published, testified, visited, talked, prayed and wept in vain. To all appearances there was no interest or impression on the minds of the people in regard to the fullness of the gospel."[7]

At best, they gathered two or three people in a small upper room on Goerck Street for meetings with the branch of about six members.[8] Pratt became discouraged and determined to leave New York City for New Orleans. As a small group met for a final prayer meeting with Parley, a monumental turning point took place.

"We began to speak in tongues and prophesy. Many marvelous things were manifested which I cannot write; but the principle burden of the prophesyings was concerning New York City . . . . The Lord said that He had heard our prayers, beheld our labors, diligence and long suffering towards that city; and that He had seen our tears."⁹

Parley felt prompted to stay in New York, "for the Lord had many people in that city." He recorded his feeling that "from that very day forward we should have plenty of friends, money to pay our debts with the publishers; means to live, and crowds to hear us. And there should be more doors open, preaching than we could fill."¹⁰

In the meeting was a chair maker named David Rogers who arranged for them to preach in a warehouse full of his chairs. When that room became too small, he helped rent an even larger room.¹¹ A Methodist preacher named Cox soon invited the Church to preach at his home near the East River, where this family and members of his congregation were baptized. Women from Willett and Grant streets invited Parley to their homes and he was invited by the Free Thinkers to lecture at Tammany Hall.

"In short, it was not three weeks from the delivery of the prophecies in the upper room till we had fifteen preaching places in the city, all of which were filled to overflowing. We preached about eleven times a week, besides visiting from house to house. We soon commenced baptizing, and continued doing so almost daily during the winter and spring."¹²

## MIRACLES IN MANHATTAN

Miracles played a part in the early growth in New York. After being crippled four years, one woman had her leg entirely healed. When her doctors were dismissed, they threatened to sue the Church for disrupting their service. Wandle Mace, who was eventually called as the first branch president in New York City, experienced a series of miraculous healings in his household.

Mace lived at 13 Bedford Street. His boy, Charles, was deathly sick with a brain fever; the doctors declared there was "no hope." Mace was introduced to Parley P. Pratt earlier by Elijah Fordham and they had met at least once to discuss religion. Now, Mace and his wife, Margaret, decided it was a "good time to try Mr. Pratt's religion." Upon request, Parley came immediately, blessed the boy, and declared that "the child should begin to mend in that very hour."¹³ He was healthy and playing by the next day.

A sick woman named Dexter, who lived above the Mace family in the same house, heard the child and requested a blessing. She had scarcely left her bed for six months; now she and her infected child were at the point of death. Parley administered a blessing with Elijah Fordham and the woman was "from that hour restored to health, and the child also." A few days later, the woman walked about two miles to the East River in the snow to be baptized by Fordham. Dexter's mother was also baptized, as were Margaret Mace, a couple by the last name of Curtis, and Ann Shaffer, who later married Fordham.

On a snowy, rainy day when the sidewalks were ankle-deep in mud, Wandle Mace's family was baptized by Parley in the East River. A few days later Mace himself was baptized and the following spring he was called as the first branch president.[14] The little branch held meetings three times a day on Sunday and once during the week. They also preached and made house calls throughout the week.[15]

The revitalized missionary activities did not go unnoticed. *The New York Evangelist* and other publications of the day continually attacked Joseph Smith as a fraud; one called him a "blockhead." L. R. Sunderland wrote an eight-part exposé about the Church that was published in the New York *Zion's Watchman* between January 13 and March 3, 1838. In response to this and earlier critics such as E.D. Howe, Parley penned a pamphlet entitled *Mormonism Unveiled*. Its revealing subtitle explains Parley's point of view: *Zion's Watchman unmasked, and its editor, Mr. L. R. Sunderland, exposed: truth vindicated: the Devil made and priestcraft in danger!*

Still, critics persisted. In *Mormonism Exposed,* Origen Bacheler refers to Parley, the local members and Joseph Smith as "perhaps the most vile, the most impudent, the most impious knot of charlatans and cheats with which any community was every disgraced."[16]

About the same time, James M'Chensey wrote another anti-Mormon book, *An Antidote to Mormonism,* and subtitled it, *A Warning Voice to the Church and Nation: The Purity of Christian Principles Defended: and Truth Disentangled From Error and Delusion.* It was published at the book store of Burnett and Pollard, 120 Broadway, three doors below Cortland Street. M'Chensey unabashedly stated how he thought New York, and the rest of America, should respond to the Mormons: "Now, we have either to admit this in full, or believe them to be the very worst dupes of darkness . . . .the combat is desperate; the battle is one of extermination. "[17]

Arriving on this religious battlefield in April 1838, Orson Pratt assumed leadership of the local church when Parley moved to Caldwell County, Missouri.[18] Under Orson's leadership, the New York Branch continued to grow. Wilford Woodruff visited the city on May 18, 1838 for three days and reported that the branch consisted of nearly one hundred newly baptized members.[19]

Meanwhile, Parley P. Pratt and the Saints were facing persecution again, this time in Caldwell County. Parley was driven from his home and put in prison for eight months. He finally returned to New York for a six-month mission in late summer 1839. Addison Everett, one of the first converts he baptized and now a High Priest, told Parley that the New York Branch had gathered for a special prayer meeting the previous July 4, to ask that Parley be released from prison. During the prayer, "the spirit of prophecy fell on him," and he declared they could stop praying as "this moment brother Parley goes at liberty." Parley had, in fact, been freed that day.[20] In addition to preaching and visiting surrounding branches, Parley completed and published a book of poetry expressing LDS ideas entitled *The Millennium and Other Poems*.[21]

## INTERNATIONAL REACH

During the late 1830s, Elders John Taylor, George A. Smith, Brigham Young, Wilford Woodruff, and Heber C. Kimball visited New York City on missions to the region and abroad. On one occasion, nearly 40 people were baptized during a "few days."[22] But by 1840, the Apostles were not the only Saints passing through New York City. On July 20, 41 members of the Church arrived in New York from Liverpool, the first of nearly 75,000 church members who would later pass through New York City on their journey west.[23]

In May 1842, the New York City Saints numbered 200. Outside Manhattan, four members were counted on Staten Island, Brooklyn had 16 members, New Rochelle had 20, and Norwalk, Connecticut had 31. There were also branches at Setauket and Hempstead on Long Island and Paterson, Lodi, Wacake, Newark, and elsewhere in New Jersey.[24] Leaders of these branches, as well as East Coast leaders from as far as Boston and Tennessee, met in a hall at 245 Spring Street for general conference every six months.

To assist the increasing number of immigrant converts making their way west, the Church stationed emigration agents in New York to act as middlemen. On December 1, 1844, Parley P. Pratt, by now effectively the apostle to New York, was called as immigrant agent. He was asked to supervise all of the New England and Mid-Atlantic branches and begin a Church newspaper, which he called *The Prophet*.

Other members of the Quorum of the Twelve Apostles joined Parley in late winter 1844 to discuss progress of the Church since the martyrdom of Joseph Smith the previous June. On April 6, 1845, the Quorum issued a 116 page booklet as an official Church proclamation was printed at 7 Spruce Street.

It was likely written to fulfill a commandment in Doctrine and Covenants 121:1-11, which states the leadership should "make a solemn proclamation of my gospel . . . to all the kings of the world . . . with loud proclamation, and with your testimony, fearing them not." The New York proclamation was directed "to all the kings of the world, to the President of the United States of America . . . and to the rulers of all nations," and commanded them "to repent and humble yourselves as little children before the majesty of the Holy One."[25]

# MORMON MUMMIES IN MANHATTAN
SCOTT TIFFANY

*In winter 1833, eleven Egyptian mummies arrived on the shipping docks of lower Manhattan. The crated curiosities were addressed to the international trade companies of Maitland & Kennedy and McLeod & Gillespie who were to sell the mummies. The proceeds would go to the family of Antonio Lebolo, who had excavated them in Thebes, Egypt around 1820 and died a decade later.*

*According to a later Mormon newspaper, a man named Michael Chandler purchased the mummies and opened their coffins in Manhattan's customs office. With two of the bodies, he discovered "rolled up with the same kind of linen, saturated with the same bitumen, which, when examined, proved to be two rolls of papyrus... he was immediately told, while in the customs house that there was no man in that city who could translate his roll; but was referred to by the same gentleman (a stranger), to Mr. Joseph Smith, Jr. who, continued he, possesses some kind of power or gifts by which he had previously translated similar characters."*

*Parts of the papyri described were eventually published as The Book of Abraham, now part of the Pearl of Great Price. Today the Church of Jesus Christ of Latter-day Saints regards this record as ancient scripture, comparable to records of the Old Testament.*

*The mummies Michael Chandler purchased may have been the largest shipment of such Egyptian oddities to arrive on American soil and were perhaps only the sixth group ever shipped to the States.*

*"Mummy watching" had gradually gained popularity in Europe after Napoleon invaded Egypt in 1798 and caught on in America in the mid-1820s. Boston, Philadelphia, and New York were among the earliest cities to sponsor mummy exhibitions. Previous to the arrival of Chandler's eleven mummies, at least four exhibits had been popular attractions in New York.*

*The August 10, 1824, issue of the* New York Evening Post *reported: "Now exhibiting from eight in the morning to nine in the evening at 328 Bway, nearly opposite the hospital, a MUMMY, just arrived from Egypt. Admittance, 25 cents; children, half price."*

*Commenting on the exhibit, an expert on Egyptian artifacts named Samuel L. Mitchill encouraged New Yorkers to "view this rare and real production, without delay." Five years later, Martin Harris consulted Mitchill about the authenticity of Joseph Smith's translation of the Book of Mormon's "reformed Egyptian" on the same trip in which he conferred with renowned professor Charles Anthon.*

*When Joseph Smith came to New York City with Newel K. Whitney in October 1832, mummy exhibitions had just peaked in popularity. Peale's Museum advertised its mummy as the "most remarkable relic of the art of embalming ever* brought to America" and the American Museum vied for visitors with "a great curiosity and well worthy the attention of every man of science and discernment." Although there is no known record of it, it is possible that Joseph Smith saw one or both of these exhibits.

It was about this same time that Michael Chandler was purchasing Lebolo's mummies, four of which Joseph Smith would eventually acquire. Chandler exhibited the lot in Philadelphia beginning April 3, 1833. He then crisscrossed the country, exhibiting mummies and selling them as he toured. After Philadelphia, Chandler and his mummies appeared in Baltimore; Harrisburg, Pennsylvania; Hudson, Ohio, and, presumably, several cities in between. By the time he arrived in Kirtland, Chandler had just four mummies left. After being told repeatedly that Joseph Smith claimed he could translate cryptic writings, Chandler must have been intrigued to finally meet the Mormon prophet.

In July 1835 Joseph Smith and a small group of Church members paid Chandler $2,400 for four mummies and at least five papyri including "two or more scrolls."

In 1833, this papyrus arrived on a shipping dock in New York City with eleven mummies, four of which Joseph Smith purchased. In 1966, a professor from the University of Utah, Dr. Aziz S. Atiya, accidentally discovered the same papyrus at New York's Metropolitan Museum of Art. Courtesy of the Church Archives, The Church of Jesus Christ of Latter-day Saints.

Their purchase price was only a fraction of the $1,800 one New York museum paid for a single mummy back in 1826. But Joseph Smith was apparently more interested in the papyri than the mummies. He said he translated part of them and then published a sample of his work in a Church newspaper, the Times and Seasons, dated March 1, 1842.

Taking note of the Times and Seasons article, the New York Herald reprinted what had been published as the first part of the Book of Abraham. On April 3, 1842, the Herald carried the entire text of chapter one along with a favorable editorial about Smith's work and a complete etching of what Smith said was an ancient depiction of Abraham being offered on a sacrificial altar.

As the technology for printing images was still evolving, printing the drawing was a significant commitment. During the entire month of April, the Herald printed only two drawings. The newspaper commented:

"This Joe Smith is undoubtedly one of the greatest characters of the age. He indi-

In March 1842, Joseph Smith printed this illustration and some text in an LDS newspaper. One month later, on April 3, the New York Herald in Manhattan printed the same image with an editorial. These were the first glimpses of what came to be the Book of Abraham in the Pearl of Great Price. Courtesy of the Church Archives, The Church of Jesus Christ of Latter-day Saints.

cates as much talent, originality, and moral courage as Mahomet, Odin, or any of the great spirits that have hitherto produced revelations of past ages... Joe Smith is creating a spiritual system, combined also with moral and industry, that may change the destiny of the race—Joe believes himself inspired and a worker of miracles."

After her son was assassinated in 1844, Joseph's mother Lucy Smith, held on to the artifacts and exhibited them for a small fee. When she died in 1856, the collection was sold to a local man named Abel Combs. After that, no known record exists for two of the four mummies.

The other two were displayed at the St. Louis Museum in 1856-57 and at the Wood's Museum in Chicago in the 1860s. Then tragedy struck. The mummies and their papyri were presumed lost in the great Chicago fire of October 8, 1871.

Whatever the fate of the mummies, some of the papyri mysteriously made their way back to New York City.

In the spring of 1966, a non-Mormon Egyptologist from the University of Utah made what he called one of the "most important finds" of his career.

Dr. Aziz S. Atiya was researching illustrations at the Metropolitan Museum of Art for a book he was writing. As he sifted through files of dusty documents and manuscripts in a museum storage area, Atiya stumbled across an image he recognized immediately.

The portion of one key figure's head was missing, as were the arms of the man being offered as a human sacrifice, but Atiya knew it was the original Egyptian papyrus Joseph Smith had published as Abraham on the altar.

Atiya dug further until he had found several related fragments and a letter, signed by Joseph Smith's wife, Emma, and his son, stating that these were in fact Joseph's papyri. At some point, the papyri pieces had been glued to paper to keep them from crumbling.

After the discovery of the papyri, Brigham Young University Professor H. Donl Peterson sought to find out how they arrived at the museum. Peterson learned that before Abel Combs died on July 5, 1892, he gave some of the papyri to his close friend and private nurse, Charlotte Benecke Weaver. After she died, her daughter, then living at 221 Ralph Avenue in Brooklyn, showed the papyri to curators at the Metropolitan Museum in 1918, perhaps for an appraisal.

Nearly three decades later, in December 1945, Ludlow Bull, an associate curator of the Metropolitan Museum, found an internal memo concerning the papyri and wrote to Charlotte Benecke Weaver's grandson, Edward Heusser, who still lived in

Brooklyn. Edward informed the museum that his family had the papyri and brought them to the museum for examination on June 11, 1946, and to discuss their possible sale.

The Metropolitan's curators, believing the fragments dated to "a late period in Egyptian history and are fragments of four different books of the Dead," purchased them for a small, undisclosed amount. The acquisition was relatively insignificant, since, as the curators explained, the museum already had "a number of complete funerary papyri in excellent condition in our collection and [we] do not really need these pieces."

The papyri may have been insignificant to the museum, but they were very significant to the Mormons. In 1967, Dr. Atiya quietly orchestrated the return of the papyri to the Church of Jesus Christ of Latter-day Saints.

In a discreet ceremony at the Metropolitan Museum of Art on November 27, 1967, President N. Eldon Tanner of the First Presidency received the eleven fragments once owned by Joseph Smith, as well as Emma Smith's letter of authentication.

Today the fragments are in the Church Archives in Salt Lake City. Presumably, they constitute only a fraction of the original documents purchased by the Mormons in 1835. According to Oliver Cowdery, Joseph Smith had enough papyri to fill "large volumes" of scripture.

The fragments found in New York City are the only ones known to exist today. Of the eleven, only one piece, now called Facsimile 1, is known to have been used directly in the Book of Abraham—the same illustration the New York Herald published in the city more than 150 years ago.

## EXODUS

After nine months in the city, Parley P. Pratt left for Nauvoo in late August 1845.[26] Taking over as Church leader and editor of *The Prophet* was an ambitious man named Samuel Brannan who was soon engulfed in a controversy over "spiritual wifery" or plural marriage. Brannan was excommunicated and then almost immediately reinstated after leaders learned more of his case.

Within the year, Brannan was asked to lead local Church members on a monumental migration. He was to charter a ship to carry East Coast Saints to the West. Brannan boarded nearly 250 members of the Church on the ship *Brooklyn* and took them on a six-month sea exodus to California. Departing on February 4, 1846 (by coincidence the same day the Nauvoo Saints crossed the Mississippi on their way west), these Church members became the first civilian group in American history to emigrate by sail to the West Coast, landing in Yerba Buena (now San Francisco) on July 31, 1846.

## PARLEY PRATT'S LAST VISIT

Parley P. Pratt apparently made few trips back to New York City after his release as editor of *The Prophet* in 1845. Parley's last trip to New York was in late December 1856. On New Year's Eve, he recorded his thoughts about being back in the city: "It leaves me among strangers . . . a pilgrim and almost a stranger in the very city where, twenty years ago, I labored, toiled, prayed, preached wrote and published the message of eternal truth . . . If I am privileged to awake in the morning of a new year, I will commence a new book or volume of my life."[27]

He did awake and on New Year's Day 1857, Parley Pratt found comfort in the now well-established branch in New York City: "Spent the day in visiting with President Taylor and others, and at 5 p.m. repaired to the Latter-day Saints' Hall, where I met with some four hundred persons, mostly members of the Church."[28]

Yet Parley's "new volume" of life was not to last. Less than five months later, Parley P. Pratt was assassinated near the border between Arkansas and Indian Territory while finishing a mission.[29] The Church mourned the loss of a great apostle. Perhaps few mourned more than those nearly four hundred members of the Church who had celebrated New Year's Day with their founding father a few months earlier.

Over the next decade, the outbreak of the Utah War and America's Civil War would dramatically alter the branch Parley Pratt struggled to create.

In 1828, Martin Harris met with Professor **CHARLES ANTHON** of Columbia University on Park Row in southern Manhattan to review a sample of Joseph Smith's translation of the Book of Mormon.

Reproduction of the Book of Mormon transcription that Charles Anthon reviewed. According to Martin Harris, the professor verified Joseph Smith's accuracy and then recanted when he learned that Smith said an angel gave him golden plates.

# NEW YORK CITY'S OCEAN PIONEERS   SCOTT TIFFANY

*Brigham Young and his company were not the first Mormons to arrive in the West—one year earlier a group of LDS sea pioneers from New York City settled in California. In 1846 nearly 250 men, women and children fleeing persecution set sail on a perilous six-month journey: 20,000 miles from Manhattan to San Francisco. These Mormons became the first American families to move west by sea.*

*"Brethren Awake! Be determined to get out from this evil nation by next spring. We do not want one Saint to be left in the United States after that time."*[1]

*Such was the cry from Apostle Orson Pratt to the Saints in New York City in November 1845.*[2] *In the previous decade, Church members had been attacked, beaten, and driven from their homes three times*[3] *Brigham Young, leader of the Church after Joseph Smith's murder in 1844, called on the faithful to leave the United States for Mexican territory in Upper California—now Nevada, California, Utah and Arizona. Members in Nauvoo would make the journey overland, while those few saints left in the northeast were encouraged to travel west by sea.*

*On a cold, gray day in February 1846, Old Slip dock of New York City's harbor was crowded with Mormon pioneers. Nearly 250 in number, most were new converts to the faith. On their first sea journey, these adventurous families entrusted their lives to a 26-year-old Mormon businessman named Samuel Brannan.*[4] *A personal friend of Joseph Smith, he directed the Church's affairs and published a LDS newspaper called* The New-York Messenger *on his own press.*[5]

*Brannan was notoriously ambitious and highly unpredictable. Less than a year before the voyage, Church leaders excommunicated him for teaching false doctrine. Brannan managed to get himself reinstated—and only six months later the Church asked him to lead the exodus from New York.*

*Brigham Young told Brannan that the rest of the Saints might meet him on the California coast. Consequently, the New York Saints packed enough supplies and machinery to establish a new colony: sheets of glass, spools of twine, more than 40 pigs, two milk cows and much else. Brannan loaded an immense printing press and enough supplies to run a newspaper for a year.*

The ship *Brooklyn* (above) carried the first group of Mormon pioneers to the West, arriving in San Francisco July 31, 1846. The ship made a return trip from New York City to San Francisco during the California Gold Rush in 1849. *Courtesy of the Church Archives, The Church of Jesus Christ of Latter-day Saints*

On February 4, 1846—coincidentally the same day the first Mormons began their overland trek West from Illinois—the ship Brooklyn set out on its remarkable journey.

In this "staunch tub," as one passenger called it, the ocean pioneers planned to follow the only-known sea route from New York to San Francisco Bay: the trade path arched south to Brazil, before venturing down around Cape Horn. To offset costs, the Brooklyn would then carry freight up to a tropical port in the Sandwich Islands, now called Hawaii. Finally, the passengers would travel to present-day San Francisco.

Crammed between decks in tiny rooms, approximately seventy men, sixty-eight women and 100 children huddled in the dark—surrounded by water leaks, stale air, and the pounding of the sea against the hull. Only the children could stand upright between decks.

Sam Brannan, meanwhile, lived next to the Captain's quarters in a pleasant space with his wife, their ten-week old son, Samuel Jr., and Brannan's mother-in-law, Fanny Corwin.

In less than eight weeks under sail, nine passengers died, and everyone knew that the most dangerous trial of the journey still lay ahead: Cape Horn. Yet in less than two weeks—a remarkable time—the Brooklyn cleared Cape Horn without further loss of life, and the Mormons were halfway to their new home.

In the Pacific, their troubles were far from over. The plan was to put ashore in the small port of Valparaiso, in central Chile, but shortly after land was spotted, a storm slammed into the Brooklyn. Running with the wind, Captain Richardson turned to Juan Fernandez Island, an almost deserted outpost nearly 400 miles off the coast of Chile. On May 4th, 1846, the Brooklyn made port. The passengers found clear, natural spring water and an oasis of orchards: pears, peaches, figs and berries.

According to one passenger, their trip across the Pacific Ocean from then on was a "dreamy, delightful period of unbroken sea voyaging."[6] On June 20, forty-one days after leaving Juan Fernandez, the Brooklyn arrived in Honolulu Harbor on the island of Oahu. Riding at anchor, framed by tropical palms, was the forty-four-gun American warship Congress.

The Mormons anxiously watched as its commander Robert F. Stockton rowed across the harbor. He boarded the Brooklyn with unwelcome news: the United States was at war with Mexico — the nation where the Mormons had hoped to seek shelter. Commander Stockton encouraged the Mormons to buy more military weapons and to move on to California—in the name of the United States.

Sam Brannan did buy more weapons, but he bought them to protect his landing party, not to help fight for the United States. "Armed to the teeth," as Brannan described it, the Brooklyn passengers set sail northeast toward their final destina-

Newsman and LDS Church leader Samuel Brannan led the Mormons on a six-month sea journey before he announced to the world that gold had been discovered in California. *LDS church*

tion: a modest Mexican whaling village known as Yerba Buena.⁷

On deck, the men began military drills as the women sewed denim uniforms. Four weeks later, on Friday, July 31, the Brooklyn entered San Francisco Bay. Upon entering the harbor, the passengers were stunned to see another battleship. Three weeks earlier, the twenty-two-gun warship Portsmouth had sailed into the bay. As the Brooklyn emerged through the fog, soldiers on shore began military procedures until they looked out and saw women on board the Brooklyn.

American Commander John B. Montgomery's greeting was met with mixed emotion when he announced that the village of Yerba Buena had been captured and was now part of the United States of America. The pioneers had returned inadvertently to the nation they were trying to escape.

The Brooklyn pioneers sailed more than 20,000 miles and endured five months and twenty-seven days at sea. Six children, four adults, and one crewmember died during the harrowing journey. These sea pioneers were the first emigrant families to sail from the East Coast to the American West.

In Yerba Buena, named for its "good herbs," the pioneers established industries and built homes. They set up shop as craftsmen, tailors, bakers, surveyors, masons, carpenters, cobblers, and attorneys. Spreading throughout the region, they established the first local bank, post office, library, and the first English public school in California.

Villagers soon changed the name Yerba Buena to match the bay: San Francisco. And in honor of the Mormons' voyage, a township across the bay was named "Brooklyn." Now called Oakland, it is the site of a soaring temple on the hill, a coincidental tribute to the New York City LDS pioneers who first settled in the West.

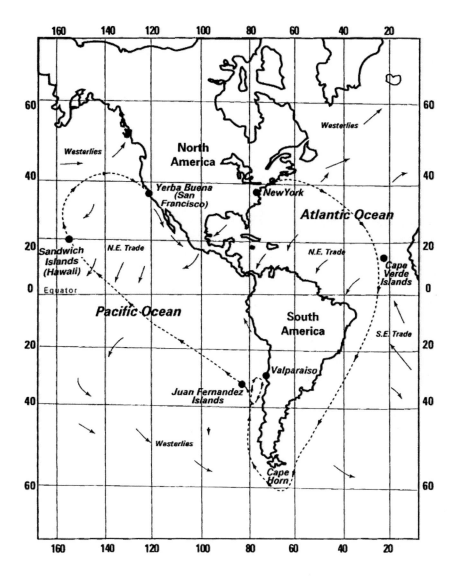

The passengers of the ship Brooklyn traveled from New York City around the treacherous tip of South America and up to California. They spent six months at sea, sailing more than 20,000 miles.

1858-1900
# RISING OR SETTING SUN?
KENT S. LARSEN II

For two decades after the organization of the Church in 1830, members relied on New York City as a center for growth, development, and publicity. But by the middle of the 1850s during the exodus to Utah, it became increasingly difficult for the Church to maintain missionary work in New York or anywhere outside the West.[1]

On the surface, it appeared as if the Church abandoned the city altogether. However, a closer study reveals a surprising level of commitment and a nearly continuous presence in New York throughout the late 1800s. In fact, New York City remained the most important center for Mormons on the East Coast. Church members passed through New York City as they immigrated to Utah and as they traveled to European missions. Others came to New York City for educational and professional reasons.

## CIVIL WAR YEARS

After John Taylor left for Utah at the outbreak of the U.S. Army's armed excursion to Utah known as the Utah War, I. Appleby and Thomas B. H. Stenhouse were left in charge of the mission.[2] Appleby was formally called to serve his second term as president of the mission in 1857 and 1858.[3] While some sources indicate the mission was then closed, George Q. Cannon succeeded Appleby from 1858 to 1860.[4]

With the breakout of the Civil War, the Church pulled its missionaries from service in the eastern states and elsewhere around the country,[5] but even during wartime, meetings must have continued: Lucius N. Scovil records in his journal that leaders in New York City discussed curtailing the meetings. And as soon as the war ended, William H. Miles reopened the mission and presided over it from 1865 to 1869.[6]

Some records indicate the mission was then closed and not re-opened until 1893.[7] However, there is evidence that missionary work in the area did not stop. Assistant Church Historian Andrew Jenson indicated that William C. Staines was in charge of the mission after 1873.[8]

John Druce was president of the branches in New York, New Jersey and

Connecticut in 1876 and 1877. About this time, Brigham Young requested that his son visit the saints in Williamsburg (now part of Brooklyn), many of whom Brigham Young had baptized while passing through on his way to England 30 years earlier.

## THE CITY AS GATEWAY

During this time, the majority of LDS immigrants arriving from Europe passed through New York City. From 1858 to 1864 just seven ships of Mormon immigrants arrived at other East Coast ports, and from 1864 to 1890, when organized Mormon immigration stopped, just one ship arrived elsewhere.[9] The number of Mormon immigrants passing through New York City between 1855 and 1890 totaled nearly 75,000.

To help the immigrants, the Church called immigration agents and stationed them in the places where members needed help, mainly where they changed modes of transportation. Church immigration agents were stationed more or less permanently in Liverpool, England (where members gathered to board ships bound for the U.S.), and in New York (where they usually arrived). Notable among these agents in New York was William C. Staines, who served as an immigration agent for the Church from 1863 through 1881.[10] The presence of these immigration agents probably also led to increased missionary activity in the city.

Immigrant converts disembarked at Castle Garden (now called Castle Clinton). There, the Church immigration agent guided them through the immigration process and across the river to Newark, New Jersey, where they boarded trains for the West. Some members who arrived without funds would stay in the New York area to earn train fare. The immigration agent would assist them in finding housing and work so they could eventually make the trip to Utah. In 1892, immigration processing moved to Ellis Island.

New York City also served as the main embarkation point for missionaries and others bound for Europe. General Authorities and other officials often went through New York City in their travels, frequently meeting with church members before continuing.[11]

## THE CITY AS DESTINATION

The city was also a destination for educational and professional activities. After completing medical school in Philadelphia, Romania B. Bunnell worked at the Eye and Ear Infirmary in New York City in the 1880s.[12] She went on to help found the Deseret Hospital in Salt Lake City and its Eye and Ear Department. Heber John Richards also came to New York City for medical training, studying at Bellevue Hospital. And Lorus Pratt, one of Apostle Orson Pratt's sons, studied art in New York City in 1876, returning to Utah to strengthen the professional arts in Utah.[13]

In the 1880s, after graduating from West Point, Richard W. Young took advantage of his proximity to New York while stationed at Gouvernor's Island to attend Columbia Law School.[14] Don Carlos and Feramorz Young, two sons of Brigham Young, attended Renassleaur Polytechnic and studied music in Brooklyn during the summer of 1876.[15]

Latter-day Saint businessmen often came to New York City for investment meetings and to make business contacts. Apostle Brigham Young Jr. came to the city in 1889 to negotiate with the Aztec Cattle Company for the Church.[16] His half brother, Apostle John W. Young, visited the city frequently in the 1870s on business for several railroad companies for which he worked. By the 1880s he became a permanent resident of the city, eventually dying in New York City in 1924.[17] Heber J. Grant also visited New York City many times on business.[18]

The presence of so many members of the Church in New York City kept the Church alive in the region. During the next century, such a critical mass of residents accumulated in the city that New York would become the first stake established east of the Rocky Mountains.

1900-1934
# SAINTS IN THE CITY
SCOTT D. TIFFANY

At the dawn of the 20th century, members of the Church in New York City were viewed by many as a small fanatical sect that stopped at nothing to gain converts. Throughout the first quarter of the century, Church members responded to news articles exaggerating their beliefs, dodged national campaigns that smeared their name, and battled stiff opposition to their dreams of building a local chapel.[1]

## MISSIONARY SCANDALS

In the spring of 1901, the conversion of two women to the "Mormon faith" made headlines throughout New York City. Elizabeth Dickenson and Mrs. Thomas Blair were "two of the most prominent women" in the Port Morris, New Jersey Congregational Church and they scandalized the religious community by renouncing their religion.

According to *The New York Times,* "Mrs. Blair shocked her friends in the church by announcing that she had become a believer in Mormonism, and resigned her position as President of the Young People's Society of Christian Endeavor. Following close upon this came Miss Dickenson's declaration and resignation, which acted like a bombshell."

About the time of this religious scandal, members of the local LDS Church moved their meetings to 172 West 81st Street where they gathered from 1901 to 1905. That year, a separate Brooklyn Branch was created, and the Manhattan Branch moved to 33 West 126th Street.

On September 13, 1913, Eastern States Mission President Ben E. Rich passed away. Walter P. Monson replaced him at the mission home located at 33 West 126th Street in Manhattan. Under Monson's direction, missionary activity in the city dramatically increased, which did not escape the attention of other churches or the press. *The New York Sun* printed a story on November 21, 1916, with the headline, "Mormons Working Here, Says Pastor." The article quoted the Reverend W. P. Neff of the Hoboken Methodist Church: "Mormon missionaries masquerading as Bible class teachers, singers and other church workers are deceiving Protestant ministers and working to convert men and women to Mormonism in their very churches."

Pastor Neff claimed that "Mormon missionaries walked up and down the aisles appealing for converts before and after the service until he himself ejected four of them."

The same *New York Sun* article reported that a female Bible teacher at a New York Methodist church had turned out to be a Mormon missionary. Consequently, local ministers were warned by the Methodist Church to "carefully examine all men and women volunteering for church work to make sure that they were not Mormons, who are numerous in the city."

In fact, New York area Church membership was only about 400 in 1913. Still, as the First World War ravaged Europe, there were many anti-Mormon activists attacking the Church. Perhaps the most notorious was former Senator Frank J. Cannon, a disenchanted member of the Church and the son of George Q. Cannon (a member of the Church's First Presidency).

In April 1914, Frank Cannon chose New York City to launch a national crusade against the Mormons. In a ticket-only rally held at Carnegie Hall, roughly 1,000 people met to hear his strategy to curb growth of the Mormon Church. Nationally, Cannon demanded that President Woodrow Wilson not appoint Mormons to political office. He also asked Congress to amend the Constitution to prohibit polygamy; denounced the president of the Mormon Church, Joseph F. Smith, as a polygamist; and accused the Church of befriending 22 senators in order to gain political clout.

Locally, Cannon demanded a New York City law banning Mormon missionaries from holding street meetings, and barring the Church from ever owning a chapel on city grounds.

After two hours Cannon put his measures up for a theatrical vote that was overwhelmingly in favor of his demands. Immediately afterward, a small group of Mormon men rushed the stage including Walter P. Monson, President of the Eastern States Mission, calling Cannon a "liar" and an "ingrate." The *New York Times* reported, "for a time it appeared likely that blows would be struck, and that Frank J. Cannon of Utah, formerly U.S. Senator and once a Mormon, would get the brunt of the attack. Women and clergymen crowded about the Senator and shielded him while he shouted stinging rebukes to his attackers."

Cannon returned to New York eight months later with news that "the Mormon Church is prepared to build a tabernacle in this city . . . The Mormons are all ready to make a determined effort here, and Mormonism will be exerting its political influence in New York before you know it."

## A BUILDING IN BROOKLYN

The Church was, in fact, hoping to build a chapel of its own, though funding was still a large challenge as local church units were required to pay half of the building costs. Commenting on the construction, the *New York Times* reprinted a letter to the editor from mission president Monson:

"Our little congregation here has had to hire a hall for many years for its meetings, and—will those who believe fairy tales about our billions please take note?—we have saved our pennies all these years, hoping our congregation could some day achieve the status of most other congregations in the city . . . When we finally get ready to put up our modest little meeting house we would not like to startle the town in which most of us have lived all of our lives with the notion that we have rushed in by underground or airship to invade it."

The Church finally purchased property for a new chapel and a mission home in Brooklyn on July 5, 1916. The home was built at 233 Gates Avenue in 1918 and a chapel next door was completed at 272 Gates Avenue the following year. On February 16, 1919, Apostle–Senator Reed Smoot dedicated the first LDS chapel east of the Mississippi River since the Mormons fled to Utah almost 75 years earlier.

Then, one year afterward, a missionary who was to greatly impact the lives of Church members in the metropolitan area arrived at the new mission home. Elder G. Stanley McAllister served in the Eastern States Mission from 1920 to 1923. After his mission, McAllister came back to New York to work at a realty firm, Cushman & Wakefield, while attending classes at New York University from 1926-28.

In 1929, McAllister went to work at Columbia Broadcasting Systems (CBS) as Director of Buildings and Plant Operations and helped secure a weekly national broadcast for the Mormon Tabernacle Choir that continues to air. McAllister eventually went on to become a prominent merchandising executive for Lord & Taylor and in 1960 was called as president of the New York Stake.

## THE ROARING 20s

While a missionary, Elder McAllister worked as mission secretary (May 1922-September 1923) under a controversial figure in American history: LDS General Authority and former Congressman B. H. Roberts, who came to Brooklyn as mission president in spring 1922.

For President Roberts, the mission home was not just a residence but, as one biographer describes it, "an embassy and the prime nerve center of the Church membership." Roberts referred to the Brooklyn home in which he lived for five years as "a spiritual and cultural center." Roberts also used the home to plan radical new missionary strategies.

In 1925, the *New York Times* reported that the Mormon missionaries were among the most effective proselytizers in the city: "Broadway has a novelty in sidewalk preachers. Many of the religious exhorters, even with the aid of a cornet, fail to draw street congregations, but many attentive listeners are attracted by a group of comely young women evangelists with up-to-date clothes and even bobbed hair. From the crowd promenading upper Broadway in the evening, sizeable audiences are drawn. When a passer-by pauses to inquire the nature of the meeting, a single word of explanation engages his attention. The word which serves to enlarge the congregation is 'Mormon.'"

In the late 1920s, Elder Wilburn West seemed to agree that sister missionaries were the keys to effective public preaching. He describes an innocent, if not strategic, game of bait and switch: "Our noon street meeting was exceptionally successful, with two lady missionaries to help draw a crowd. Sister Lillian Mortimer, a newly arrived missionary, has an exceptionally fine voice. When she sang, a crowd gathered. Then an elder would speak."

At the beginning of the Great Depression, Elder West was serving in Brooklyn as secretary of the Eastern States Mission. Since the mission cook had Thursdays off, Elder West and a companion were at the mission home on August 9, 1929, preparing their "usual Thursday evening supper of bread and milk" when the doorbell rang. As the mission president, James H. Moyle, and his wife were out to dinner, the young elders answered the door. They were shocked to find the prophet of the LDS church on their doorstep.

President Heber J. Grant explained that he had just failed to negotiate an important loan for a church subsidiary and was "discouraged and lonely and could not bring himself to go to a hotel and spend the night all by himself." When the missionaries tried to explain they had little to eat, President Grant replied, "I am especially fond of bread and milk." Still, the young men managed to find some peanut butter and grape jelly, "something special for the Prophet!"

Throughout the 1920s, Church members met for Sunday services at a variety of places, from the refined surroundings of Carnegie Hall on 57th Street, to a beer hall off Broadway on the Upper West Side. In 1928, the Church found a semi-permanent home on the ground floor of a hotel located at 2166 Broadway between 76th and 77th Streets.

They also met for a time in a former YMCA building at 316 West 57th Street, which they shared with art, drama, and business schools as well as Stillman's Gymnasium. Members commented that during Sunday meetings there was "nothing unusual about a bunch of dancing girls over there coming in with leotards." The YMCA had a seating capacity of 500 with an office and a social room. Separate services were held in German at the same facility, and two other branches met in Brooklyn, at the Church's building at Gates and Franklin next to the Eastern States Mission home.

## A NEW STAKE

By the early 1930s, the New York metropolitan area had nearly 1,600 Church members. Many of these were from the western United States who had come to New York to pursue career opportunities during the "roaring 20s." Another significant source of Church growth in the area were a number of immigrants who had come from Germany after the First World War. These German members were the first of many groups of foreign-born Saints who would figure prominently in the Church's make-up in New York down to the present day.

On April 26, 1931, the New York Mission District was formed, covering greater New York, Long Island, and parts of New Jersey as an independent unit from the Eastern States Mission. In fact, many New York members felt they were ready to become a stake—a unique claim, as there were no stakes east of Colorado. But no stake would be formed as the distance from Church headquarters in Salt Lake City seemed too great.

However, the Church continued to grow steadily in the New York area. By 1934, the metropolitan area had 2,000 members—a 400% increase since 1924. Unlike other mission districts of the time, which were usually led by missionaries, the New York Mission District was staffed entirely by local members. Eventually, Church leaders in Salt Lake City came to a different view about this arrangement.

In December 1934, President Heber J. Grant, First Presidency counselor J. Reuben Clark (a former New York City resident), and Presiding Bishop Sylvester Q. Cannon traveled to New York City to organize the first New York Stake. This was a signal event in Church history. The New York Stake was the first stake created east of Colorado since the exodus to the western United States and only the third (after Los Angeles and San Francisco) to be formed in the "mission field" outside the areas of LDS pioneer settlement.

A priesthood session was held on Saturday December 8 at the Brooklyn chapel and on Sunday, December 9, 1934, the conference formally organizing the stake was held at the 316 West 57th Street facility. Interestingly, this location is only a few blocks from the current location of the Manhattan New York Temple and New York New York Stake center at West 65th Street and Broadway.

The stake's original wards were Manhattan, Brooklyn, Queens, and East Orange (New Jersey), with branches in Oceanside (Long Island), Bay Ridge (Brooklyn), and Westchester. Initially, the New York Stake included New York City, all of Long Island, the northern half of New Jersey and all of Westchester County.

# B.H. ROBERTS:
## FATHER OF MODERN MISSIONARY WORK SCOTT TIFFANY

*As a member of the presidency of the Quorum of the Seventy and assistant Church historian, Elder B. H. Roberts was given free reign to work as president of any American mission of his choice. Roberts chose the Eastern States Mission because it had more than "33 millions of people—truly a noble field" and was based in New York City. At the age of 65, he arrived at the mission home in Brooklyn on May 29, 1922.*

*"My mission here is to convert the Jews," he said. "More Jews live in Brooklyn and New York than anywhere else in the world. I do not want to leave until we have a branch of Jewish converts meeting here."*

*Roberts' dream was not achieved. However, he fulfilled a life-long desire to defend Jesus "as the Christ" to thousands of Jews by writing a detailed series of articles later published as a book called* Rasha the Jew. *More than one million copies of the first two articles were published and distributed throughout New York City.*

*During his tenure as president, Roberts radically altered the face of missionary work throughout the city, the Eastern States and, ultimately, the entire Church. President Roberts demanded that the missionaries work in pairs of two, and he created the first formalized series of "investigator" missionary lessons. He honed proselytizing skills to a near science, developing some of the earliest materials to train missionaries in a "systematic method." Much of what he wrote was incorporated into the first official* Missionary's Handbook *published by the Church in 1937.*

*After one performance review of the missionaries, President Roberts "hit upon the idea of establishing a mission school for imparting such instructions and creating a background of general knowledge and specific instructions which would lead to a general improvement in efficiency and morale of the missionaries." He developed a series of four-week concentrated training sessions in which groups of missionaries from throughout the twelve states he supervised came to "Missionary School" in Brooklyn: "I wish to impress upon all those who come to the school that they are coming here for a period of INTENSE WORK. . . they must not think of coming to New York as coming upon a pleasure trip."*

*Indeed, the missionaries were trained, lectured, scolded and tested from 9 a.m. to 10 p.m.*

*Apparently President Roberts was not much easier on the missionaries when they were working in their fields of labor. He was known to stall letters from home, delay monthly checks to "test their faith," and lecture parents who sent more support money than the allotted $40 per month. As biographer Truman Madsen says,*

*B.H. Roberts was "firm in rebuke and sparing in praise."*

At least one missionary who worked closely with him called Roberts "tender and sympathetic to his missionaries," but members of the Brooklyn Branch were put off by Robert's lack of warmth and personal interaction. In a meeting held to confront him with their concerns, President Roberts said:

"I am not cold but I know I appear at times indifferent. In all my life I have had little time for play or for pleasant times to cultivate friendships. . . I am writing every free minute I have. I have much to do before I die."

And so Roberts wrote. He spent many isolated hours writing at home and researching at the New York Public Library. "I am a hermit," he once confided in a letter. His mission secretary, Elder G. Stanley McAllister, recalled, "the light showed under his door until 4 or 5 in the morning." By the end of Roberts' five-year tenure, he had written thirteen tracts and reprinted three of his own books with revisions.

President Roberts also wrote a number of proselytizing tracts which he "tested" in sermons at the Brooklyn chapel, inviting ministers of other faiths, newspaper editors, Church members and people off the streets. McAllister says, "crowds gathered in the Chapel and it was impossible to get seats unless you were there an hour before the service."

After Roberts' release as mission president, President Heber J. Grant gave Elder Roberts a six-month commission to finish his monumental book, The Truth, The Way, The Life. While living at 308 Riverside Drive in Manhattan, he finished the 747-page masterpiece, which Roberts said reflected "all of my thought, research and studies." Despite his labor, the Church deemed the book too controversial and declined to publish it.

In October 1927, B.H. Roberts returned to Salt Lake City to resume his duties in the presidency of the First Quorum of the Seventy. He left New York on what he called a "rising market" of missionary work. The successful creation of the first New York Stake seven years later was due, in part, to his efforts.

This large area included a population approaching ten million, but the stake population was just about 2,000 members. Manhattan, with its many inactive members, accounted for nearly one-third of the stake membership.

The first stake president was Fred G. Taylor, who had been serving as president of the New York Mission District. His counselors were Howard S. Bennion and H. H. Haglund. James S. Knecht was called as the first stake patriarch. Among the other leaders of the new stake were the famous scientist Harvey Fletcher, called to the high council, and Bishop Ernest L. Wilkinson of the Queens Ward, who would go on to a prominent legal career and serve many years as president of Brigham Young University.

The *New York Times* covered the event in a respectable three-column article with pictures of President Grant and the new local leaders—a stark contrast of coverage compared to the same newspaper three decades earlier, when Mormons made headline news with just two conversions.[2]

**FRANK CANNON**, son of Apostle George Q. Cannon and a strong critic of the Church, held an anti-Mormon rally at Carnegie Hall in 1914.
**STANLEY MCALLISTER** served as a missionary in New York (in the Eastern States mission) from 1920 to 1923. After his mission he moved back to the city and, in 1960, became president of the New York Stake. Photo courtesy of the New York New York Stake.
**B. H. ROBERTS** president of the Brooklyn based Eastern States Mission from 1922-1927. As president, he developed standards and procedures that revolutionized the way missionaries worked throughout the church.

Latter-day Saints gather outside the Brooklyn chapel on the day of its dedication, February 16, 1919. Elder Reed Smoot of the Quorum of the Twelve Apostles dedicated the building, the first LDS Church built east of the Mississippi after the Saints left Nauvoo. Courtesy of the Church Archives, The Church of Jesus Christ of Latter-day Saints.

Around 1925, Latter-day Saints gather outside the Brooklyn chapel, on the corner of Gates and Franklin Avenues. Courtesy of the Church Archives, The Church of Jesus Christ of Latter-day Saints

The chapel in the Brooklyn meetinghouse. Photo courtesy of the New York New York Stake stake archive, from 50th Anniversary celebration.

The New York Stake was created December 9, 1934 at Stillman's Gym, 316 West 57th Street, which is the YMCA building in this picture. Photo courtesy of the Milstein Division of United States History, Local History & Genealogy, the New York Public Library, Astor, Lenox and Tilden Foundations

1934-1964
# A STAKE IN BABYLON
KENT S. LARSEN II

On December 9, 1934, LDS Church president Heber J. Grant stood at the podium of a rented hall at 316 West 57th Street and took what seemed like a big risk for the Church: he turned the New York Mission District into the New York Stake.[1] The new stake almost immediately faced serious challenges.

**THE DEPRESSION**

When the New York Stake was formed in 1934, the United States was already in the midst of the Great Depression. Church members in New York suffered as the minimum wage fell to $15 a week—for those who could find work. According to Manhattan Ward bishop William L. Woolfe, that wage often wasn't enough to pay the rent. Instead, renters paid what they could, when they could, and landlords didn't evict them or ask anyone to leave, knowing that they wouldn't get a new tenant. Woolfe said he went an entire year without paying rent during the worst of the Depression.

Meanwhile the growth of the Church in the city essentially stopped. Initially organized with 2,000 members, by 1937 the stake had declined to 1,885, perhaps because of the formation of the Metuchen branch outside the stake in 1936. Hard times prevented Utah-based Church members from moving to New York City to pursue schooling or careers. Meanwhile, Church members with specialized training, including scientists Harvey Fletcher, Carl Christensen, Melvin Cook and Preston Robinson, stayed near New York City because of better job opportunities.

In response to the economic crisis, the Church started the welfare program, and the New York Stake was asked to participate. Stake members pooled their resources and purchased an entire railroad carload of wheat, which was divided among the members. The wheat was stored in their homes and apartments.

However, Woolfe said that the wheat wasn't used quite as the Church anticipated. After World War II ended, the Church asked its members for donations to alleviate starvation in Europe. In New York, Church members donated the same railroad carload of wheat.

One way the New York Stake addressed the Depression was through a stake employment office run by Roscoe Turner, Sr., a convert from the South. Turner used a variety of methods to find employment for Church members – telephone calls, letters, stickers, even going so far as to tell companies in the city that Church members would be high-quality employees who were "sober on Monday mornings, who weren't quarrelsome, and who were conscientious." Woolfe, a member of the stake presidency during the Depression, said that the employment office placed 300 people a year, on average.

In 1936, the stake's first president, Fred G. Taylor, was released and renowned scientist Harvey Fletcher was called in his place. While Fletcher led the stake, another branch was created in northern New Jersey; a portion of the stake was split off into the Metuchen Branch (part of the Eastern States Mission); and the Oceanside Branch, previously a dependent branch of the Queens Ward, was made an independent branch.

But growth did not come quickly. Woolfe described a pattern in which ward membership often changed because a respected member moved to another ward or branch and other members followed. But larger factors would soon alter the Church in the city even more.

## WORLD WAR II

With the advent of the war, the activities of the Church in New York City changed dramatically. The Hill Cumorah Pageant, which New York City members helped organize, was shut down and the scientific and military expertise of many stake leaders was absorbed into the war effort. The war also increased the number of visitors to the city, bringing in new faces and taking others away.

In support of the war effort, the New York Relief Society helped members add black window shades to conform to blackout regulations. Members lived through gas rationing and meat shortages. Some worked in war-related businesses. Joseph Strobel converted his factory to produce airplane parts and employed several Church members there, while scientists Henry Eyring, Harvey Fletcher, Carl J. Christensen and others were drawn into war-related scientific projects. The war brought other scientists and engineers to New York City, including Corbett Aamodt, who worked on the Manhattan Project. Their efforts had a direct effect on the war since research by Carl Christensen led to the discovery of a German submarine in New York Harbor.

The war also affected the local Church buildings. In 1943, the U.S. Navy WAVES took over the hotel where the Manhattan ward met, forcing it to move back to Steinway Hall on West 57th Street. The ward stayed there until the end of the war, when the Church was able to purchase a building on West 81st Street.

During the war, the wards served as a social center for LDS servicemen who passed through on their way to Europe. One group of 14 LDS servicemen from California attended the Manhattan ward while studying an electronics course in New York. They brought along with them a nonmember named Earl Tound who, when forced to remain in New York because of a medical condition, continued attending the Manhattan Ward and was eventually baptized.

## POST-WAR RENEWAL

The end of World War II allowed the Church to improve its facilities in the city. Seeking a more substantial presence, the Church purchased a new mission home at 973 Fifth Avenue in 1948. The building was designed in 1903 by noted architect Stanford White and was built as a wedding present to the Count and Countess de Heredia of France by the Countess's father, General McCook. It featured imported furnishings from France and Italy, including old masters paintings. The home remained the headquarters of the Eastern States Mission until its sale in 1973.

In 1946, the stake put on a centennial celebration commemorating the sailing of the ship *Brooklyn* from New York City in 1846. That celebration included a Sunday evening pageant written by New York University professor and Church member Howard Driggs.

The same year the stake suffered the loss of some prestigious and long-time members when University of Utah president L. Ray Olpin persuaded three members to move their families to Salt Lake City and join his faculty. Henry Eyring, Carl J. Christensen and Preston Robinson all left that year.

Following World War II, the Church's leadership asked the stake to purchase a welfare farm as part of its welfare program. However, the stake had difficulty finding a suitable property. Finally, a working but somewhat run-down farm was purchased in 1953.

Located some 50 miles west of New York City off of Route 31 in New Jersey, the farm was used throughout the 1950s and 1960s, and the stake spent a considerable amount of effort improving the farm. Eventually, stake leaders became frustrated with the difficulties that the farm faced, and the farm was sold in 1970 at a large profit, leading some members to conclude that New York Mormons were better at investing than at farming.

## GRADUAL GROWTH

From the beginning of the stake in 1934 until the early 1950s, the stake remained basically the same size with four wards and three branches, although some boundaries and names were changed. Then, in the mid 1950s, the stake finally began to grow, principally in the city's suburbs.

The Church also began to see New York as a place to demonstrate the accomplishments of its members. In 1958, the Mormon Tabernacle Choir came to New York to perform in Carnegie Hall. About this time, Sister Ellen N. Barnes of the General Board of the Relief Society, then residing in Washington, D.C., established the Relief Society Singing Mothers, which came to New York to sing in the Grand Ballroom of the Waldorf-Astoria Hotel as part of the National American Mothers Annual Awards Banquet. Later the Utah Symphony came to New York, performing in Carnegie Hall.

In 1960, the Church's growth in the city reached another milestone when the stake was divided for the first time. The Short Hills and North Jersey Wards and the Montclair Branch were combined with the Metuchen, Monmouth and Trenton Branches from the New Jersey District of the Eastern States Mission to form the New Jersey Stake. Southwestern Connecticut was transferred to the New York Stake from the Eastern States Mission. Stake President George Mortimer continued as president of the New Jersey Stake, while his counselor, G. Stanley McAllister, was called as president of the New York Stake.

## THE WORLD'S FAIR

In the 1960s, the stake growth mushroomed due to the LDS Church's sponsorship of the Mormon Pavilion at the 1964 New York World's Fair. The Mormon Pavilion was the brainchild of G. Stanley McAllister. He persuaded Church leaders in Salt Lake City to attempt this new approach to reaching non-members, and he spearheaded the complex task of negotiating the Church's participation in this world-famous event.

Unlike the growth of the previous decade, the baptisms from the World's Fair came in all areas of the stake. In the first year the Mormon Pavilion saw 3.1 million visitors, with as many as 34,000 a day. That generated 250,000 missionary referrals, many of which were local.

Those referrals had an almost immediate effect on baptisms. Mission President Wilburn West reported that where the New York Stake had 165 baptisms in 1963, it nearly tripled to 483 in 1964.

In Manhattan, Bishop Earl Tingey said his ward saw almost 100 baptisms in 1964, and 197 the following year. The Church assigned 12 Spanish-speaking missionaries to New York City during the second year of the World's Fair because Spanish speakers' interest in the Church was so high. The Church also purchased a brownstone adjacent to the Manhattan chapel during the Fair to accommodate the swelling size of the Manhattan Ward, which reached 1100 members of record by the time it was split in 1965.

On Long Island, growth attributable to the World's Fair led to the formation of a new stake (now the Plainview New York Stake) the following year—the second time the New York Stake had been split in seven years.

The Mormon Pavilion was also used to help strengthen the youth of the Church along the East Coast. Winifred Bowers reported that the stake held a three- or four-day youth conference during the Fair, attracting youth from as far away as Florida. The youth visited the Mormon Pavilion, saw the rest of the Fair, and heard from speakers, including a representative of the Church's First Presidency.

The World's Fair left the New York Stake a very different stake from what it had been 30 years earlier. In place of one small, fledgling unit far from Church headquarters that struggled for 20 years before major growth, there were three rapidly-growing stakes. The New York Stake itself was smaller and included a new demographic: Spanish-speaking, urban residents. In the process of local growth, the stake also made an important impact on the worldwide Church.

**PRESIDENT HEBER J. GRANT**, who organized the New York Stake in 1934.
**RENOWNED SCIENTIST HARVEY FLETCHER** was called to be the second president of the New York Stake in 1936. He is the grandfather of D. Fletcher, a stake member who today is in the Manhattan First Ward. Courtesy of the Church Archives, The Church of Jesus Christ of Latter-day Saints.
**SCIENTIST HENRY EYRING'S** family lived in the stake, in Princeton, New Jersey, until they moved to Utah in 1946. One of his sons, Henry B. Eyring, grew up in New Jersey and is today an Apostle in the Quorum of the Twelve. Courtesy of the Church Archives, The Church of Jesus Christ of Latter-day Saints.
**GEORGE MORTIMER**, stake president of the New York Stake until it was reorganized in 1960. President Mortimer was then called as stake president in New Jersey. Courtesy of the Church Archives, The Church of Jesus Christ of Latter-day Saints.

## VISITING THE MORMON PAVILION: THE MORMONS' GLOBAL INTRODUCTION AT THE WORLD'S FAIR OF 1964 TAYLOR PETREY

The 1964 World's Fair was held at Flushing Meadows Park in New York City's borough of Queens. The Fair lasted two seasons, 1964 and 1965. One of its memorable features was the participation of religious organizations, including Catholics, Protestants, Christian Scientists, and the Church of Jesus Christ of Latter-day Saints.

The Church sponsored a visitors' site that came to be known as the "Mormon Pavilion." It was so successful as a global missionary tool that it changed the face of missionary work forever in New York City and the Church as a whole. The idea to participate in the fair came from New York Stake President Stanley McAllister. Through the help of LDS missionaries and hundreds of New York Latter-day Saints, the Pavilion became the proselyting opportunity of the century.[1]

### THE MORMON PAVILION

The Mormon Pavilion was among the first things people saw upon entering the Fair. It was a 12-story replica of the façade of the Salt Lake Temple. Standing 127-feet in the air, it was the tallest structure in the park except for the massive symbol of the Fair itself, the Unisphere.[2]

When Church leaders from Salt Lake City and local members met to dedicate the structure for the fair, the New York Times reported the meeting was "the largest assemblage of Mormon officials to gather in the East since the Mormons went west in 1846"[3]

The Mormon Pavilion and its expansive gardens became a popular and picturesque tourist spot, visited by nearly six million people. The Pavilion was featured on post cards and in an estimated 1,075,000 photographs.[4]

### PAVILION ART

Inside the Pavilion, the LDS Church pioneered new uses of art and technology to promote its image. Church officials commissioned and acquired new statues, dioramas, and displays for its 15,000-square foot exhibition space. All of the artwork was original and on display for the first time.

Among the most noteworthy acquisitions was The Christus by Italian sculptor Aldo Rebechi. The statue is a reproduction of the original carved by the famous Dutch sculptor Bertel Thorvaldsen. Today the piece is well known in LDS culture, but at the time the Church had not featured artwork with physical depictions of Jesus Christ.[5]

Another well-known piece of Mormon culture was born at the World's Fair—the film Man's Search for Happiness produced by the Brigham Young University Motion Picture Studio, under the supervision of Elder Harold B. Lee and Church President David O. McKay. The film's message was intended to complement the theme of the World's Fair, "Peace Through Understanding."

**PAVILION TOURS**

*Full-time missionaries gave scripted guided tours starting with* The Christus *and then to view other art, the film, and large dioramas about LDS Church history and the life of Christ. The tour did not provide time to ask questions, but visitors could fill out a registration card with comments or request a visit from missionaries.*

*One frequent topic of the day in 1964 and 1965 was the issue of Civil Rights. Missionaries were often asked about the position of African Americans in the Church, since blacks could not hold the priesthood at the time. Meanwhile, a lack of diversity at the Pavilion and in the Church at that time created unique challenges for members and missionaries who worked at the Fair.*

*During the entire 1964 season of the World's Fair, no tours were officially offered in any languages other than English. Some missionaries happened to speak a second language and gave spontaneous tours. By far, Spanish was the most-requested foreign language. When Church leaders realized the need, the first 12 Spanish-speaking missionaries were sent to New York City for the Fair.*

*These efforts and the Church's involvement in the Fair were symbolic of the Church's shift from a provincial Utah organization to its presence as a worldwide church. The Mormon Pavilion helped the Church's reputation and strengthened its core membership on the East Coast and, particularly, in New York City.*

Church President Heber J. Grant (front left) with members of the first stake presidency: Fred G. Taylor (front right), (back row, left to right) Ivor Sharp, Howard S. Bennion and Hakon H. Haglund. Photo courtesy of the New York New York Stake.

1960 New York Stake conference with Apostle Spencer W. Kimball. Earlier that day Stake President George Mortimer said the congregation looked like the scattering of Israel, and charged the members to fill the imposing hall. Photo courtesy of the New York New York Stake.

This former Jewish synagogue at 142 West 81st Street was purchased by the LDS Church and used as a meetinghouse from 1945 until 1975, when the stake center was built at Lincoln Square. Photo courtesy of the New York New York Stake.

The 1964 World's Fair in New York City was a turning point for the Church in the metro area. LDS units exploded with new members who had been referred to the missionaries after their experiences at the Fair. Notably, the Spanish-language Spanish-American Branch in Manhattan and the Rego Park Branch in urban Queens were formed to accomodate new demographics in membership.

The Mormon Pavilion at the 1964 New York World's Fair introduced thousands of vistitors to the LDS Church. Stake President Stanley McAllister spearheaded the project. A New York high council member at the time, Apostle, Tom Perry helped coordinate local participation.

## 1964-1997
# WELCOME TO THE WORLD
JAMES LUCAS

### IMPACT OF THE MORMON PAVILION

On a global scale, the Church did not keep precise statistics on the number of missionary referrals or baptisms attributable to the Mormon Pavilion at the 1964 New York World's Fair.[1] However, the Pavilion's local effects were clear. Every unit in New York City saw numbers of new converts. In addition, the Pavilion had two specific impacts that may have seemed small at the time, but which proved to be especially significant.

The first of these was to launch a branch in the heart of Queens, the home of the Fair. Elder L. Tom Perry, who served on the New York Stake high council at the time, estimated that this branch, located in Rego Park, owed 75% of its membership to the Mormon Pavilion.[2] While there was a ward housed in a traditional colonial style chapel in the Little Neck area of northeastern Queens before the World's Fair, it had served an automobile-based suburban membership primarily of transplanted westerners. The new Rego Park Branch was the first significant establishment of the Church in urban Queens. Today, the area originally covered by this one branch contains the largest concentration of Latter-day Saints in New York City.

The second, and even more significant, development was the establishment of the first Spanish language unit in the city in May 1965. Although there were some Hispanic members before then, Spanish-speaking converts from the Mormon Pavilion were the main impetus for the creation of the Spanish-American Branch which met in the Church's brownstone building on West 81st Street in Manhattan. As of the year 2004, there were over 40 Spanish language units in New York City and adjoining areas. The original Spanish branch created in 1965 (now the Manhattan Fourth Ward) may be seen as the mother congregation of half of all the present Latter-day Saints in the metropolitan area.

### A STAKE CENTER

This growth led to impossible strain on the existing Church facilities. Small chapels were built in Rego Park and Staten Island. However, the Church's most important solution was to build a major new facility in Manhattan.

The West 81st Street building had become inadequate to accommodate the units meeting there. Furthermore, its location on the west side was regarded as undesirable by many members living on the east side of Manhattan, who often held their meetings at the mission home then located at 973 Fifth Avenue. Church officials initially looked at sites near Fifth Avenue for a new chapel. (Until recently, the office building at 9 West 57th Street featured unused exterior escalators leading down to a very visible but closed lower level which was originally designed to house Church meeting facilities.)

The Lincoln Center for the Performing Arts had recently been completed, but Lincoln Square was not, at the time, a prime real estate area. The neighborhood was in a general state of disrepair. In fact, Lincoln Center had been originally proposed principally as an urban renewal project. The slum-like tenements that were demolished to make way for the construction of Lincoln Center were first used as the set for the 1961 movie version of *West Side Story*. A parking lot and some dilapidated tenements occupied the block along Columbus Avenue between West 65th and 66th Streets.

One may well use the term prophetic to describe any decision to build a major facility over that particular site. In 1970, George Mortimer, a local Church leader and the Church's attorney, accompanied President Harold B. Lee in inspecting possible sites for the new Manhattan building. Brother Mortimer described their visit to the Lincoln Square site: "I want to walk out on it," said President Lee, getting out of the cab. After standing on the ground about three minutes, he declared, "George, this is the place the Lord wants. Buy it."[3]

With a marquee temple now standing on the property, it may fairly be said that the Church probably possesses few properties of the quality and visibility of the Lincoln Square site. The building dedicated by President Spencer W. Kimball on May 25, 1975, symbolized a renewed commitment of resources by the Church to America's premier urban center.

## THE "SUBWAY" STAKE

The New York Stake created in 1934 covered a vast area comprising not only New York City, but much of New Jersey and suburbs of New York City to the north in New York state and east to the end of Long Island. New Jersey became a separate stake in 1960; a suburban Long Island stake was formed in 1967. Although the remaining stake consisting of New York City and the northern suburbs was technically headquartered at the new Lincoln Square stake center, suburban wards provided the bulk of the stake leadership.

In 1978 the total representation of New York City residents in stake leadership consisted of two regular high counselors and one alternate, one counselor in the Young Men, Primary, and Sunday School presidencies, the Relief Society garment representative, and one member of the stake activities committee.

Thus on April 30, 1978 when Elder Robert D. Hales, a native of Queens, created the Kitchawan Stake (subsequently renamed the Yorktown New York Stake) covering the northern suburbs, the New York City stake leadership transferred almost en masse to the new stake. Elder Hales pointedly joked that church members needed to remember that the Kitchawan Stake was the new stake, not the city stake. It was the remaining New York City Stake that needed to be organized almost from scratch.

Another challenge seemed even more daunting. The city "subway" stake was reportedly the first stake in the Church consisting only of the inner city without the "support" of wards from adjoining suburbs. Its membership was very diverse in many respects. Ethnic and linguistic minorities, particularly Hispanics, were numerous. In addition, singles and younger adults constituted an unusually large part of the stake membership in comparison with the perceived norms of the Church.

The new stake president was Frank Miller, one of the few New York City resident members of the high council from the prior stake leadership. A Salt Lake City native who lived in Brooklyn, he established a policy of broad inclusiveness in the new stake organization. Hispanic members served in the stake presidency, high council, and stake auxiliary presidencies regardless of English language proficiency or residency status. Single members also served throughout the stake, with many single men serving on the high council and as bishopric counselors.

The diversity of the stake received a further significant impetus a few months after its creation when President Spencer W. Kimball announced the historic revelation extending the priesthood to worthy men of all races. The long-term impact of this revelation on the Church in New York City can be seen today in the numerous majority black Church units in Brooklyn, Queens, and the Bronx, and the fact that an estimated one in every five New York City Latter-day Saints is black.

Another major impetus toward diversity came a year later in April 1979, when President Kimball issued a special appeal to accelerate missionary work among linguistic minorities in urban areas where the Church was established. Missionaries trained in Chinese, Korean, Polish, Greek, and Russian were added to the Spanish-speaking missionaries who had served in New York City since the creation of the first Spanish-speaking branch in the mid-1960s. Shortly thereafter, a Chinese-speaking branch was formed in Brooklyn and a Korean-speaking branch was formed in Queens.

# FRANK W. MILLER NEW YORK STAKE PRESIDENT 1978-1985

*Drawn from interviews in March 1997 and February 1998 by* Jim Lucas *with* Frank Miller

**JIM** *Now, we come to the time when a new stake was created in Westchester. Tell us the story of the creation of that stake and of the new stake leadership in New York City.*

**FRANK** *The application had gone in three or four times to, as it was put, "create a stake in New York City." Actually, it was to create a stake in the northern suburbs, where most of the people and leadership lived, and leave the existing stake in New York City. The application had been turned down three times. Then Robert Hales came in April 1978, and was given the assignment to create the stake if he felt it was the right thing to do. But if not, he was not to do it.*

*Elder Hales came on a Friday and interviewed people in the southern part of the stake for New York Stake leadership. At that time, the boundary for the Westchester and Manhattan First Wards was changed to the Westchester/Bronx county lines, which sent a few people from the Westchester Ward into the Manhattan First Ward.*

*[President Miller was called as president of the New York Stake, and Al Woodhouse and Manuel Nieto were called as his counselors.]*

**FRANK** *We didn't have a complete organization. First we had to select bishops to replace the two men called as my counselors. We had to fill a high council—we ended up with only ten at the time; six of them had to be ordained high priests. We called a counselor in the two ward bishoprics to be bishops, and each of their counselors had to be ordained high priests. So we had ten people presented to be high priests that day.*

*We didn't have a complete auxiliary, but at least we had the basics—stake and assistant stake clerks, executive secretary—a bare-bones structure. Thora Allan was called as Relief Society president. Bill Quayle was Sunday School president. Clara Neu became the Primary president. She had never had an administrative position in the Church, but had always been connected with music. Jean Woodhouse was the stake Young Women president, and George Arrington was the stake Young Men president. . .*

*There is something else interesting about this time. When Bishop Nieto was called to serve in the first stake presidency, he asked Elder Hales for a blessing to help him with the language. Prior to this, as I was working with the young men and the scouts in the stake, I had many dealings with Bishop Nieto. Whenever I want-*

ed to talk to him, he would call his second counselor, Luis Rojas, in to translate. The day the stake was organized, we discussed and called a stake clerk, Larry Stay, who spoke very fluent Spanish.

But later in the evening, after President Nieto's blessing, we called Luis Rojas—who had acted as translator for Brother Nieto—to the high council. He came in to be interviewed by the stake presidency, but couldn't understand. President Nieto had to translate for him that evening. The process of communication in organizing the stake was very interesting.

**JIM** I've wondered about two decisions that were taken then. One was that people didn't have to speak English to serve in the stake, and the other was that people didn't have to have all their immigration papers in order before they could serve in Church callings. Were those deliberate decisions or did it just sort of happen that way?

**FRANK** The first was a deliberate decision. We had to find a way for people who don't speak English to serve. A sister (Florencia Rodriguez) from the Manhattan Spanish ward was called as Clara Neu's counselor in the stake Primary, and she later served as president. She didn't speak English at all, but we felt the language problems could be solved.

On immigration, we followed Church guidelines. Up to the mid-1970s, the policy had been that anyone illegally in the United States could not receive the priesthood, go to the temple, or serve in church callings. But the policy had just been changed, as it became clear that many of these people would never have a chance to go to the temple, which for the men required ordination to the Melchizedek Priesthood. Some had come here specifically to go to the temple. So the rules were relaxed, also about serving in callings.

**JIM** Could you take us through the Frank Miller years of the New York City Stake? How did things progress; what were some of your continuing challenges and memorable experiences?

**FRANK** In 1978, when the suburbs were sent packing, the New York Stake was just the five boroughs of New York City. There were only about 1,800 members in six units (three Manhattan wards, the Brooklyn Ward, the Staten Island Branch, and the Brooklyn Spanish Branch). In 1979, at a regional representatives seminar, President Kimball talked about taking the gospel to all nations of the world. And initially the idea was to form branches in the great cities of the world, which could draw people to them. President Kimball specifically mentioned New York City, and challenged the five language groups represented by members here.

The stake started looking around. There were already two Spanish-speaking units—Brooklyn, which had been made a separate independent branch the same day I was called as stake president, as one of my recommendations; and a Manhattan unit—a dependent branch of the Manhattan First Ward, which met in the Bronx in a school, with the sacrament meeting being held in the library where 52 people could physically sit down. The average sacrament meeting attendance was 55.

The first priority was to get a building in the Bronx. After some finagling with the Church real estate department (before there was a physical facilities department headquartered in Minneapolis), we were able to buy a used building in early 1979. Jimmy Wright in Salt Lake sent some people here, who agreed that the Olmstead Avenue Chapel was a good deal. This was actually the school of a Presbyterian congregation, and the cafeteria/gymnasium area was made into a chapel. Shortly thereafter an English and a Spanish-speaking unit were formed in the Bronx.

In the stake there was also a member of the Brooklyn Ward, Brother Kang Woo Lee, who had been one of the original bishops when the Seoul Korea Stake was formed. He came to me and said that he felt sure there were a lot of Korean people in the city who were members of the Church but did not come out. He suggested advertising a special meeting in the Korean newspaper, to be held in the fourth floor of the Lincoln Center building, which had now become our stake center. He also knew that the man in charge of all Church real estate in Korea was coming to general conference, and suggested inviting him to New York the week after that for the special meeting.

I agreed, and he paid for the advertisement in the Korean newspaper, with the result that 20 or 30 people came out. He suggested trying it again the next week. After five or six weeks, it was decided to form a Korean Branch, which was done in June 1979 with Kang Woo Lee as the first branch president, and Korean members serving as the leaders. [Editor's note: at the time of this publication, Brother Lee is serving in the Manhattan New York Temple presidency] *Jim Lucas was called as their high council adviser; and later it was Scott Rasmussen, who had served a mission in Korea.*

**JIM** *When I was called, I was very young and inexperienced, and spoke no Korean. The thing that saved me was that Brother Lee spoke very good English, and that Scott Rasmussen came to Columbia Law School shortly thereafter, and stayed on in the city. He would hang out with them and informally help me as translator.*

**FRANK** *There were all kinds of young people in the new stake, and we had no preconceived notions when we called someone to a position. We just called the people we had. There were single high councilman, members of bishoprics who were single, as well as Relief Society presidents.*

**JIM** *I was far from the only high priest in his 20's in those days. Now, tell us about the Chinese unit.*

**FRANK** *At the same time the Korean branch was formed, we realized that we had as many members who were from China. It seemed right to do the same thing there. We called Kai Wan Mui—who had been a branch president in Hong Kong before coming to the United States—to be the president of a Chinese branch here in 1979. In both these cases we had seasoned leaders in the city.*

*At the outset of the organization of the Chinese Branch—which, like Hong Kong, was Cantonese-speaking—the vast majority of members were Muis. President Mui had eight children, some of them married. Shirley and Pauline came from Queens. Isabel was living on Long Island, I think...*

**JIM** *During this time, the Spanish-speaking membership of the Church started to grow significantly, I believe.*

**FRANK** *The first Spanish-speaking unit was the Spanish American Branch in Manhattan, after we disbanded our group in Brooklyn in 1965, to enable the establishment of a branch. In fact, we sent a brother over to be a counselor in the new branch presidency. Another Spanish-speaking unit was started in the late 1960s/ early 1970s in Brooklyn because of the need to take into account the distances members had to travel. That became an official unit in 1978 when I was called as stake president. By the time I was released as stake president, and growing out of discussions at regional meetings, there were nine Spanish-speaking units in the region.*

*Most of the leadership in these units came from the Manhattan Spanish Ward. The Bronx Spanish unit was formed in 1979, when a building was purchased. In the Elmhurst Spanish unit in the Long Island Stake, Brother Ramírez, a former high priest group leader in the Manhattan Spanish Ward, was called as branch president. The Caldwell New Jersey Stake started forming units with people from our stake who were released from their calls in the Manhattan Spanish Ward to serve in the new units. One of them was Elder Rodriguez, the elders quorum president in the Manhattan Spanish Ward, who was transferred to the Patterson-area unit.*

*One of the things I instituted as stake president was looking the other way on membership issues. We found that the kids in seminary from the Spanish-speaking units didn't all read Spanish. They read English because they had been born and raised here. There were problems with homework when they were expected to attend seminary in a Spanish-speaking unit. So, working with the youth committee, it was decided that young people could attend the English-speaking seminary outside their own units. The youth were concerned that during their teenage years they learn the most they could about the gospel, to prepare for missions, and in general, to grow spiritually...*

**JIM** *Another example of this was the symbiotic relationship between the Korean Branch and the Manhattan First Ward, which held a joint Primary and youth program.*

**FRANK** *Yes. And along those lines, in the summer of 1985, the stake created—not a singles ward, but—a family ward.* The idea was presented to the First Presidency, after we had looked around and found that it was difficult for the three Manhattan wards (the Manhattan Third Ward had been formed in 1980, when the consolidated meeting schedule came into existence, and it was then possible to fit three wards into the Lincoln Center building) to run separate youth programs. It took a lot of people and a lot of time for very few youth. It made sense in Manhattan to have all the youth attend one ward, where the activities could be concentrated.

Mike Young—my counselor then, who succeeded me as stake president—looked at the demographics of the wards and found that there were not that many families in the Manhattan First and Third Wards with older children. The first ward had lots of law students with small children, but few were school-age yet. . . . We recommended that anybody with children in the first grade through high school become members of the Manhattan Second Ward. That affected, I think, only three families in the Manhattan Third Ward and two in the Manhattan First Ward. This allowed each ward to still have a young Primary. The singles said one of the disadvantages of a singles ward was that you don't see any children. So each ward could have a young Primary, but no youth program. All efforts for that program were concentrated in the Manhattan Second Ward, where it became stronger. I think this worked quite well although I wasn't around long enough to really know as I became part of the newly formed New York New York East Stake shortly thereafter.

**JIM** *How long did you serve as stake president?*

**FRANK** *Seven and a half years.*

**JIM** *Can you think of other significant events that occurred during that time?*

**FRANK** *One of the big things we did was the commemoration of the 50th anniversary of the stake . . . we decided to have a special sacrament meeting.* It happened that the exact day of the organization, December 9, was again a Sunday in 1984, 50 years later.

A sacrament meeting for the whole stake was planned. There were sacrament tables all through the second and fourth floors, and three on the third floor. People acting as priests and deacons—many of them Melchizedek Priesthood holders—were at each of the tables. A prayer was said at a microphone and piped throughout the building. Sacrament trays had been brought in from outlying branches and more were ordered from Salt Lake. Some of these had to be sent by Federal Express because the original order still had not arrived after six weeks. There were all kinds of logistical problems.

Several speakers covered the history of the stake, followed by a slide show with as many pictures as could be gathered together. Afton Miles organized that...

Different people portrayed participants in the organization of the stake such as J. Reuben Clark, who had been a law student in New York. Clara Neu came back as organist for the event. Afton Miles led the choir in a special number with Tom Vogelman on the piano joining Clara at the organ. All the people who participated in the preparation through to the presentation, including serving the sacrament, were listed in an insert. The closing prayer was given by a member of the Chinese Branch... There were about 66 people on the planning/presentation side and 70 people participating in serving the sacrament. There were well over 1,000 - 1,300 or 1,400 people as I recall in attendance that day. New Jersey, Long Island, and Yorktown Stake members had also been invited although they are no longer part of the New York New York Stake... The program brought a lot of people back together.

**JIM** *You mentioned that when the Yorktown (originally Kitchawan) Stake was organized out of the New York New York Stake, there had been some concern among the brethren about having an entirely inner-city stake.*

**FRANK** We had a different stake from the rest. We didn't have executives leading ours... Our high council was not made up, for the most part, of business professionals. We had George Mortimer who was an experienced professional and some young up-and-coming people... but there were also factory workers, school teachers, graduate students serving in leadership positions. Don Allan [an artist] wasn't called originally but shortly thereafter as assistant stake clerk, although he was only here six months a year, but served a very useful purpose.

Our people were not necessarily managers in their daily work, so they had to rely on the Lord. Therefore, we were very successful. It turned out that our stake led the mission in baptisms. In my seven and a half years as stake president, our membership went from 1,800 to 4,000. We created a sixth branch at the time I was called. When I was released there were 11 branches. There were two buildings when I began and four when I left. Plus, in that time period, many people attending the Manhattan Spanish Ward were sent out to help form wards in Elmhurst (Queens), and in Patterson, Jersey City, and Newark (New Jersey), all having been trained in our stake. Our stake was a success.

Sure, there were problems running things efficiently. Our reports weren't always on time. In fact, they were rarely on time. It was interesting when President

*Thomas S. Monson (then Elder Monson of the Quorum of the Twelve) came out for stake conference in 1982. . . Although nothing had been mentioned before about reports being late or slow, he made the comment while I was driving him to the airport that reports weren't the only thing. Working with people and their growth were what mattered. . .*

We had counted once that active members in our stake were born in 50 different missions.

**JIM** *I remember hearing at the time that the Spanish Ward had members from 23 different countries.*

**FRANK** *That's where a lot of diversity came from. And the Brooklyn Ward had members from 35 different countries. On the subject of diversity, people might think that all Spanish-speakers are similar but cultural, even language differences are wide ranging. A word used in El Salvador could have a quite different meaning in Argentina. Everybody learned a lot.*

Our youth and seminary programs were quite good. A lot of missionaries were sent out...

**JIM** *Did you personally find it difficult presiding over a stake where a large number of members spoke a language that you didn't?*

**FRANK** *I found it difficult presiding over a stake, period. Let me tell you two different experiences I had as a stake president. I had learned all the interview questions in Spanish as well as English, so I could look people in the eye when I was asking them a question. One time there was a problem in the Manhattan Spanish Ward. I was asked to come and intercede. I was in a room across from the bishop's office with the people involved. As they were telling me the story, I understood what the problem was. I didn't need the interpreter. My response had to be interpreted, but I experienced the gift of comprehension at that time.*

Paul Gunther got a missionary training manual for Spanish and organized classes for us. We weren't all so successful, I have difficulty with languages, but somehow the comprehension was often there.

Another time I was interviewing a sister from Switzerland, then a member in Brooklyn, for a temple recommend. She spoke German, French, and Italian as well as English. I had interviewed her in English before. She was elderly though, in her 70s, and losing her faculties, especially in English. Bishop Quayle's son had been on a mission to France and came in to serve as an interpreter. I greeted her in German, because I knew some from having lived in Germany and studying it in college. That started her train of thought in German. When I asked her questions in English, which Billy translated into French, she would answer in German. And

*I understood. She would have been fine in French had I not spoken to her in German. The interpreter, of course, had no idea what was being said. Funny things can happen.*

**JIM** *Tell us about what led up to the division of the stake and to your release.*

**FRANK** *We had thought of creating a Spanish-speaking stake. Nine units in our area were Spanish-speaking. It seemed the way to go. . .*

*Franklin D. Richards, who was then senior president of the Seventy, and Paul Thompson, our regional representative, called me to meet with them at Newark Airport after a conference they had attended in a New Jersey stake. After I had argued the case for a Spanish-speaking stake, I was told that the stake was to be divided on a geographic rather than language basis. We were to put in the papers, and make it happen NOW. And that's what we did.*

*We proposed, and the Church approved, the creation of a Brooklyn New York Stake, with 60% of the members in Brooklyn and some from Queens. Two of the three units in Queens already had members living in Brooklyn, including a bishop in one of the Queens units. Staten Island was also included in the new stake. . .*

*Richard Scott, then a member of the Quorum of Seventies before being called as an Apostle, was assigned to do the division. He spoke fluent Spanish and was there to go over things with the Plainview and New York stake presidencies before the division. One idea was to cut the boundary at the East River, which I said made no sense. A lot of the Manhattan Second Ward was in Astoria and Long Island City and could get to the New York stake center more easily than to Rego Park. So it was decided to go by subway lines. That meant Astoria and Long Island City remained part of the New York New York Stake [as the new stake would be called, not the Brooklyn New York Stake]. Transportation is always a key factor. . .*

*A year later the new stake presidents, Mike Young and Mark Butler, changed [the stake boundaries]...Now all of Queens is part of the Queens West District instead of the New York New York Stake.*

Frank Miller was born and raised in Salt Lake City and attended the University of Pennsylvania, after which he married his high school sweetheart and settled permanently in Brooklyn in 1964. He was branch president of the Brooklyn Branch and then bishop of the Brooklyn Ward for 11 years, from 1965 until 1976. He was called as stake president of the New York Stake in 1978 and served until 1985. Frank's wife Alice is a methods and resource teacher for parents and teachers who are working to include children with disabilities in a classroom. In 1985 she was selected as New York State Mother of the Year.

## GROWTH AND CHALLENGES

Despite its challenges, the New York City Stake saw remarkable growth from a number of sources. Improvements in the city's economy in the 1980s helped bring an increased influx of Church members from other parts of the United States to pursue careers and education. Columbia University's law school went from having less than a handful of LDS students in the 1970s to consistently always having from 20 to 30 in the late 1980s to the present. Another significant influx of Church members came from Latin America, where the Church had begun to realize major growth in the 1960s. These Latin American immigrants provided a leadership core for the increasing number of Spanish language units and may now constitute a quarter or more of the Hispanic Latter-day Saints in New York City.

However, the largest source of Church growth in New York City came from new converts. With the liberalization of U.S. immigration laws in the 1960s and the city's improved economy in the 1980s, a new wave of immigration to New York City began. Whereas previous immigrants had come from various parts of Europe, major migrations now came to New York City "from all parts of the world," as Joseph Smith had put it in his 1832 letter to his wife Emma.

It was among these new immigrant communities that the LDS missionaries found their principal reception. In addition to the Latin American groups, significant numbers of converts were found among immigrants from the French and English-speaking Caribbean and Africa. A smaller number came from Asia and Eastern Europe. By November 17, 1985, only seven years after the previous stake division, the New York New York East Stake was formed covering Brooklyn, most of Queens, and Staten Island. The New York Stake was comprised of Manhattan and the Bronx.

Such rapid growth brought many challenges. Experienced leadership was thin, and convert retention difficult. In addition, supplying suitable meeting places was a problem. Constructing traditional Church buildings in New York City was very expensive, and the Manhattan-centered subway system made commuting to meeting houses in the other boroughs difficult.

Then, in the early 1990s, Church leaders implemented an unexpected reorganization on the Church in New York City. The New York New York East Stake was dissolved on May 19, 1991, and a mission district formed in its place. A mission district was also formed in the Bronx, which was thus removed from the New York Stake. Wards from southern Westchester County were added to the New York Stake, creating a bi-polar entity. Initially, it appeared that there would be a reversion to the old pattern of having the suburban wards dominate the stake leadership.

## MICHAEL YOUNG  NEW YORK NEW YORK STAKE PRESIDENT
1985-1989

Michael Young was called as stake president in 1985, the year in which the New York Stake was divided in two. Prior to that time, the stake under President Frank Miller encompassed virtually all of New York City: Brooklyn, Staten Island, the Bronx, Manhattan and part of Queens.

Young was called to preside over Manhattan and the Bronx, and Mark Butler took the leadership of the New York East Stake comprising the other boroughs (save for the greater part of Queens). The newly reorganized New York Stake consisted of three wards, English and Spanish language branches in The Bronx, and Hispanic and Korean branches.

The immediate challenge facing President Young was to make up a $70,000 deficit that had developed largely through inexperienced unit leadership, lack of attention to the budget, and unsound bookkeeping practices. Fortunately, he was able to persuade the Church to forgive the debt and at the same time stake clerks were assigned to supervise ward and branch financial clerks. The new stake began its life afresh without the stultifying weight of financial burden.

President Young was 36 when called as stake president by Richard G. Scott of the Quorum of the Twelve. He speculated that the members, seeing 'kids' had been put in charge, realized the new presidency needed help. When interviewed, he repeatedly expressed thanks for the support Church members gave him.

When he became stake president, five of the six units were crowded into the stake center, making the need for property obvious. Yet the scarcity of eligible sites and the high prices hampered building expansion.

Possible sites in the Bronx or the Village seemed too costly or undesirable because of run down neighborhoods. President Young felt the urban Church had to be served despite the cost. He believed that if Church members in large cities were to have experiences comparable to suburban members, extra expenditures and adaptation to unusual conditions would be necessary.

The most obvious answer was to expand the existing stake center where the top two floors were privately owned. The owner, Joel Banker, offered to sell that space when the health club housed there proved to be impractical, but what seemed like a reasonable price in New York seemed out of sight to the Church's building department. To make the offer more appealing, President Young and his counselor Eliot Brinton proposed turning the space into a temple. They even projected a plan closely resembling the one adopted later for the Manhattan Temple.

Soon after his call, President Young turned his attention to the youth programs. Encouraged by his wife Suzan, he appointed some of the best young leaders as scoutmasters. Frequent camp-outs, many on Governor's Island, led to an increase in Eagle Scout awards. Meanwhile Suzan organized Friday night events for the young women to match the boys' camping. To increase mission calls, President Young raised a substantial missionary fund that guaranteed no worthy young man would be prevented from serving because of finances.

The Youngs had moved to New York from Washington D. C. where Michael had clerked for Supreme Court Justice William Rehnquist. After being hired by Columbia University Law School in 1978 as an expert in Japanese law, the family spent two years in Japan where he had served his mission. With their three small children they first contemplated living in New Jersey, but fell in love with New York and moved into the city.

Michael Young was made a counselor to President Frank Miller in 1983. Then President Young was released from the stake presidency in 1989 when he took a two-year position in Washington, D.C. Subsequently he was selected as dean of the George Washington University law school. When he was interviewed in 2004, Michael Young was in his third day on the job as the new president of the University of Utah.

A few months after her baptism, Lirio de Belén Pacheco took her boys back to the Mormon Pavilion at the World's Fair, where she had her first introduction to the Church. Photo courtesy of América Cruz.

Program cover for the dedication of the Manhattan stake center in 1975. Image courtesy of the New York New York Stake.

When the new stake center opened in 1975, it featured a "Mormon Visitors' Center." The center taught visitors about Family Home Evening using hi-tech dioramas with talking mannequins and a robot named "Botch" that showed a film on its chest. Photo courtesy of the New York New York Stake.

From 1975 to 1983, the stake center's family history center was located on the third floor in what is now the nursery room. After closing temporarily, the center was moved in 1989 to the second floor, where it remained until construction began on the temple. Photo courtesy of the New York New York Stake.

## ELIOT A. BRINTON  NEW YORK NEW YORK STAKE PRESIDENT
1989-1991

Eliot Brinton took an interest in medical research while a medical student at the University of Utah. After a residency at Duke University and a fellowship at the University of Washington, he was offered a junior faculty position at the Rockefeller University in Manhattan. He and his wife Bethany both hesitated to take the position because of the challenges of city living with three (later six) young children, but they were reassured by their Durham, NC, friends, Bill and Judene Jack, that New York was a fine place for child rearing and Church service.

Eliot served as counselor to Michael Young throughout his term as stake president, and when President Young moved to Washington, D.C. in mid-1989, Elder Russell Nelson called Eliot as stake president. At the time, there were three English wards, one Hispanic ward, and a Korean branch in Manhattan, and one English branch and two Hispanic wards in the Bronx. Although space for needed additional meeting facilities, not readily found elsewhere, was available in the vacant upper floors of the stake center, President Brinton felt inspired to press instead for creation of a temple within the Lincoln Center building. The high cost and somewhat alien living conditions in Manhattan made it difficult to attract Church members, especially families, to New York. Believing a temple would provide a magnet for members and a foundation for Church growth in the city, President Brinton made his case on every possible occasion. He even presented the idea directly to President Hinckley during his visit for the regional Church conference in Radio City Music Hall.

Eliot Brinton is best remembered for organizing the first singles ward in the stake. He held a special love for singles, having served in both stake and ward singles programs in Salt Lake City and Seattle. He believed that the singles' greatest needs were opportunities for service and spiritual growth, which would also, paradoxically, better fulfill their social needs than overtly social activities. When the first singles ward was organized, just before President Brinton's departure from the city, many single members opposed the action, voicing concerns that it would stigmatize them and take them away from their married friends. Nevertheless, President Brinton felt directed by the Spirit to proceed even though he did not foresee the subsequent multiplication of singles units in Manhattan nor the contribution they would make to the explosive growth of the Church in New York City.

*The wards organized the surging number of young single adult Latter-day Saint professionals and graduate students and fostered an increasing number of Manhattan marriages.*

*President Brinton recognized the need for quality home teaching while acknowledging the challenges imposed by the city environment. He often cited Bishop Bill Jack (whom he served as counselor in the Manhattan Second Ward), who said that New York home teachers did not leave the ninety and nine to seek out the one, but left the one to find the ninety and nine! Many members went for years without home teaching contact, so President Brinton instructed home teachers to make (and count) postal visits of inspirational messages to those unavailable or unwilling to receive in-person visits.*

*He was known for his faithful presence on the overnight stake temple excursions to Washington, D.C. Michael Young commented that typically the bus leaving at midnight Friday would have 35 or 40 Spanish-speaking members and his counselor Eliot Brinton, among only four or five English-speaking members. President Brinton was a favorite of the Hispanic members because of his love of the language and the people, and his participation on stake temple trips.*

*After 25 years away from Utah, the Brintons returned to the Salt Lake City neighborhood in which Eliot was raised, coincidentally to a house formerly owned by Elder Harold B. Lee, who selected the Lincoln Center site for purchase. Eliot currently directs the Metabolism Section of Cardiovascular Genetics at the University of Utah School of Medicine, and he and Bethany were pleased to help persuade the Board of Regents to select Michael Young as 14th president of the University of Utah.*

## THE EVOLVING CHURCH AT THE END OF A CENTURY

Church growth continued at an increasingly rapid pace in New York City in the 1990s. From about 3,200 members in 1980, Church membership in New York City increased to 6,500 in 1990 and to 17,000 at the end of 1998. There were nearly 20,000 Latter-day Saints in New York City at the end of 2000. From 1980 to 2000, the number of wards and branches in New York City increased from 13 to 50. The five Church meetinghouses in 1980 grew into 19 in 2000, with several more under construction. These new meetinghouses included the construction of large new multi-unit chapels on Kingsbridge Road in the Bronx and in Inwood in northern Manhattan. Because of real estate and construction costs, local members often claim the chapels are the most expensive meetinghouses ever built by the Church in the United States.

Most of the new meeting spaces have been clever renovations or "co-habitations" in existing buildings, including churches of other faiths, office buildings, a union hall, a funeral parlor, and a restaurant. The most significant of these is the renovation of a complex of former Bulova Watch Company offices and schools in Woodside, Queens, and is the second largest Church facility in New York City after the temple/stake center complex at Lincoln Square in Manhattan.

The Church organization in New York City reflected these advances. On November 9, 1997, the suburban Westchester units of the New York City Stake were combined with the Bronx District to form a new Westchester New York Stake, leaving Manhattan alone to form the New York New York Stake. This time, in contrast to the earlier division, a majority of the city stake's leadership came from Manhattan, leaving the Westchester Stake with the greater staffing challenge.

A year later the Brooklyn New York Stake was created, on November 22, 1998, encompassing Staten Island and most of Brooklyn. Queens was divided into two mission districts, Queens and Richmond Hill (the latter also including some parts of Brooklyn) with five units in eastern Queens assigned to the suburban Plainview New York Stake and Lynbrook New York District.

The turn of a new century finds the Church in New York City significantly changed from its character throughout most of the 20th century. As recently as 1980, the Church in all five boroughs was centered on a Manhattan base of transplanted westerners, with 38% of the New York Latter-day Saints living in Manhattan. By 2000, that percentage had declined to 20% — far behind Queens and Brooklyn, homes of 32% and 30% of LDS New Yorkers respectively. Perhaps more significantly, the ethnic makeup of LDS New Yorkers has changed to the point where an estimated 50% are Hispanic and 20% are black. Of the 50 units in New York City in 2000, 21 were Spanish-speaking, two used American Sign Language, and one each operated in Chinese and Korean.

In addition to the diversity among the units, New York City wards and branches exhibit considerable internal diversity. English language units outside of Manhattan often consist of a dizzying mix of American whites and blacks, West Indians, Africans, English-speaking Latino and Asian members, and other immigrant groups from places as varied as the Philippines, Russia, Brazil, and Utah. Most of the city's Spanish language units include members from throughout Latin America.

Early in the 21st century, the Church faces many challenges in New York City. Some are to be found wherever the Church is experiencing continued rapid growth, including training leadership, convert retention, and housing Church functions. Others are more particular to New York City. These include building a stable foundation on a growing but constantly transient membership base and integrating English-speaking second-generation Hispanic members into residential, rather than ethnic-based, Church units. On a larger scale, the development of the Church in New York City presages the character of the entire Church in 10 or 15 years.

Statisticians at Brigham Young University predict that 70% of Church will reside in Latin America by 2020.[4] The ability of New York City Latter-day Saints to surmount these challenges could point the way to the establishment of a truly worldwide Zion in the 21st century.

## JOHN STONE  NEW YORK NEW YORK STAKE PRESIDENT
1991-1997

*John Stone began serving as a counselor to Eliot Brinton in the presidency of the New York Stake in the summer of 1991. Three months later, in September, President Brinton was released and Elder Russell Ballard called President Stone to be president. At that time, the stake was comprised of the Westchester Ward; an English-speaking ward and a Spanish-speaking branch in the Bronx; three English-speaking wards (including a singles ward) and a Spanish-speaking ward in Manhattan; and a Korean branch in Manhattan whose branch members lived primarily in New Jersey and Queens.*

*President Stone's tenure was characterized by considerable growth in the stake's population and in the number of units that comprised the stake. During the six years he served, from 1991-97, a Spanish-speaking and an English-speaking unit were created in Yonkers; a second Spanish-speaking unit was formed in the Bronx; English- and Spanish-speaking branches were formed in northern Manhattan; a branch was created in Harlem; and a second singles ward was formed in Manhattan.*

*Also at this time, the Korean branch was divided into two distinct branches, with one branch meeting in New Jersey and the other in Queens.*

*The growth in the stake was particularly pronounced among the singles population. The explosion in the number of singles had much to do with the fact that young Latter-day Saints increasingly viewed the law schools at New York University and Columbia University as desirable programs, and these schools were becoming increasingly interested in attracting students from Brigham Young University. Also, Church members on the whole were obtaining increasingly broad educations and were becoming more aware of the arts and the opportunities available in New York. At the same time, they were becoming more qualified to pursue those artistic opportunities.*

*One of the greatest challenges the stake faced during President Stone's tenure was having adequate space for weekly worship and activities. For the majority of the time he was stake president, he searched for land for additional meeting space, including hundreds of hours searching for a suitable location on the east side, and considerable time scouring lower Manhattan for possibilities. While this search did prove successful in Harlem during his tenure, the hunt was fruitless on the Upper East Side and in lower Manhattan during the 1990s.*

*The rapid turnover of stake membership and the time constraints Church leaders faced because of their professional responsibilities also presented a challenge to the stake, particularly in terms of creating a sense of community among stake members. In spite of those obstacles, a great number of Church members felt welcome in the stake.*

*President Stone is fondly remembered for his language skills and his efforts at using them in his calling. Throughout his tenure he made particular efforts at speaking to the Spanish-speaking members in their own language. Many Sundays he would make a grand tour of the stake, beginning at the stake center in Manhattan, traveling to the school in Inwood where two branches were meeting, up to Olmstead in the Bronx, on to the units in Yonkers, and ending up in his home ward in Westchester. At each stop that included Spanish-speaking units, he would delight the congregations both with his Spanish and with his genuine warmth.*

*An economist by training, President Stone came to the New York area in 1969 to take a job with the Federal Reserve Bank of New York. He and his wife, Helen, raised their five children in Scarsdale, Westchester County, where President Stone served as bishop from 1978 to 1983. Two and a half years after being released as stake president, in July 2000, President and Sister Stone were called to preside over the Greece Athens Mission. President and Sister Stone returned to the States in July 2003, before receiving their new assignments, in April 2004, as Manhattan New York Temple President and Matron.*

# PART 2: NEW STAKE, NEW CENTURY

BUILDING FAITH:
# MANHATTAN REACHES NEW HEIGHTS
SCOTT D. TIFFANY

The most recent stage of Church growth in Manhattan has seen of startling developments. Since its division in November 1997, the stake has arranged hallmark events in legendary locations—Madison Square Garden, Carnegie Hall and Radio City Music Hall—and nearly doubled its active membership.

Yet perhaps the most visible sign of growth is the construction blitz of LDS buildings—unprecedented perhaps in the world and certainly on the 13-mile stretch of Manhattan island. How this phenomenal growth occurred is a remarkable story of toil and timing.

For current stake president Brent J. Belnap and his wife Lorinda, the story of the New York New York Stake comprising only Manhattan began in a clash of conflicting emotions nearly six months before the stake's division. In June 1997, after living in New York City for over a decade, Brent, who was then serving as bishop of the Manhattan Third (Singles) Ward, was ready for a major career change. In the middle of a job search and unhappy as a senior associate at a large law firm, he had always wanted to work overseas. He was delighted when he got a job offer at a major law firm in London.

Before accepting the offer, Bishop Belnap went to the Washington, D.C., temple over the July 4th weekend to seek inspiration concerning this opportunity. While inside the celestial room, the strong feeling came to him that leaving New York City was not the right thing to do. And so, with three small children and unhappy with Brent's job situation, the Belnaps chose to reject the London job offer and stay in Manhattan.

In late October 1997, Bishop Belnap received a strong but unsettling confirmation of something he had felt earlier in the year. "I walked into our stake center late one evening for some appointments with ward members," he recalls. "Posted near the elevator were flyers announcing that at the upcoming stake conference in November we were going to have a visiting General Authority. As I read the flyer, I received an unmistakable impression that I was going to be called as stake president."

Approximately two weeks later, prior to the start of stake conference, Bishop Belnap was asked to meet with Elder Marlin K. Jensen, who was accompanied by (then Area Authority Seventy and soon thereafter member of the Second Quorum of Seventy) Elder D. Lee Tobler. (a longtime resident of Queens) The General Authorities called him to be the president of the New York New York Stake, which was divided to create the Westchester New York Stake. With this division, the New York New York Stake would consist of only the borough of Manhattan for the first time.

At the time it was divided, the stake consisted of Manhattan and the southern portion of Westchester County. (The Bronx had split off from the stake on April 30, 1995, when it became its own district.) John Stone, who would later become the Manhattan New York Temple president, was serving as stake president at the time of the division. At the same time that Bishop Belnap was called to be stake president, Douglas R. Jackson, who was serving as bishop of the Manhattan Eighth (Singles) Ward, was called as president of the new Westchester New York Stake, to which were added the units previously included in the Bronx New York District.[1]

President Belnap called C. Scott Baxter, a counselor to President Stone (and a former roommate) as his first counselor. As his second counselor President Belnap called David Santamaría, who was then serving as the high priest group leader in the Manhattan Fifth Branch.

The announcement of the stake's division was made in one English session of stake conference in Manhattan and one Spanish-speaking session in the Kingsbridge Chapel in the Bronx on Sunday, November 9, 1997.

The new stake faced many challenges. Prior to the division, a number of the stake leaders resided in Westchester. As a result, many important stake auxiliary positions needed to be filled, including the entire Relief Society, Young Men and Young Women presidencies and part of the stake Sunday School presidency, along with several new high councilors and assistant stake clerks.

"The task was daunting but we knew we had people who could do the job, and there was a strong sense of excitement in the stake," recalls President Belnap.

Perhaps the largest obstacle was the lack of Spanish-speaking leaders on the ward level. Whereas previous stake presidencies felt impressed to integrate Spanish-speaking Church members as stake leaders, the new stake leadership in Manhattan was encouraged to let Spanish-speaking members stay in their home units in order to strengthen them.[2] This emphasis on building multicultural units became a guiding principle for the new stake.

In the upcoming years, the New York New York Stake would also become known for exceptional musical events, expanded single adult wards, meetings in legendary locations and its burst of new buildings.

## A PROPHET IN THE GARDEN

Approximately two months after the stake was reorganized, a member of the Area Presidency informed President Belnap that the office of the First Presidency was planning a special regional fireside on Sunday, April 26, 1998—the same weekend as the new stake presidency's first stake conference. President Gordon B. Hinckley would speak.

With the assistance of Church member David Checketts, then president of Madison Square Garden, the celebrated facility was secured for the prophet's visit. Thomas Epting, stake executive secretary at the time, handled many of the technical logistics, which he called an overwhelming responsibility. The stake shouldered the primary responsibility for the event, coordinating logistics for the 24 stakes, districts and missions invited to attend—from translation to press, programs, ushers, signs, security, a 150-voice choir, parking for 100 buses, lunch for the prophet and a fireside for 800 full-time missionaries afterward at the stake center—all of which was pulled together in under three months.

Before daylight on Sunday, April 26, an estimated 24,000 Church members began arriving at Madison Square Garden from all over the East Coast. The hall quickly reached maximum capacity, filling all of the skyboxes and even the overflow theater, leaving hundreds of Church members outside.

The prophet was accompanied by his wife, Sister Marjorie Pay Hinckley, and two members of the North America Northeast Area Presidency, Elder Marlin K. Jensen and Elder Donald L. Staheli, together with their wives. Also seated on the stand, which was located on the floor of the arena, were local stake, mission and district presidents, together with a choir comprised of members of the New York New York Stake, under the direction of Patrick Perkins. Special guests, including many U.N. ambassadors, were hosted at a VIP event before the fireside, and many of them remained to hear President Hinckley speak. Also seated in the audience that day were CBS news anchor Mike Wallace and Mitt Romney, future governor of Massachusetts.

In order to broadcast the proceedings of the special fireside simultaneously to the many members seated inside the arena who did not speak English, the New York New York Stake obtained special permission from the FCC for the unprecedented use of low-frequency radio. This meant anyone with a portable FM radio sitting inside Madison Square Garden could tune in to listen to the prophet in his or her own language. The proceedings of the fireside were translated simultaneously into 11 languages—with all translation supplied by New York metro region Church members.[3]

In his talk, the prophet, taking a page from Charles Dickens, explained some of the "Great Expectations" which the Church had of its members.

"Since its earliest days much has been expected of our people," he said. "Some complain that ours is not an easy religion. It is not."

## BUILDING THE KINGDOM

The Madison Square Garden fireside was a landmark event for the Church in the Eastern States. But some 30 blocks to the north, the Church was quietly working on plans that would eventually have a far greater impact.

For many years following the 1975 completion of the stake center at West 65th Street, members of the Church in Manhattan had met in the same building across from Lincoln Center. Active membership had grown from 1,000 members in 1975 to approximately 1,400 members in 1990 to approximately 2,900 at the end of 1997.

The logical place to expand was on the top floor of the existing stake center. This floor, which had been vacant for several years, had once housed several large racquetball courts and a gym facility for the residents of the adjacent apartment building. To accommodate the now fast-growing stake, the Church purchased back the long-term lease on the upper floor soon after the stake. The spacious top floor would actually be divided into two separate floors—a fifth and sixth floor. The fifth floor would be completely renovated to build another chapel and cultural hall. Classroom and office spaces would be built on the sixth. Two complete ward buildings were stacked one on top of the other.[4]

Construction took several years to complete and was plagued with numerous delays. One of the largest hurdles, in addition to adding an entire new floor, was the installation of two new elevator shafts to access the upper floors of the building.

## A CHURCH UPTOWN

While construction issues were being resolved at the stake center, the Church had an even larger construction project in the works: For about a year prior to the stake's division, the only units of the stake to meet anywhere other than the stake center were the Manhattan Fifth and Sixth Branches in Washington Heights. (The new Manhattan Ninth Branch in Harlem started meeting inside Sylvia's Restaurant shortly before the stake was divided.) The Washington Heights units rented an unruly space at the Herbert L. Birch Manhattan Early Childhood Center, on Fort Washington Avenue at 186th Street.

On June 14, 1997, ground was broken on property acquired in 1993 for the first new Church meetinghouse to be constructed in Manhattan since the stake center was completed in 1975. The new facility was built at 1815 Riverside Drive, and Payson Street in Inwood. With a future stake center in mind, the Church included a full-scale chapel, cultural hall, classrooms and office space for up to four wards.

Construction on the 23,000-square foot building began in earnest in November 1998, following extensive delays in resolving local community board concerns and zoning issues, driving foundation pilings and prefabricating the necessary structural steel. Chief architect Frank Fernandez and his firm, Fernandez Architects and Planners, were based in Irvington, New Jersey. Mr. Fernandez is not a member of the Church, but following his work on the Inwood chapel he designed the Manhattan New York Temple at Lincoln Square.

According to Mr. Fernandez, the steeple section of Inwood's main entrance was inspired by the tower and steeple of the Salt Lake Temple. The Inwood facility was built with a parking garage that had no entrance. The Church purchased the property behind the chapel with the intention of creating a driveway at a future date.

An open house for the new facility was held March 25, 2000. Members from the two local units were responsible for hosting the event, which included presentations in classrooms about the Church's teachings and a welcome ceremony for local dignitaries in the chapel. Sunday meetings were held in the building for the first time the following day. Bishop Richard C. Edgley of the Presiding Bishopric dedicated the Inwood building Sunday, June 11, 2000.

Shortly before the Inwood building open house, in November 1999, the Manhattan Sixth Branch became the Inwood First Ward. The Inwood Second Ward was created from the Manhattan Fifth Branch in April 2000. Unit boundaries remained the same, covering the Washington Heights and Inwood neighborhoods of Manhattan.

As these wards were being formed in upper Manhattan, the foundation was being laid for another future important unit in lower Manhattan. The Chinese group, which had met as a dependent body of the Manhattan Second Ward and later the Manhattan Fifth Ward, separated from the fifth ward and began meeting on its own in Chinatown at 401 Broadway, just below Canal Street, in a small office on the 12th floor (later the 10th floor).[5]

Many stake members thought that the growth in membership and the simultaneous construction on the stake center's upper floors and the Inwood meetinghouse was a grand beginning for the new century. As it turned out, the building boom in Manhattan was just beginning.

## A CHURCH IN HARLEM

As the Inwood construction began in winter 1998, 75 blocks to the south the Harlem First Branch was undergoing major changes. In December the branch moved from meeting two hours each Sunday at Sylvia's Restaurant to meeting in a former single-story Jehovah's Witnesses Kingdom Hall at 58 West 129th Street, between Lenox and Fifth Avenues.

"We were very grateful for the building," says Ron Anderson, branch presi-

# NEXT DOOR NEIGHBORS

*The Inwood chapel was built on the site of an apartment complex that was torn down in the early 1980s because a stream beneath the building eroded its foundation (to overcome this obstacle, the chapel's foundation is built on about 130 concrete-filled steel piles, some as deep as 70 feet into solid bedrock).*

*For nearly 20 years, stake members Arthur and Jessica Sherry watched the development of the Church's lot from next door. They moved into 1825 Riverside Drive in May 1981, the same month their first child, Rachel, was born. Arthur recalls that the building on the present Church lot was condemned and that most people had moved out. Anyone left had to "step down from the front door" to get into their apartment because the foundation was sinking into the underground stream.*

*Following are some of Arthur's recollections on watching the construction of the Inwood chapel next door.*

Q: After the building was torn down what happened to the property?

A: In early 1983, a local resident named Brian Murtaugh held a community meeting at the Episcopal Church asking what to do with the site. Maggie Clark, Ted Galligher and about 50 other locals were there. Maggie put up her hand and said, "Why don't we throw some wild flower seeds and maybe they'll take." Maggie went to Keukenhoff Gardens in Holland that summer and brought back some bulbs. The Horticulture Society gave our group shovels and hoses and the Green Guerrillas gave us more bulbs...Later that year Maggie found a contractor who had topsoil that he had to get rid of. He came by with 38 dump truck loads full and a front-end loader to spread it all around.

Q: What do you remember about the garden?

A: I loved that garden, playing with Rachel and her little friends. There was a large pile of sand in the back where they built castles and dug almost all the way to China. A small forest was well under way in the back when we received word that the landlord wanted the lot unencumbered so it could be sold.

Q: What happened to the garden?

A: We had to get off the property by November 1997. The Boy Scout Troop 525 helped us haul the plants away and we started working with the community board for the William Tighe Triangle where nearby Ring Garden now stands near the intersection of Broadway and Dyckman streets...We raised new funds and started over. As you can see today our efforts have been well rewarded and the Ring Garden had a recent makeover.

Q: The lot stood vacant for more than a decade. How did the Church purchase it?

*A: In 1994 I was talking with Stake President Stone and he mentioned that they were looking for a site to build a new church uptown. He went through a litany of possibilities that were falling down like dominoes. Then I mentioned the old garden site. It was convenient to the A train and Broadway bus lines and with Fort Tryon Park across the street, what could be better?*

dent at the time. "Just having our own building, our attendance jumped from about 30 people to about 50 people. So there was huge increase in the level of activity and in the enthusiasm of the branch."

However, the building was far from ideal. It was small, only 25 feet across and less than 100 feet deep, and there were no windows. The carpets were in terrible condition, the pipes were rusted, the ceiling leaked and both the heating and the air conditioning were broken. The building had only a partial basement and lacked adequate meeting space for a growing branch.

"For a long time we were holding nursery in the hallway," recalls President Anderson. "And the rest of the Primary was meeting in the bathroom."

Branch members, he says, were still grateful to have their own meeting space and they knew the situation would be temporary. Renovations were to be made almost immediately and, longer term, Church leaders planned to overhaul and expand or even entirely replace the building. However, budget and building problems led to delays and it was more than a year before some basic problems were fixed.

Despite the deficiencies of their facility, branch members received good news. In June 2000, while in Manhattan to dedicate the Inwood building, Bishop Richard C. Edgley of the Presiding Bishopric visited the Harlem First Branch building. He reviewed the proposed architectural plans that called for entirely replacing the building with a grand multi-story meetinghouse and came to an unexpected decision: the Church would buy an different lot for a new chapel. He told local leaders that the Church would allocate more money than usual to find a home for a new meetinghouse in Harlem.

Several properties were reviewed. Ultimately, Church leaders agreed that a "marquee" location at 360-368 Lenox Avenue on the northeast corner of 128th Street and Lenox Avenue, in the heart of Harlem and just around the corner from the previous structure, would provide the easiest access for members and the greatest visibility for the Church.

Church leaders finalized the purchase of the new location in spring 2001, but obtaining the necessary permits to demolish the existing buildings and start construction did not go as smoothly as hoped. Soon after the purchase of the condemned tenement apartment buildings, construction workers discovered that a former resident was still living in one of the buildings.

Given New York City's strict eviction laws, the Church faced a lengthy legal process in order to find the former resident a new home and tear down the buildings. One positive outcome from the many delays and setbacks, however, was the stake's creation of the Harlem Bridge-building Committee, which met with many local political and community leaders in a focused effort to build good relationships within Harlem. Finally, the old buildings were demolished and a groundbreaking ceremony was held September 7, 2003. Nearly 70 branch members attended as did Manhattan Borough President C. Virginia Fields. Full construction began on the four-story meetinghouse in July 2004. Meanwhile, as Harlem members grew ever closer to having a home of their own, the stake was buying property for other units.

## A CHURCH DOWNTOWN

Stake leaders were quietly looking for property on the southern end of Manhattan. In spring 2001, as the stake was purchasing property for a new full-size meetinghouse in Harlem, the Church finalized the purchase of some downtown property with a remarkable history.

The site, running between West 14th and 15th Streets, near Union Square in lower Manhattan (between Sixth and Seventh Avenues), was home to a Catholic convent that needed to be closed and relocated. Acquisition by the Church was a complicated endeavor.

The Archdiocese of New York received a competitive bid that would have required redesigning the space for commercial and residential development. However, the Sisters of St. Zita's Convent, who believed the convent to be "sacred ground," wanted the facility to pass into the hands of a religious organization that would respect Christian teachings consistent with its time-honored mission of service.

In January 2001, the Sisters of St. Zita's welcomed a bid from the Church, but the offer was soon mired in a lengthy legal battle with the commercial bidders. Finally, in April 2002, the Church won the bid and acquired the former convent.

At the time, seven wards and one branch met at the stake center at 2 Lincoln Square. The plan was to move two wards and one branch downtown to the building on the 15th Street side of the property. In fall 2003, the Manhattan Fifth Ward and Manhattan Sixth Ward became the Union Square First and Third Wards, respectively, and the Manhattan Seventh Branch became the Union Square (Deaf) Second Branch. These three congregations met for the first time in their new building on Sunday, November 23, 2003. The meetinghouse was dedicated as an LDS house of worship on January 18, 2004.

Whereas the original façade of the building was left largely intact, the interior was extensively remodeled. The renovated building occupies five floors and includes a chapel on the top floor, a large number of classrooms, offices for as many as four congregations on the main floor, a library for instructional materials, a mini family history center for genealogical research, a baptismal font, a large hall in the basement for social events and an outdoor courtyard behind the building for recreational activities.

A regional Employment Resource Center for the Church and the Church

## SELFELSS SERVICE: ST. ZITA'S CONVENT AND THE LDS CHURCH AT UNION SQUARE TODD W. FLYR

*Prior to its acquisition and renovation, the building now occupied by three LDS units served as the home of St. Zita's Convent and Home for Women for the Catholic Archdiocese of New York. In 1890, an Irish immigrant nurse named Ellen O'Keefe was concerned about the many women in New York City who were homeless, poor and otherwise unable to sustain themselves. To help solve the problem, she used her own money to rent a home on West 24th Street, which became known as "St. Zita's Home for the Friendless Women of New York City".[1]*

*The Home operated under the concept of self-sufficiency. Women who were able assisted with laundry, including "altar linens, surplices, albs, etc.," and other similar work for the Archdiocese.[2]*

*In Catholicism, each convent has a patron saint. Because this convent served as a "domestic helper" with church laundry work and mending, St. Zita, the patron saint of domestic servants, was chosen as its patron saint.[3]*

*With the help of donations, the convent eventually moved to its long-standing location at 143 West 14th Street. It later expanded to include the building immediately to the north, at 144 West 15th Street. In 1903, Miss O'Keefe began the religious training necessary to become a nun and she founded a religious order, The Sisters of Reparation of the Congregation of Mary.[4]*

*At any given time, the sisters accommodated and cared for up to 100 women, and provided assistance to as many as a thousand women per year. Women could stay as long as they needed. Those who could work were required to do so, but the nuns also provided care for the invalid and sick, even arranging free medical care. For many years, a nun was required to sleep by the front door every evenings, in keeping with the policy that the Home was open to women arriving at any time—day or night.*

*The women admitted to the Home included those were ill or elderly, those evicted by landlords and those who were victims of domestic abuse. No judgment was made concerning why a woman needed shelter and care.*

*In addition to its role as a shelter for women, St. Zita's was also a fully functioning convent. This meant that it had catechetical responsibilities.[6] This work included the training of altar boys, as well as the preparation for children and teens for Catholic communion and confirmation. Additionally, women who were interested could train to become nuns. This involved a lengthy multi-year process that ended with the making of "perpetual vows" of poverty, chastity and obedience.*

*By the 1990s, the number of sisters joining the religious order had declined, and the remaining sisters grew too old to continue providing sheltering services. Consequently, it was decided by the Archdiocese that the convent should be sold and the remaining handful of sisters relocated to a different convent in upstate New York, in Monsey.*

*Many LDS Church members who attend church in the building also look forward to serving the local community. They say they are happy to see the histories of two religious faiths in New York City merge in a tradition of service.*

Educational System also call the building home. The employment center, which serves members of the community during the week, is one way in which a tradition and spirit of service and self-sufficiency continue within the building.

### A CHURCH ON THE EAST SIDE

In early 2002, following more than a decade of searching for a new meetinghouse location on Manhattan's Upper East Side, the Church purchased property, a school for troubled youth run by the Jewish Child Care Association, at 217 East 87th Street, between Second and Third Avenues. Unlike other recent purchases in Manhattan, very few legal battles were involved. Demolition of the existing building commenced in 2003, following the departure of the previous owners and operators of the school. However, construction halted for almost a year, until October 2004, while work on the Manhattan temple blazed ahead.

### THE PROPHET VISITS AGAIN

On Sunday, March 24, 2002, President Gordon B. Hinckley addressed a large number of Saints in a special meeting that was broadcast live from the New York New York Stake center to meetinghouses in the greater New York area. The purpose of his visit was to finalize plans for a new temple in Manhattan, given the many delays that had plagued the White Plains (later redesignated the Harrison) New York Temple after it was publicly announced during the general priesthood session of general conference on Saturday, September 30, 1995.

Shortly after President Hinckley's visit in April 2002, the Church acquired the two storefront street-level leases immediately below the existing stake center in order to make room for the new temple, which would not be publicly announced until August 2002.[6]

At about the same time that the Church was acquiring the Lincoln Square leases, the stake moved forward with plans to rent a larger facility closer to the heart of Chinatown for the new Canal Street Branch. The Branch, created on Easter Sunday, March 31, 2002, had fully outgrown its location at 401 Broadway. After several lengthy renovation delays, the new meetinghouse facility at 41 Elizabeth Street was dedicated in June 2004, shortly after the dedication of the Manhattan New York Temple. In fall 2004, the first bishops' storehouse in Manhattan was completed, in the parking garage of the existing Inwood building.

Through all of the many meetinghouse construction projects, special visits and large stake activities, the main focus of the stake, in ways intentional and not, was the temple. Stake temple trips, special firesides, family history seminars and high council talks, not to mention the regular emphasis placed on priesthood advancements, missionary work, convert retention and member reactivation, regularly focused members' attention on the temple. During this time, the stake participated in the dedication of a temple in Boston and was blessed shortly thereafter with a visit from President James E. Faust of the First Presidency, who promised that members of the Church in the New York City area would have a temple in their midst sooner than they would be ready for it. In hindsight, such emphasis on the spiritual center of the gospel from so many directions was perhaps needed, not just in preparation for the eventual dedication of a House of the Lord in Manhattan, but also to fortify the members of the Church in New York against an unspeakable horror that would affect in a major way the city and the world.

President Hinckley speaks to a full house at a fireside in Madison Square Garden, April 26, 1998. Nearly 25,000 Church members from the metro region attended. Photo courtesy of Public Affairs, The Church of Jesus Christ of Latter-day Saints.

President Gordon B. Hinckley speaking at Madison Square Garden, April 26, 1998. The event marked the first stake conference of the newly reorganized, Manhattan-based New York New York Stake. Photo courtesy of the New York New York Stake.

Mike Wallace greets President Hinckley at a reception in the prophet's honor, April 26, 1998. Photo courtesy of Public Affairs, The Church of Jesus Christ of Latter-day Saints.

Brent Belnap was sustained as stake president of the New York New York Stake when it was reorganized in November 1997. Like hundreds of other Church members, his family attended the ceremony in which the Angel Moroni was placed on top of the Manhattan temple's steeple on October 9, 2004.

The Inwood building on Riverside Drive was dedicated in June 2000. It is home to the Inwood First Ward (English) and the Inwood Second Ward (Spanish). Photo courtesy of Maria Hunter.

The steeple for the Inwood chapel was brought in on a truck and lifted to the top of the building with a crane in March 2000. Photo courtesy of Emily Orton.

Harlem Branch choir at the groundbreaking for the Harlem chapel to be built at 128th Street and Lenox Avenue, September 7, 2003. Photo courtesy of Lisa Anderson.

# THE CITY MOURNS

Along with fellow New Yorkers and the rest of the world, Church members were stunned by the terrorist attacks on the World Trade Center on September 11, 2001. Everyone was affected in some way.

## HOW 9/11 CHANGED US BY JOANNA LEGERSKI

Directly after the attacks of September 11, 2001, LDS ward, branch and stake leaders if possible immediately used phone trees to account for membership of their units. Within about 48 hours, they found that not one member in our stake was lost or injured. But the emotional losses were severe. The whole city grieved, some openly through public memorials. Others grieved silently. Some suffered survivor's guilt. Many sought out their families, while others struggled with the despair of feeling more alone than ever. For a month after the attacks, the streets seemed silent; it took a long time for impatient cab drivers to start honking their horns again.

Everyone seemed to reassess his or her life. Some chose to stick it out, some left the city, some went back to school or sought religion; others got married, got divorced or had babies. Perhaps these life changes would have occurred anyway; but for many in and out of the Church, there seemed to be a sense that 9/11 impacted people in a way that made them look more deeply at their relationships, read their scriptures in a new light and strive to become better individuals.

In the days and weeks following 9/11, a central objective for everyone became getting to a destination and returning home safely. Security was high and so was stress and anxiety. Those of us working in tall buildings quietly began to leave extra pairs of sneakers and flashlights near our desks. Once home, people tended to stay home. Bomb and anthrax scares threatened the subways, trains, tunnels and bridges. Trains were delayed and sometimes evacuated, leaving passengers stranded—a constant reminder that our city and lives had changed.

The youth of New York City and of the Church felt the anxiety, too. As in other dense metropolitan cities, the majority of the population in New York

City uses public transportation. Schools are not always within a student's immediate neighborhood but may be across town or even in another borough. After the terrorist attacks, most LDS seminary students could not attend seminary class because the trains were running so erratically.

September 11, 2001 was a Tuesday. A stake youth activity had been planned for Saturday, September 15. Although it would have been easy to cancel the activity, ward and stake leaders decided to go ahead as planned. Forty of the youth and their leaders journeyed far from the plumes of smoke to swim in the ocean at Robert Moses State Park. It was the first time many youth had a chance to play and "be kids" since the attacks.

Difficult as it was, the city seemed to be full of resolve—resolve for our community to find footing and move ahead. Church members across the country encouraged local members by sending hundreds of cards, toys and letters of love.

Less than a month after the attacks, Church members in New York City welcomed an opportunity to hear general conference. The following spring, President Gordon B. Hinckley visited to speak at the Manhattan stake center. Many hearts were open towards his words of encouragement and vision. He promised a temple and now, less than three years after the attacks, we have a temple of our own. A palace of peace has been created in the stake center, and perhaps within ourselves as well.

*As the first anniversary of the attacks on the World Trade Center approached, the New York New York Stake LDS History Committee gathered the impressions of stake members who had lived through the event. They were asked what had they experienced and how had their lives been changed. Out of many, here are four responses.*

## REFLECTIONS OF THE STAKE PRESIDENT: BRENT J. BELNAP

The tragic events of 9/11 have become a defining, pivotal moment for us all. Whether one personally witnessed the towers in flames, or watched helplessly as they fell, or feverishly contacted other members to ensure they were still alive, or came to the stake center to help, or stood in line for hours to donate blood or to volunteer at a local fire station, or comforted co-workers and friends, or sorted through enormous piles of goods and letters received from hundreds of Church members around the world, or quietly hung the flag outside their apartment windows—none of us can ever really be quite the same.

Even with all that occurred last September, many within the stake worked diligently to ensure that life's rhythms proceeded as normally as possible. On September 15, the Saturday immediately following the disaster, the stake youth held their annual fall opening social event at the beach—away from the still steaming wreckage of what was once the World Trade Center. The following day, declared by the First Presidency to be a solemn day of observance in every sacrament meeting around the world, the Manhattan First Ward held its ward conference leadership meetings as previously scheduled in the stake directories. Bishop Glade Holman and others of the Manhattan Fifth Ward, which had been created less than a year before and included the bulk of Church members residing closest to Ground Zero, worked overtime locating every possible known member and housing those who were permanently displaced. One of the biggest worries of displaced endowed members was obtaining clean temple garments. Within a few days, the Boston temple presidency generously donated and delivered a load of various sizes and styles of fresh, clean garments.

Once the telephone trees in each ward and branch confirmed that no one in our stake had been killed in the disasters, and the flood of offers of assistance from members of the Church in literally every state and a dozen or more foreign countries began tapering off, I found myself waiting for the proverbial "other shoe" to drop—for people working throughout the city, but particularly in and near the WTC, to be laid off and to begin moving away in droves. While the after-effects of 9/11, mostly in increased unemployment and the resulting relocation, have been real, I count it as no small miracle that this has not occurred in any large degree anywhere in our stake. Quite the opposite in fact. There has been no noticeable statistical drop in attendance, and there are reports of "September 11 members"—those who began attending and participating again following the attack. If anything, we are more united as a local body of Church members than ever before. I sense more than before in many of the talks given and testimonies borne in the meetings that I visit, that we are more prone to acknowledge God's protective hand in our lives, to speak of the gift of the resurrection and eternal life, and to give thanks for the blessings of health and life and family.

### NEIGHBORHOOD RESIDENT: SUSAN ROBISON

*Susan Robison was living in Battery Park City across the street from the World Trade Center when the attack occurred. Her husband, whose office was in the towers, had returned late from a business trip to Asia and stayed home that morning. Sister Robison told her story to Sara Anderson.*

I went downstairs, out into the street, and looked up; and I could see the north tower where the plane had hit the building. I watched that for a couple of minutes then came back up to tell Ron. And we of course turned on CNN to see what they were picking up. Then all of a sudden, we heard this huge roar, and it was the second plane coming right over our building. And then we heard a huge explosion. So we knew that the first plane—that something was wrong. Then a couple of minutes later, our son, who works in the Financial Center, came running into the apartment in tears, "Where's Dad? Where's Dad?" And fortunately, his dad was standing right there. So we all hugged for a few minutes and then decided we'd go up on the roof to see what we could see from there.

You could see the towers and planes burning, and all the smoke, and everything that was happening. But the most difficult thing was that we saw bodies falling. And these were people whose lives were ending. It was like being a witness to a murder. You can imagine these people and the choices that they had. A wall of fire, or leaping from a building. What choice really is there? That was the time it really hit, in terms of what an immense and horrific event this really was. While we were on the roof we saw the first tower fall.

Once the first building fell, all the clouds of dust and smoke and ash started coming towards us, so we went back inside our lobby. Clouds of smoke and ash came by, and people were coming off the street through the door. Our doorman was pulling people in and then closing the door quickly, but the air became increasingly more difficult to breathe. And that was the only time I thought, "well, maybe we aren't going to make it through this."

Our apartment faces southwest, so we look right out on the Hudson River and can see the Statue of Liberty; and the contrast of looking at the Statue on such a bright, beautiful, sunny September day and knowing what was going on was the dichotomy that didn't compute emotionally.

Before we were actually evacuated, we looked out our window and could see the barges coming in to evacuate the people; and you could see all the strollers that were left along the promenade. You couldn't take the strollers because there wasn't enough room. All they could do was to carry the children onto the boats.

The boats that came to evacuate people evacuated them right before our apartment building in Battery Park City. The barges and police boats came in and took the people that had come down to the Battery, and took us over into New Jersey. There were many, many police cars there, and many, many ambulances because of course they were thinking there would be a lot of injured people and the New York hospitals would not be able to handle everyone, and so New Jersey and the surrounding communities were prepared and ready. But the very eerie thing is that there were no injured. The bodies never came.

That night, I fell apart. We were in a hotel in New Jersey and I was just so grateful that Ron was safe. It really hit me of what might have been and how fortunate and blessed we were. The next morning when Ron went to his office, I literally could not move. I mean, it sounds weird but you know, you tell yourself, "This is silly, Susan. Get up and get with it;" and yet my body was just not willing to move. I pretty much laid there for most of the day watching the news.

I thought I could donate blood. Of course, they had been receiving a lot of offers; but the woman at the desk was nice and took my name and asked for a phone number. I didn't have a number to give since I had been evacuated, so I gave her my cell number. Later that night I got a phone call from her while I was at the hotel. She just said, "I realize this has been a traumatic experience for you and I wanted to make sure you're doing all right." That touched me a lot, that a stranger, somebody I didn't know, would take the time to call.

## IN MEMORIAM: IVHAN CARPIO

*Ivhan Luis Carpio Bautista, 24, of the Richmond Hill Third Branch in Queens, was working at the Windows on the World restaurant at the top of the World Trade Center on September 11, 2001, when the Trade Center was struck by terrorists. He had planned to take the day off, as it was his birthday, but agreed to cover a co-worker's shift instead.*

*Ivhan moved to New York from Peru only two years ago, and since his arrival had become nearly fluent in English, found a job that he loved, moved into his own apartment, and been accepted to the John Jay College of Criminal Justice. He worked as hard and as often as he could, always willing to cover others' shifts, so that he could pay for a niece's schooling in Peru.*

*Ivhan was the only member of the Church in his family, having converted shortly after his arrival in New York City; and although he was a recent convert, he held two callings in the Richmond Hill Third Branch: young single adult representative and second counselor in the Young Men presidency. Ivhan thoroughly loved serving the members in his branch in any capacity. In fact, he showed up to nearly every church activity, if only to help out with the smaller details like setting up chairs. He regularly went on splits with the missionaries, and was saving for his own full-time mission.*

*Blair Garff, district president of Richmond Hill, arranged to fly Ivhan's family in from Peru for a memorial service, which was held on October 3, 2001.*

## WORKING AT THE HOSPITAL: DEBBIE BINGHAM

*Debbie Bingham is the Director of Maternal Child Health Nursing for St. Luke's and Roosevelt Hospitals in Manhattan. She shares her recollections of working at the hospital during the tragedy.*

On September 11, 2001, at 8 a.m., I was attending a meeting at the outpatient clinics of Continuum Health Partners on 14th Street near Union Square, only a few blocks from the World Trade Towers. I was stressed about the things I needed to do at work that day and I had the added stress of parking my car due to the alternate side of the street parking rules in New York City.

At about 8:49 a.m. the person next to me got a page and after a brief conversation whispered to me and that she could not believe what her friend just told her: she had been driving down the West Side highway and saw a plane crash into one of the World Trade Towers. She asked "What should we do?"

Just as she finished asking me everyone around the room started getting pages and answering their pages in a muffled voice. Seconds later someone said out loud, "A plane just crashed into the World Trade Center" and then the meeting abruptly ended without any of us saying anything more to each other. Almost in unison we stood up, grabbed our belongings and scattered in different directions to get to our respective hospitals—we knew we had to be at the hospitals ready to respond to a huge disaster.

Once out of the building the street was chaotic, sirens blaring, people running. We ducked into a nearby subway station just as a train arrived. We got on one of the last trains to leave the area that day and we were quickly whisked away further uptown toward Roosevelt Hospital on 58th Street and 10th Avenue. The people on the train did not appear to know that anything unusual had just happened above ground. When we emerged from the subway at 57th Street, the city was calm and quiet. It was like any other normal morning: shopkeepers were opening their store gates and well-dressed business people were focused and rushing to get to work on time.

I was struck by the beauty of the day, the air was crisp, cool, clear, and the sky was a striking blue. As we half-walked and sprinted to get to the hospital I saw several people getting cell phone calls and their looks of disbelief as they learned the unbelievable news.

Once at the hospital I reported to the disaster command center and I was dispatched to the St. Luke's hospital on 113th Street and Amsterdam. As a disaster leadership team we quickly focused on implementing our disaster plan: we decided which patients could give up their hospital bed, canceled all non-emergency surgeries, expanded blood bank donor services, identified needs of staff and additional staff resources, and a multitude of other tasks to help us get ready for thousands of patients. We were focused and working in high gear.

In my role as the Director of Maternal Child Health Nursing for both St. Luke's and Roosevelt Hospitals, I also had the unique opportunity to watch over the safety of all the mothers who were currently in labor, those that might go into labor, and the needs of children. It was a mixed blessing that on this particular day many women were in labor and would be giving birth. It gave me a unique perspective to witness the hope of new life on a day when so many were killed.

As the day wore on, the news came that the second tower was struck, that the Pentagon was hit, that a plane had crashed in the fields of Pennsylvania. My mind and heart could barely comprehend the magnitude of the senseless horror of it all. All of this destruction was so unexpected at the start of such an ordinary and beautiful clear day.

Since the hospitals I work at are further uptown from the World Trade Towers we did not receive as many victims as the hospitals nearer the attack. We were preparing for the overflow of patients we were confident would come once the downtown hospitals filled up. It was not until late in the afternoon that I began to comprehend that the thousands of victims that we were preparing for would not arrive, for they had been killed.

## DOWNTOWN TRADER: KRISTOPHER WOOLLEY

*While living in downtown Manhattan, Kristopher was working as a trader at CSFB at the time of the World Trade Center attacks. He and his wife Heather now live in Boston, where Kristopher attends Harvard Business School.*

I work on a trading floor, and it's very open; there are no cubicles, its loud, phones are ringing. And I was turning around to mention something to a colleague, but I noted that behind him in the window there was paper fluttering, and I thought it was a ticker tape parade. It looked like really small pieces of paper but it turns out they were 8.5 by 11 office paper, floating. We walked over to the window and then the view of the whole building kind of opens up as you get closer to the window. And sure enough, there was that dark, black smoke coming out from Tower One.

I walked to the window to watch when out of the left side of the window, just off our building, came flying in this plane really low. I had dual vision; I was watching the TV, but then out of the corner of my eye there is a plane; and then it came on the TV. It was a surreal experience witnessing both live and on TV the second plane. We watched it plunge right into that side of the building that we face.

I saw Patti, and she was crying. Tears were already coming down, and she said "oh, my goodness. So many people are dying right now." At that point, we all knew how serious it was; just so many people were literally dying, right then. Then it turned chaotic. It was Go time. Everyone knew it was time to evacuate the building. Not that at that point we even suspected that the two buildings would fall; but it was like, "Gotta get out. Gotta get off the island." Manhattan was like the Titanic.

So Larry and I went over to Battery Park where we figured if there were any more situations like that we would be at least in the open. There wouldn't be any building or shrapnel or things blowing on us. I still had a sense of security when Larry started speculating. "Those buildings are going to fall from the weight." Sure enough, that first tower just crumbled right in front of us, and we all watched it. And then, everyone took off, and that black pile of smoke came in. It was far enough away that there weren't pieces of things falling on us. But the smoke—I had no idea that the smoke would get us that quick and turn what was blue sky into almost no visibility. It was so thick, and there was stuff floating in it. And it looked kind of like what volcanic ash would be like. It's in your hair, in your sleeves. I had my sleeves rolled up and it was in my shoes and pants and shirt. And my contact lenses were so irritated.

As we got onto the FDR highway, it literally looked like there was a marathon. There were thousands of people from Wall Street and different spots down there just evacuating lower Manhattan. And it was hot. It was going to be a hot day that day. I remember men had taken off their shirts and tied them around their heads; and women were breaking the heels off their shoes and walking bare foot, or they put their walking shoes back on that they had taken to work. It was just a sight to see—like refugees walking and walking. Everyone was all dirty from the smoke. And now we were sweaty because we'd been running and it's getting warmer.

And as we got to the Brooklyn Bridge, we heard the sound again. The sound was probably the most frightening part of the whole experience for me. Because it wasn't screechy, it gathered momentum. It got louder and louder like clapping thunder with a bowling ball hitting bowling pins. Things just started clapping and snapping and breaking. It was really, just a really, really distinct sound. So we kept walking and just as we were getting to the Brooklyn Bridge we heard the sound again, and Tower One fell. We all looked over our shoulders and they were gone.

I've thought of quitting it all and going to work for the CIA. My feelings were so intense the days and weeks after, I was, like, what's it all worth. Why be here? I thought a lot of people would move from lower Manhattan or from New York City. I thought people would just mass exodus to other cities and states. But I find myself calmed down now. Days have turned into weeks, and weeks have turned into months. And I'm not going to learn Arabic or go join the CIA and try to be a counterintelligence agent, and try to put an end to this evil in the world.

There are going to be some dreadful events. Even worse than this probably. But you know, it all goes back to the gospel and the Restoration and the plan of salvation and where we stand in the whole history of the events of the world. And I feel calm. Come what may, I feel calm. And I feel like this has been a blow to everyone, and me personally; but it hasn't shaken me and I'm not afraid. I'm not leaving New York. My testimony's not shaken. In fact, it's solidified my resolve to be here right now, at this point in my life to be doing what I'm doing.

Memorial quilt made by members of the New York New York Stake after September 11, 2001.

# A TEMPLE IN THE CITY

**THE COMING OF A TEMPLE** SCOTT TIFFANY

On November 10, 1869, the New York Times printed a misguided headline, "A Mormon Temple to be Erected in This City."[1] As it turned out, it wasn't until 2001 that the idea of a temple in New York City quietly began to take root. On June 19, 2001, Manhattan's LDS stake president, Brent J. Belnap, received an unexpected telephone call from a member of the Church's Quorum of the Twelve Apostles in Salt Lake City.[2] Elder Robert D. Hales, who grew up in the New York City area, said that he had some questions regarding costs and convenience associated with the previously announced Harrison temple in neighboring Westchester County.

Elder Hales seemed particularly interested in the travel logistics and associated costs for members residing within the metropolitan area. He inquired how much it would cost members living in New York City to travel to the new temple, how many members would need to rent cars versus those who owned them, and what the difference in time and money was for members between the announced temple in Harrison and the recently dedicated Boston temple.

As a former resident of the area, Elder Hales was familiar with the difficulties and time constraints of getting in and out of the city. As there was no direct public transportation from any of the five boroughs to the Harrison temple site, he seemed concerned to learn that the cost in time and money to members to rent a car and travel 20 to 30 miles north was only slightly less than the relative cost of traveling all the way to Boston.

After answering several very specific logistical questions, it occurred to President Belnap that something much bigger was afoot than working out how much it would cost members within the city to get to the Harrison temple. President Belnap recalls saying, perhaps too directly, to Elder Hales, "It sounds like you are considering building a temple in Manhattan." The conversation suddenly turned very quiet and the speakerphone in Elder Hales' office clicked off. There was silence on the other end of the phone line for what seemed to President Belnap like an uncomfortably long period of time.

Thinking that he had said something very wrong, President Belnap felt terrible for being so blunt. He finally ventured to add, "Forgive me if I've asked the wrong question." After another pause, Elder Hales softly replied, "No, President, you've asked exactly the right question."

Elder Hales then confirmed something that would change the lives of Church members in the metropolitan region: a temple somewhere in Manhattan was a topic of discussion among Church leaders in Salt Lake City.

With the idea of a possible temple in New York City out on the table, the conversation now got down to brass tacks. Elder Hales talked quite openly about the pros and cons of a possible temple in New York City. Among other things, the two men discussed potential impacts on the members, travel costs and associated logistics, and potential locations.

At the time, President Belnap believed that the actual location was still in question. Previous proposals in the last two decades to build a temple at the existing New York New York Stake Center had been discarded for a variety of reasons. Still, this seemed like the most logical choice, as the building was centrally located near Lincoln Center and on a highly visible piece of property, unlike other prospects in the city. Elder Hales suggested that having a temple in such a central location would allow members from the suburbs to come into the city, attend the temple, and still have time to shop or attend a cultural event.

One consideration was that the stake had only recently completed a much-needed expansion into the fifth and sixth floors of the stake center, having installed a second chapel and additional classrooms and offices. Also, the Church no longer controlled the ground-floor leases between the stake center foyer and the American Folk Art Museum space (the ground leases were later acquired in the spring of 2002).

Plans for a temple within the existing stake center were further along than President Belnap had first realized. In August 2001, less than two months after the phone call from Elder Hales, Elder W. Craig Zwick and Elder Spencer J. Condie of the North America Northeast Area Presidency presented a rough schematic drawing of a "small" temple within the fifth and sixth floors of the existing stake center.

But President Belnap was asked not to tell anyone of the project. Under normal conditions, not discussing a possible temple in Manhattan would be hard enough. But maintaining silence about this hopeful message became particularly difficult after the events of September 11, 2001.

After the destruction of the World Trade Center, President Belnap received an odd invitation from an unlikely source. Holly Hinckley, a member of the stake and granddaughter of President Gordon B. Hinckley, asked President

Belnap to schedule an appointment for him and his wife to meet briefly with her grandfather in Salt Lake City.

As the Belnaps were already traveling to Salt Lake City for the upcoming October 2001 general conference, an appointment was scheduled on the Friday before the conference. Given the "unofficial" nature of the request, President Belnap made the appointment through the president's secretary, assuming that the purpose of the meeting was to discuss the impact of 9/11 on Church members in New York City.

On Friday, October 5, 2001, in Salt Lake City, Don Staheli, the president's personal secretary, ushered President Belnap and his wife, Lorinda, into President Hinckley's office, where a map of New York City was rolled out. Most of their 15-minute meeting focused on the feasibility, desirability and necessity of having a temple in New York City.

The Belnaps left the prophet's office feeling that the prayers of the local members had been answered. The following two days, while seated inside the Conference Center, they quietly hoped for, and even expected, an announcement to be made in general conference—yet nothing was said over the pulpit about the temple. Presumably, the idea of a temple in the city was not yet fully decided.

A few weeks later, on Saturday, November 10, 2001, following the Saturday training session of stake conference, President Belnap dedicated the new fifth and sixth floor chapel and meetinghouse space in the stake center. As Church members celebrated the event, President Belnap was also pleased. Yet at the same time, he attended the dedication with the odd, hidden hope that the new chapel would soon be dismantled to make room for a temple.

Two months later, his hopes were confirmed. On Saturday, January 12, 2002, the LDS Church's Presiding Bishop, H. David Burton, came to New York City to visit sites for the temple and three sites for proposed new chapels in Manhattan. In connection with this visit, President Belnap was asked to put together a thorough, confidential analysis of the transportation and financial issues of getting to the Harrison temple versus traveling to a temple in Manhattan from New Jersey, the five boroughs, Long Island, upstate New York, and Connecticut. Not even President Belnap's counselors were privy to the plan.

"Although I was as guilty as the next person in expressing aloud how nice it would be to have a temple here in Manhattan, I stopped making off-hand comments once I knew that a temple was a distinct possibility," said President Belnap. "Once I stopped joining in on the casual conversation, I thought for certain that people could read my mind. Thankfully, no one ever asked me point blank whether a temple was coming to New York City."

The stake's focus for 2002 was "Preparing for a Temple in Our Midst" and the topic of a temple was a focal point in stake and ward lessons, meetings and service projects. Wishful speculation about getting a temple in Manhattan had now floated within the New York New York Stake for a long time, especially after September 11, 2001, and a series of legal setbacks that had delayed the groundbreaking for a temple in Harrison.

After attending a regional meeting in Boston, President Hinckley came to visit potential temple and meetinghouse properties in the New York City area. On Saturday, March 23, 2002, the prophet, his personal secretary, his security guard, Elder Zwick, President Belnap, and Richard Hedberg first visited the Harrison temple site in Westchester County. President Belnap recalls the prophet was intimately familiar with precise details about the site: he rattled off information regarding square footage, drainage, utility lines and elevation, and could identify exactly what the orange spray paint lines on the property meant.

After this visit, the group traveled to view the new Inwood chapel and met Bishops Mark E. Johnson (Inwood First Ward) and Matthew B. Day (Inwood Second Ward). From Inwood, the group drove past the proposed sites for new chapels in Harlem, on East 87th Street, and in a convent near Union Square. As they traveled down Second Avenue, the prophet remarked how unhappy everyone looked. They also drove by Ground Zero where the World Trade Center towers once stood. The prophet commented "how terrible and how horrendous" the events were that took place on September 11th. Late in the afternoon, the group ended their day at the Manhattan stake center to review that location.

After walking through the building, the group met in President Belnap's office to review and discuss what they had seen. According to President Belnap, it appeared certain that a decision to build a temple in New York City had been reached. On the following day, Sunday, March 24, 2002, President Belnap supposed a temple announcement might be made at the special regional meeting being broadcast to the area that would approximate the future temple district. Many local members also hoped the prophet would shed light on a temple in Harrison or even in Manhattan.

On the day of the special regional meeting, however, nothing was said formally. Addressing a full house in the New York New York Stake Center, the prophet did promise that "within two years," members in the city would have access to a temple, and challenged the members to begin preparing themselves. Otherwise, he offered no specific details. However, a series of rapid decisions and communications from Salt Lake City soon brought answers.

In July 2002, a little more than three months after President Hinckley's visit, stake members were surprised to learn that the new chapel and meeting space on the fifth and sixth floors of the stake center would be closed for "renovation."³ Rumors spread quickly of what might be in store. Many Church members hoped a temple would finally be in their midst.

The answer came on Wednesday, August 7, 2002. With no press conference and no special meetings, the First Presidency announced in a press release that a temple would be built in New York City in the present stake center. At the time, President Belnap was vacationing with his family in Utah. Arriving late one evening at his parents' home in Ogden after spending the day in Salt Lake City, he was surprised to learn that he had an urgent message from President Hinckley's personal secretary asking him to call President Hinckley that evening at his home.

President Hinckley told President Belnap that an announcement had gone out earlier that day. The Manhattan New York Temple was now official. The next morning, President Belnap fielded a phone call from a reporter from the New York Times while sitting in the lobby of the Joseph Smith Memorial Building in Salt Lake City.

On August 9, 2002, more than 130 years after its first article announcing a temple in New York City, the New York Times ran a headline about the Latter-day Saints constructing a house of worship: "Mormons Plan a Temple Opposite Lincoln Center." This time, the article was accurate.

# A PROPHET'S PROMISE   PRESIDENT GORDON B HINCKLEY

Highlights of remarks made during a special regional meeting broadcast, originating from the New York New York Stake Center in Manhattan, Sunday, March 24, 2002

Now, one of the reasons I've come here [to New York City], the only reason I've come here, was to see what we could do to move along a temple in this area. We've got a beautiful temple in Boston. We've got a beautiful temple in Washington, and each city is a long ways from New York. We've got all you people here who ought to have the privilege and the opportunity of going to the House of the Lord. I don't know [why] we've had so much trouble. We bought that site in Harrison and we've had it for about six years. We've had hearings and hearings and hearings. I'm tired of hearings. I'm anxious to hear some speakings, in a positive way, to get that building moving....

I can only give you this promise, that somehow, whether it's there [in Harrison] or someplace else, I'm going to see that we get a temple built in this New York area while I'm still alive.... I am going to say that within two years we'll have a temple...ready for dedication. Now don't hold me to the exact date, but I just feel so very strongly that you are deserving of a House of the Lord, that you are deserving of a temple to which you may go and do your work and receive the blessings that are to be found there and only there, and that's why I am in New York, not to talk with you this morning but for a greater purpose....

Now, I want to say to you, that in view of what I have just said, that you get yourselves ready. I'm giving you advance notice to get yourselves ready, to be worthy to go to the House of the Lord.... Get a recommend, a temple recommend as we speak of it, in your pocket, in your purse, so that you may go to the House of the Lord.

You men who are here today, if your lives are not in order, you put them in order. If you are not the kind of man that you ought to be, change, repent, lay aside the past, look up and stand taller, and be a better son of God. Walk in the dignity of the Holy Priesthood. Put on you the armor of righteousness.... and be ready to go to the House of the Lord.

No man who abuses his wife is worthy of that privilege. No man who abuses his children is worthy of that privilege. No man who is dishonest, no man who is a poor neighbor, is worthy of that privilege. My brethren, get yourselves ready and if any of you women are in the same category, you can change, beginning today. Be ready when a House of the Lord is reared somewhere, I don't know where, in this part of the world where you can get to it....

Well, I'm just telling you to get ready, because I feel satisfied that it's coming. I don't know where that temple will stand. I don't know whether we'll be able to build [on] the property that we've owned for six years where we've been opposed *time after time after time for a reason we cannot understand except that there's an adversary who makes his power felt. Brigham Young once said, "We never announce the construction of a temple that the bells of hell don't begin to ring." And some of us have heard them. Well . . . somehow we're going to do it. We're going to exercise our faith. We're going to pray for it. All of us. I urge you, I plead with you, to do so and it will come to pass to bless your lives.*

## A PEOPLE PREPARE ALLISON CLARK

After the temple was publicly announced on August 7, 2002, a flurry of activity spread through the stakes and wards of the proposed new temple district. Wherever a new temple is being constructed, a temple executive committee serves as the steering body for all temple-related activities. In this case, the first temple committee meeting was held in September 2002, presided over by Elder Spencer J. Condie, North America Northeast Area President.

The committee was comprised of the current Area President, a Public Affairs representative (Bruce L. Olsen), a Temple Department representative (Robert K. Reeve), and a local committee coordinator (Brent J. Belnap). With Elder Condie's release as the Area President in the summer of 2003, Elder Glen L. Pace succeeded him. When Elder Pace became ill in the fall of 2003, Elder David R. Stone, second counselor in the Area Presidency, assumed that role. Members of the committee appointed from the temple district took responsibility for audiovisual arrangements, community relations, reservations, food, missionary activities, music, physical facilities, public affairs, history, dedication recommends, security, translation, and volunteer services.

Under the supervision of this committee, large numbers of Church members from all over the temple district volunteered their services. Projects ranged from cleaning the temple construction site to orchestrating a youth jubilee at Radio City Music Hall. Staffing the five-week open house gave hundreds of members an opportunity to serve in the temple prior to its dedication. In the New York New York Stake alone, over 400 members volunteered in some capacity, along with more than 2,000 youth from the region for the jubilee.

Lynn Fisher, a member of the New York New York Stake, was asked to help clean the tile in the bathroom of the baptismal area. She said that, beyond the dirt, dust, and grime of the construction site, "every once in a while I caught a glimpse of the beauty of a temple; like a beautiful piece of millwork hidden behind some plywood just waiting to be put in place."

Sandra Turley, president of the Inwood First Ward Primary, recalls the children writing thank you cards for the construction workers: "Our Primary made a large poster with individual letters from each child pasted on. The children loved writing to the workers and shared their encouragement and love in a way only children can." Later, at a special stake activity the Primary children counted the protective foot coverings used to cover the feet of the folding chairs at the temple dedication.

Each of the 14 stakes or districts in the temple district was asked to provide at least one altar cloth for use on one of the four altars of the temple. Tara Skouson of the New York New York Stake oversaw the altar cloth project both for her stake and for the temple district as a whole. Her stake took a collaborative approach to making the altar cloths. Rather than have one individual crochet the entire cloth, about 30 individuals created one crocheted square that became part of the larger whole.

While the Church Public Affairs office and the local temple committee were responsible for organizing the open house, local volunteer members were essential in executing the work. Members from the Brooklyn New York Stake helped verify addresses, proof the VIP letters of invitation and stuff them into envelopes. Open house tickets generated through the two reservation call centers were printed and mailed by a Church volunteer. Brother Ray Oser in New Jersey managed the entire reservation ticketing system and personally printed and mailed all the individual tickets.

To staff the open house for the VIP week and the four weeks of public tours, volunteers were organized by Steven Quinn, Blair Garff, and Malcolm Draper. Each stake within the temple district was assigned shifts (morning or afternoon/evening) to staff each day of the open house. Sixty volunteers were assigned for the morning shifts lasting from 9 a.m. to 3 p.m., and eighty for the afternoon/evening shifts lasting from 3 p.m. until the closing at 9 p.m. six days a week. From 250 to 300 volunteers were at the temple each day. The volunteers were responsible for a range of tasks including ushering, greeting, operating elevators, giving shoe covers, and serving refreshments. The approximately 550 tour guides were selected by the bishops and stake presidents within the temple district. Many bishops reported that people felt it a special privilege to be asked.

The preparations made the temple the focus of church life for over a year, culminating in the intense six-week period beginning May 1, 2004, with the open house, and culminating June 13, with the dedication. Through their work, the Saints laid personal claims to the temple well before it opened for formal sessions.

### EFFECTS ON LOCAL FAMILY HISTORY WORK  LINDA CAMERON

When construction of the Manhattan New York Temple was announced in August 2002, leaders of the New York New York Stake established a family history goal: before the dedication in 2004, members of the stake would prepare 4,000 names for temple ordinances—roughly equal to the number of current members of the stake. Every unit helped spark ward members' efforts to achieve this goal in different ways. Some units held linger-longers, family home evenings, or other family history-related ward activities. Two wards called a small army of family history consultants and assigned each of them to focus on a portion of the ward roster. One ward organized a service project to tackle one member's massive family file. Several units held Sunday family history classes.

Most importantly, all of the stake's family history consultants provided members with help, support, and one-on-one contact. Because of these efforts, many members in our stake became enthusiastic about family history work. By the time of the temple dedication, family history work had been completed for 3,140 ancestors. Stake members are continuing to work on the original goal and intend to complete it by the end of 2004.

## TEMPLE OPEN HOUSE: HOTTEST TICKET IN TOWN
RICHARD BUSHMAN

"The hottest ticket in town," an article in *USA Today* called reservations at the Manhattan New York Temple open house. Judging by attendance, thousands of New Yorkers and people from far off places agreed.

The first tours were given on Saturday, May 1, 2004. The special guests invited for the occasion included the construction workers and their families. Many of them knew the temple inside out already, but not all had seen it furnished and beautified. This was a chance to show their handiwork to their families. The others to come on that first day were nearby residents invited to "Neighbor Day."

Tours from May 3 to 7 were part of "VIP week," attracting leading politicians, business leaders, and academic figures. At the Friday reception, Latter-day Saint Senators Harry Reid and Gordon Smith, and Member of Congress Eni F. H. Faleomavaega were present to greet New York congressional leaders Senator Charles Schumer and Congressman Charles Rangel. Tour guides were pleased to show State Representative Keith Wright through the building. Michael Wallace, host of *Sixty Minutes* and a friend of President Hinckley, chatted for over an hour with friends in the Church. Many United Nations ambassadors attended the reception.

Temple tours ended in the cultural hall decorated for the first week with sprays of cherry blossoms and greenery. Tables and sofas provided comfortable locations for people to talk following the tours. Many lingered to ask questions and become better acquainted with Church members.

The tour's 13-minute introductory video included many New York touches. Local Latter-day Saints were interviewed on the street about their reactions to the temple. The Church's beginnings in New York State and Joseph Smith's 1832 visit to New York City helped explain why Latter-day Saints honor New York.

The boundaries for the temple's "neighbors" ran from about 60th to 70th Street on the west side. An individual invitation was sent to each of the 1400 apartments in six residential buildings within those limits. To reach the temple's commercial neighbors, New York New York Stake volunteers hand delivered invitations to about 150 businesses, all of which are part of the larger "Lincoln Square Business Improvement District," a neighborhood consortium in which the Church participates.

Tours for the general public began on Saturday, May 8, and ran through Saturday, June 5. As many as 3,000 people a day came to the site. The size of the temple elevator limited each tour to about 15 people. To allow as many as possible to visit, guides remained at each stop for no more than four minutes on a tour that lasted three-quarters of an hour.

Governor Olene Walker of Utah and Senate Majority Leader Joseph L. Bruno of New York were among those to tour the temple. Four members of the Quorum of the Twelve, Elders Boyd K. Packer, L. Tom Perry, Russell M. Nelson, and Richard G. Scott, viewed the temple in the first week of public tours. Among those in attendance during most of VIP week to welcome guests were Elder Earl C. Tingey of the Presidency of the Seventy, Sheri L. Dew, CEO of Deseret Book and former member of the General Relief Society presidency, Elders H. Bryan Richards and David R. Stone of the North America Northeast Area Presidency and their wives.

Over 53,000 people toured the Manhattan temple during the open house. The cards they were invited to fill out at the end revealed that the vast majority were from the metropolitan New York area and neighboring states, but many came from far away, including visitors from 29 different states and Canada, Puerto Rico, Italy, Peru, and Australia.

The overwhelming response of the visitors was that of gratitude for being able to come, and pleasant surprise at the beauty, serenity, and peacefulness of the temple, especially the celestial room. Many said their knowledge of the Church's beliefs increased as a result of the tour: "I really enjoyed the tour and found it both informative and interesting. I came away with a better understanding of both the church and the temple." An intriguing comment came from one visitor: "Very clean, American place. I am continually reminded yours is truly a religion of our native soil. Thanks for your hospitality and blessings!"

Visitors found their own individual reasons for enjoying the tour:

"I was amazed at the happiness and joy all of the volunteers here demonstrate—even I felt a sense of peace and happiness as I passed through the temple."

"I came to this temple to understand or at least try to understand why the family who came with me was and is so pleasant and kind and I got a lot of my questions answered. Thanks for the opportunity to see a great group of people and a great culture."

"The tour of your temple is something I will never forget. I now understand why Mormons all look so happy and serene. How wonderful to believe that marriage and family are until eternity."

"Who knew all this peace and beauty [existed] in Manhattan."

"This must be the quietest building on Broadway."

"Thank you for having us. We see the roots of our Jewish faith carried on in yours."

"This is a very special ethereal place. I am a Catholic."

"I am thanking God right now to you and your church for teaching family unity and the importance of morality. These are the very fundamental ingredients for a good life in harmony and in walking in God's light."

"I'd love a celestial place at my church!!"

"Thank you for allowing a non-Mormon like myself to visit your temple. It is truly a beautiful and holy place."

"Today, God confirmed to me once again that he will be with us as long as we have faith in him—regardless of our religious affiliation."

"I had not been in a temple in five years as I've been highly inactive. The visit helped me feel the Spirit and remember when I went to the temple for the first time to be a missionary. Beautiful!"

Many LDS Church members traveling to New York took the occasion to visit the temple as well. One member from California explained: "I saw the Statue of Liberty for the first time today which was most impressive and symbolic. However the temple tour was even more meaningful. Thank you." Some members seemed to have come to New York specifically for the temple open house. A couple in Nevada noted that, "We met here—on the 3rd floor—back in 1975! It is wonderful to see it now."

## ENCAPSULATING THE PRESENT FOR FUTURE GENERATIONS: THE TEMPLE CORNERSTONE RICHARD BUSHMAN

The cornerstone of the Manhattan New York Temple is neither in a corner nor is it a stone. A marble plaque with the inscription "Temple Dedicated 2004" in large gold letters is affixed to the partition between the temple and meetinghouse elevators in the lobby of the building. The cornerstone box was sealed behind this plaque by President Gordon B. Hinckley on Sunday, June 13, 2004, as part of the first dedicatory session.

The previous day at 8 a.m. a brief ceremony was conducted in the foyer of the temple itself to place the items in the cornerstone box where they will presumably lie for 50 to 100 years. Under the direction of Elder A. Kim Smith, Area Authority Seventy, various members were called up to place items in the box.

Amber Blakesley, the person responsible for graphic design of the contents, was called up first, and then other members of the history committee who had helped assemble the materials. The entire temple committee was called forward and from among them, Stephen Quinn, Blair Garff, and Malcolm Draper, who played a large part in organizing the open house, placed items. The new temple presidency headed by President John R. Stone with Rodney A. Hawes Jr., first counselor, and Kang Woo Lee, second counselor, also placed items.

Following Church guidelines, the list of contents included the standard works, a book by Gordon B. Hinckley, *Stand for Something*, a hymn book in Spanish signed by many Spanish-speaking members, a *New York Times* for June 12, 2004. In fulfillment of the suggestion for a local history, *New York Glory: Religions in the City,* edited by Tony Carnes and Anna Karpathakis was added to the list. The book contained an article by New York New York Stake member James Lucas, "Mormons in New York City."

Richard Bushman, patriarch in the New York New York Stake, chaired the history sub-committee responsible for organizing the cornerstone. He invited each of the 14 stakes and districts and 4 missions in the temple district to submit three pages (six sides) for inclusion in a cornerstone scrapbook. The entries included local histories, photos of buildings, names of leaders, and pictures of members. One unusual example from the Richmond Hill District had three- and four-line testimonies from hundreds of members closely packed onto six pages.

Another scrapbook held temple memorabilia from the open house along with a small group of documents to capture the flavor of the Lincoln Square neighborhood including programs from the Metropolitan Opera and the New York Philharmonic, which perform across the street. A subway map and a subway MetroCard were inserted to show future generations how many local members reach the temple. Even the special recipe for the cookies at the open house found a place in the box.

A small tin container held a silk handkerchief with the words of "The Spirit of God Like a Fire Is Burning" printed in gold. It was prepared for the temple dedication by Claudia Bushman, Amber Blakesley and Sumer Thurston Evans in the tradition of a similar handkerchief made for the Kirtland Temple dedication by William W. Phelps at the request of Joseph Smith.

The following morning, President Hinckley was the first to place mortar along the edge of the plaque. A choir led by Peter Asplund opened the ceremony, and then members present, including two children called from the audience, took their turns with the trowel and mortar provided by Cory Karl, manager of temple construction. Elders Hales and Stone and their wives wielded the trowel followed by the new temple presidency. President Hinckley joked that despite all his practice he still was not expert at troweling in mortar.

## SERVICE PROJECT ON THE "BIG STAGE" ALLISON CLARKE

June 12, 2004—the day before the dedication of the Manhattan New York Temple—is a day that will stand out in the hearts and memories of thousands of youth in the temple district for years to come. That afternoon they gathered together for a once-in-a-lifetime activity: performing at Radio City Music Hall at the request of President Hinckley. He wanted to hold this Youth Jubilee in honor of the temple's dedication to provide an opportunity for the youth to celebrate and praise the Lord through dance and song.

"The largest cast ever to appear on the stage of Radio City Music Hall," was the way Dave Checketts, former head of the famed theater, characterized the Youth Jubilee presented on a Saturday evening with President Gordon B. Hinckley in the audience. "Stupendous, wonderful, absolutely wonderful," were the words President Hinckley used to describe his reaction as he left the hall.

It was the marquee that first caught President Hinckley's attention as he approached the world-famous hall. To see "Manhattan Mormon Temple, Standard for the Nations Youth Jubilee, Church of Jesus Christ of Latter-day Saints " up there in bright lights made him feel that the Church had finally arrived in New York City.

A regional committee designed the night's program and local leaders implemented the plan in 14 weeks. Under the direction of a team of talented professionals, the event was broadcast to Church buildings with satellite reception throughout the temple district.

Jubilee events had been organized previously for the dedication of temples in Ghana, Alaska, and Copenhagen, and for the re-dedication of the São Paolo Temple in Brazil. Sister Claudia Bushman of the New York New York Stake, producer of the program, indicated that in early phases of planning there was some thought of securing either Yankee or Shea stadium in New York City or Giants Stadium in New Jersey, or using other outdoor venues such as the Great Lawn in Central Park or Corona Park in Queens. However, by early March, Radio City Music Hall had been selected.

At the outset it was decided to divide the temple district into six units and assign each group a theme to be developed into eight-minute segments. The groups assigned to each theme did not necessarily correspond with the cultural heritage of many of the youth in those stakes or districts, giving the youth an opportunity to explore the music and dance of other cultures. The stakes and districts were assigned into segments as follows:

Pioneers: Morristown and Caldwell New Jersey Stakes, and Paterson New Jersey District, directed by Robyn Smith and Gail Spjut.

European: Plainview New York Stake and Lynbrook New York District, directed by Vivian DeRosa.

Harlem: New York New York and Brooklyn New York Stakes, directed by Matt Toronto.

Latin: Scotch Plains and East Brunswick New Jersey Stakes, directed by Julie Pearson and Tara Cobia.

Asian: Queens New York West and Richmond Hill Districts, directed by Samantha Stentzler.

Broadway: Newburgh, Westchester, and Yorktown New York Stakes, directed by Dorothy Bench, Sue Garff, Tom Pratt, and Kevin Kelly.

Sister Bushman estimated that nearly 1,000 adult Church members and about 2,400 youth were involved in bringing this project to life. "This is a larger scale than any of us are accustomed to working in," she said, "but we all consider it a great opportunity and a blessing to sing and dance for the prophet in Radio City Music Hall."

While as many as 600 youth at a time got on and off the stage, video clips showing New York Church history, local youth, and General Authority speakers from the New York area held the audience's attention. Apostles L. Tom Perry, Robert D. Hales, and Henry B. Eyring reminisced about their own time growing up or working in the New York metropolitan region.

Erik Orton, an experienced Broadway producer who served as artistic director for the event, described preparation for the project as "very overwhelming," but noted that the volunteers and youth involved "took ownership" of their parts and enjoyed being involved. The morning after the Jubilee he wrote to the production team, "I can't speak for everybody, but I must say Saturday evening truly felt like a revelation to me. . . . As I was writing in my journal last night, the phrase that came to mind was 'one heart and one mind.'"

The youth seemed to feel the same spirit. Katherine Gámez, a 14-year-old member of the Manhattan First Ward, commented upon the effect of all gathering together to rehearse on the stage of Radio City Music Hall: "When we did the practices before I didn't know people much, and I felt distance from other kids. But once we went to the stage, I felt that we were a team and felt more close with the other kids."

Matt Toronto, a Broadway performer from the Inwood First Ward, directed the Harlem segment presented by a combined cast from the New York and Brooklyn Stakes. To help choreograph the Harlem section, Matt turned to five seasoned dancers and performers from the Inwood First Ward.

One of these five, 16-year-old Navild Acosta, attends a performing arts high school in Manhattan. Navild commented that it was "pretty special" to be the "only 16-year-old choreographing for the show," yet she felt that she was "respected like the other choreographers."

Navild indicated that the six choreographers began meeting weekly in early May to set the dance until they had established the choreography for all the pieces. The choreographers began meeting with the youth from the two stakes in two separate groups to teach them the movements. The groups rehearsed for two hours each Saturday from mid-May up to the very date of the Jubilee.

Youth from the two stakes first practiced the Harlem segment together on the Saturday prior to the Jubilee, when all the youth crowded into the Inwood building in upper Manhattan. Navild commented that the most satisfying rehearsal of all was the one held on the day of the Jubilee itself, as all the youth from the entire temple district came together.

Youth from throughout the stake concurred that the Jubilee was a memorable experience. Miguel Rojas, a 17-year-old priest in the Inwood Second Ward, reported, "I came to the USA just two months, I don't understand the language but still I went to the Jubilee. I have the opportunity to meet all the young men and women from the stake. When I arrived to the Radio City Music Hall I was nervous but later I realized that I was going to do this for the prophet, then I start relaxing. When I saw all this young people together I realized that if they are faithful they will make the Church more strong in the future."

During a one-hour interlude following the Jubilee, box lunches were passed up and down the aisles to the youth participants. Then President Hinckley spoke to the audience about how the temple decision was made. He read from his personal journal for March 23, 2002, when he was inspired to build the temple in Manhattan following the model of the Hong Kong Temple, where the church building also has multiple uses.

Many of the participating youth reported being touched by President Hinckley's fireside comments. They took his message about making a difference to heart. Judith Feliz, a 13-year-old member of the Manhattan Fourth Ward, commented, "I am going to remember the message that if I don't make my decisions in time, time will make my decisions for me." Alan Garcia, a 16-year-old member of the same ward said that he "liked the challenge that President Hinckley gave to us, to make a difference."

## MANHATTAN TEMPLE DEDICATION REACHES OVER 10,000
RICHARD BUSHMAN AND ALLISON CLARK

On Sunday, June 13, 2004, President Gordon B. Hinckley dedicated the Church's 119th temple, located at the corner of 65th Street and Columbus Avenue across from famed Lincoln Center in New York City.

This temple is unusual because it is constructed within a standing structure—and in the middle of a city that is recognized as the financial and arts capital of the world. Perhaps President Hinckley had this in mind when he observed during his remarks that, "as I walked through this magnificent building created within an old building, I said to myself, 'This is Zion in Babylon...This is such a place of beauty. A miracle, I think, has occurred here." It was a miracle he had predicted himself in March 2002 when he announced to local members that they would have a temple somewhere nearby within two years.

The sun shone all day on the crowds lined up outside the temple for admission to the dedicatory sessions. One group lined up on 65th Street on the south side of the temple with blue recommend tickets in hand waiting to take the stairs to the temple rooms. Another assembled along 66th Street on the north side with green recommends for the seats in the chapel, cultural hall, and surrounding classrooms. Those with white recommends for the celestial room entered through the front door on Columbus Avenue.

As they entered, the groups going into the temple donned white plastic shoe coverings to protect the carpets. A large team of ushers and security people under the direction of Stephen Quinn, Blair Garff and Malcolm Draper shepherded them to their seats.

Four dedicatory sessions were held, starting at 9:00 a.m., 11:30 a.m., 2:00 p.m. and 4:30 p.m. Each session lasted for almost an hour and a half. That left a little more than an hour to clear the building of one session and to seat the next group before the following session began. President Hinckley was the hero of the day, officiating at all four sessions with only brief rests in between.

Elders David R. Stone of the North America North East Area Presidency and Robert D. Hales of the Quorum of the Twelve spoke at each session. Sister Rosalie Stone also spoke in multiple sessions. In at least one session, Elder Hales, who was raised in New York, spoke of modern pioneers who moved east—rather than west—to establish the Church in this area. For each session, Elder Hales led the hosanna shout and the waving of white handkerchiefs, and President Hinckley gave the concluding remarks and offered the dedicatory prayer.

Additional speakers included Sister Helen Stone and President John R. Stone in the first session, Brother LaVell Edwards and Elder Cree-L Kofford? in the second session, Sister Beverly Hawes, President Rodney A. Hawes Jr., and President Brent J. Belnap in the third session, and Sister Kum Hee Lee and President Kang Woo Lee in the fourth session. Stake presidents from the temple district were assigned in advance to offer the invocation and benediction at each session.

Members of President Hinckley's immediate family in attendance included Virginia and James Pearce, Kathleen and Richard Walker, Clark and

Kathleen Hinckley, and Jane and Roger Dudley, plus several grandchildren and their spouses.

Each session featured a different regional choir from the temple district, organized by Bishop J. David Skouson, chair of the temple committee's music subcommittee. For the first session, Janeel S. Smith led the "east" choir from the Plainview New York Stake and Lynbrook New York District; Jeff Osborn led the "north" choir from the Newburgh, Yorktown and Westchester New York Stakes for the second session; Nancy Thorne led the "west" choir from the East Brunswick, Scotch Plains, Morristown and Caldwell New Jersey Stakes and the Paterson New Jersey District in the third session; and David Skouson led the "south" choir from the New York and Brooklyn New York Stakes and the Queens West and Richmond Hill New York Districts in the fourth session.

Two stationary video cameras inside the celestial room relayed each session to members seated in the rooms of the temple and the adjacent meetinghouse. Meanwhile, in 15 other meetinghouses throughout the temple district, members viewed the dedicatory sessions live via satellite. Each of these broadcast locations was considered an extension of the temple for the occasion. Only baptized and confirmed members of the Church, people who were worthy of temple recommends, were admitted to view the dedication, including children eight years of age or older. In the course of the day, 10,649 people participated in the four dedicatory sessions.

During the second session, the dedication was broadcast in Spanish to parts of the temple and most meetinghouse locations to accommodate the large Spanish-speaking population within the temple district. With the help of translators in Salt Lake City, all of the dedication was made available during various sessions and in various locations in one or more of the following languages: Mandarin, Cantonese, French, Haitian French Creole, Korean, Portuguese, Russian and Spanish. The third session was closed-captioned and also translated at the Lincoln Square meetinghouse into American Sign Language for hearing-impaired members.

Following each session, members lingered on the sidewalk greeting friends. Many participants had returned to New York City from distant places. Former mission presidents and stake presidents attended. The requests for recommend tickets came in from all over the country. A former mission president from Sydney, Australia, returned to New York to serve as an open house tour guide and attend the dedication.

President Hinckley's words about "Zion in Babylon" could be taken as a challenge to temple district members. "Of all the cities in the world, I can't think of anywhere that needs a place of peace and refuge and repentance more than New York City," said local committee coordinator President Brent

J. Belnap of the New York New York Stake. President Hinckley extended strength to the Saints in the words of the dedicatory prayer:

"We remember before thee those who preside in other temples, those who preside in stakes and wards, in districts and branches, in missions, in the quorums of the priesthood, in the Relief Society and other organizations of thy Church and kingdom. May all work with an eye single to thy glory that light and truth and knowledge of things divine may crown their lives."

President Hinckley offered a vision of how this temple and its surrounding Zion might bless the city and the world. Praying for local leaders, he said:

Watch over them and shelter and protect them, and lead them with revelation that will bless thy people everywhere, that thy work will be seen as a bright and shining star in a world oppressed with darkness. Father, there is so much of evil in the world, of strife, of man's inhumanity to man. We pray that peace may come where there is war, that conciliation may come where there is conflict, that neighborliness and love may replace hatred and enmity.

New York City's first temple ordinances began on Monday, June 14, at 11:00 a.m., with an endowment session for stake and mission presidents from the temple district.

### THE FIRST MANHATTAN TEMPLE PRESIDENT AND MATRON: JOHN AND HELEN STONE SARIAH TORONTO

As a stake president in the New York City region during the 1990s, John Stone had good reason to think there may not be a temple in Manhattan any time soon. In his office desk one day he found a letter that a prior stake president had written to Church authorities in Salt Lake City, asking them to consider the possibility of a temple in the area. The reply from Salt Lake was a request for that stake president to focus on other considerable matters before him.

One of the most pressing concerns for local Church leaders for a number of years has been space for weekly worship and activities. "Physical facilities have always played catch-up to the membership in Manhattan," President Stone said, and for most of the time he was stake president he searched for meeting space. While this search proved successful in Harlem, the hunt was fruitless on the Upper East Side. These efforts eclipsed any thought of a temple.

Now that a temple has been built, President Stone calls its existence a "miracle." With a growing membership in the metro region, two new meetinghouses and plans for two more in Manhattan alone, President Stone says the new temple represents "a multiplication of the Church's commitment" to the region.

Having lived in the area more than 30 years, President Stone speaks from experience. An economist by training, President Stone came to the New

York area in 1969 to take a job with the Federal Reserve Bank of New York. He and his wife, Helen, had one child at the time and the trio set up house in Scarsdale, Westchester County. The Stones called Scarsdale home for the next three decades, during which time they raised five children. Two of the children continue to live in the New York metro area—Greg in Manhattan and Megan on Long Island.

President Stone, who joined the Church as a teenager in El Paso, Texas, is no stranger to Church service, both in the New York area and farther afield. He served as a Young Men's president, and from 1978 to 1983 he was bishop of the Westchester Ward. During the summer of 1991, he was briefly a counselor in the stake presidency of the New York New York Stake, which at the time was comprised of the Westchester Ward and all units in the Bronx and Manhattan.

In September 1991, he was called as president of the stake, a role he filled until November 1997, when the stake was split into two separate units. Two and a half years later, in July 2000, President and Sister Stone were called to preside over the Greece Athens Mission. The mission included the countries of Greece and Cyprus, where young missionaries served, as well as Egypt, Lebanon, Syria and Jordan, where couple missionaries labored. President and Sister Stone returned to the States in July 2003 before receiving their new assignments as temple president and matron in April 2004.

Given President Stone's background and Church experience in the metro region, the new temple president is uniquely positioned to comment on the effect the temple will likely have on the Church membership. "It will grow," he says because "people feel safe and uplifted when there's a temple. That's why we need it."

In the mid-1800s the area that was to become Lincoln Square was a suburban hamlet called Bloomingdale Village. The church in this illustration is at what is now West 68th Street and Broadway (originally Bloomingdale Road). Photo courtesy of New York Public LIbrary.

The Lincoln Square area began to change rapidly with the construction of the Ninth Avenue Elevated, shown here at West 69th Street and what would become Columbus Avenue. Photo courtesy of New York Public LIbrary.

From the 1880s to the early 1940s, Lincoln Square was dominated by the Ninth Avenue El station located in front of the block now occupied by the Manhattan temple and stake center. The neighborhood, of mixed Irish and African-American working class populations, was nicknames "San Juan Hill," in honor of the African-American Tenth Cavalry of the U.S. Army, which had fought in that famous battle during the Spanish-American War. Photo courtesy of New York Public LIbrary.

By 1970, the building pictured here on the corner of West 66th Street and Columbus Avenue had been torn down and replaced by the parking lot on which President Harold B. Lee stood when inspired to have the Church acquire the site. This corner is now occupied by the apartment building next to the Manhattan temple and stake center. Photo courtesy of New York Public LIbrary.

Fifth-floor construction where the terrestrial and celestial rooms of the temple were to be built. The space housed racquetball courts when the building was first built in the 1970s. Photo courtesy of the New York New York Stake.

Artist's rendering of the Manhattan New York Temple. © Courtesy of the Church Archives, The Church of Jesus Christ of Latter-day Saints.

President Gordon B. Hinckley at the dedication of the cornerstone of the temple. © Courtesy of the Church Archives, The Church of Jesus Christ of Latter-day Saints.

Logo of the Youth Jubilee, which took place at Radio City Music Hall on June 12, 2004.

Marquis of Radio City Music Hall, where youth from the temple district performed in the Youth Jubilee, comprising the largest cast ever to perform on that historic stage. Photo courtesy of James Ransom.

John and Helen Stone, president and matron of the Manhattan New York Temple. Photo courtesy of John and Helen Stone.

# PART 3: IT'S A WONDERFUL TOWN

# GROWING UP IN THE CITY

**STROLLERS ON THE ISLAND** JOANNE ROWLAND

Transporting the baby around town is one of the chief problems of young parents living in New York City. Most people do not have cars and rely on public transportation. They arrive for church services via foot, bus, subway, or taxi. There are very few places to park near the Manhattan chapels. There is, however, a very big stroller "parking lot" each Sunday.

One Sunday, a Primary president was explaining to the children what the exit plans were in case of emergency in the stake center's meeting space on the third floor. "If there is a fire in the building, we will leave Primary with our teachers and meet our parents downstairs outside the building," she explained.

"Will we take the strollers?" asked one child.

"No, we will leave the strollers," she answered.

Then another child asked, "But what if there is a baby in the stroller?"

For those hearty enough to stay after the birth of the second child, the big question becomes whether to purchase a side-by-side double stroller or a front-to-back double. Whatever the decision, young parents agree that some errands can no longer be done without someone to stay at home with the children because revolving doors do not accommodate any type of double stroller.

One mother of a large family explained that once her family became too large to fit into one taxicab, they decided that they would no longer go anyplace unless they could walk. Fortunately, within a one-mile radius of their apartment was the church, Lincoln Center, the Juilliard School, Carnegie Hall, Broadway, Central Park, the American Museum of Natural History, the Metropolitan Museum of Art, the Museum of Modern Art, and several branches of the New York Public Library, a few of the cultural perks of growing up in New York.

How old is a New York City child before he or she can leave home unaccompanied? If two well-acquainted families live in the same building, young children will learn to ride the elevator alone to visit the other family. One

New York mother was heard to say upon returning from a summer trip to visit family in Utah, "My three-year-old daughter can ride the elevator by herself, but she is afraid of grass."

Adults accompany children to school during most of the elementary school grades. Somewhere in those years, a child will be allowed to go alone to the corner deli to make a purchase of milk or ice cream or some other necessity, or perhaps return a library book if the library is within two or three blocks of home. Somewhere in fourth or fifth grade, children are allowed to go to school alone or with siblings or friends. At age 11 or 12, children might be allowed to travel to the church alone for daytime activities.

Some children who live in large building complexes with attached playgrounds have some latitude and freedom to go outside and find a playmate. However, it is not uncommon for a child's social life to consist mainly of the formal, pre-planned "play date" with parents initiating the invitations and arranging the drop off and pick up of the invited child and the reciprocal invitation. Birthday parties become important social events.

The trade-off for the labor-intensive early childhood transportation arrangements is that when the children are teenagers, they are not getting driver's licenses or riding with friends who are inexperienced drivers. Teenagers get around by themselves on public transportation.

Growing up in New York City, Latter-day Saint children also establish their spiritual identities and make decisions about standards at an early age. At school, they meet children of all different faith backgrounds. They learn something about other religions when their Jewish and Muslim friends are excused from school on their religious holidays.

The children and youth organizations in the English language Manhattan wards tend to be bottom heavy. By December of each year the Primary nurseries are full of eighteen-month to three-year-old children. From there on up, the classes tend to diminish in size year by year. Senior Primary classes often combine two classes into one. It is not uncommon for a young girl to be made president of a Beehive class of which she is the only member or a young boy to be the only twelve-year-old passing the sacrament.

English speaking young people come to New York City for school or first jobs and often do not stay more than two or three years. In Spanish-speaking wards, flight to the suburbs or back to the West occurs less often. Many Spanish-speaking members are first generation Americans, and some return to their homelands for short periods, but for most, New York City is the ultimate rather than an interim destination.

Kamla Fennimore and Jordan Gunther lived New York City Mormon lives from a young age. Their families not only held on; they enjoyed being city

Saints. Following are some of their experiences in their own words.

## KAMLA FENNIMORE

*Kamla Fennimore, daughter of Bishop Tony Fennimore and Sharon Fitzpatrick, is currently a member of the Manhattan Eighth Ward. She graduated in 2003 from Brigham Young University with a Bachelor of Social Work. She has just finished her Masters in Social Work at Columbia University and is now job hunting. She served in the Japan Tokyo North Mission from 2000 to 2002.*

I was born on Manhattan's Upper West Side three months short of the 1980s. My parents were still hippies, despite the impending decade of materialism. They brought me home from the hospital to 251 West 98th Street, where I continued to reside until I came of legal voting age. My neighborhood was a melting pot of people varying in culture, faith and lifestyle.

The tenants of my building ranged from schizophrenics to refugees to child abusers to AIDS patients to my Mormon family. It was not a surprise to come home and encounter homeless people sleeping in the lobby, doors axed down, drug dealers doing business or the police in their pursuit. My building was located two blocks from projects and two blocks from penthouses. Living between affluence and poverty enabled me to see the traps of both extremes.

Growing up, I thought my world was one of contradictions, but I learned it was one of duality. I was lost somewhere between protests and bake sales; Chelsea clubs and girls camp; living amidst church names and wanting to disown them. You always knew you were different; it was something that you felt more than you were told. And you learned that opposition empowered you. Resistance is what gave you your strength, and if you didn't embrace your trials, they could never become your teachers.

Sometimes I am asked in adulthood "what it was like." Not quite grasping it myself, I pause before responding, not sure whether to share the stories people may or may not want to hear. "It was great" is easier to say. And so I smile and feel a little guilty.

## JORDAN GUNTHER

*Paul and Lynda Gunther reared their eight children in an apartment building adjacent to the Lincoln Square church. Their son Jordan served a mission in the Dominican Republic. He now works as a claims adjuster for the car insurance company, Progressive. Jordan and his wife Jera are members of the Inwood First Ward. Jordan serves as second counselor in his ward Young Men presidency, and Jera is second counselor in the stake Young Women presidency.*

Growing up in New York as a Church member made me feel like a pioneer. I did not pull a handcart across the plains or face much persecution, but I feel I helped to blaze a trail for members who will follow me in New York.

My family moved to the city in 1975 when I was three or four years old. We lived in an apartment house on the same block where the stake center and temple are now located. It was easy for my parents to send us to church activities next door rather than having to accompany us on the subway or bus. There used to be a visitors' center in the church, and my siblings and I loved to go over to the church and watch Church commercials on Boch, a robot that had a screen where his stomach should have been. It was a sad day when the Church got rid of Boch.

My first church "responsibility" was to clean the church chalkboards once a week. Tom Vogelmann would let me into the building, and I enjoyed making the church a nicer place to be.

I served as deacon and teacher quorum president as well as first and second counselor—by default since I was the only deacon and teacher at the time. I enjoyed preparing and passing the sacrament every Sunday. I had no supervisor, only a word of advice from my father and the bishop every once in a while. I tried my best to be a good example.

I was the only Church member in the several schools I attended, unless one of my siblings happened to be there at the time. I found that I was respected for what I believed. Those who smoked and drank alcohol would ask me why I didn't do those things. This led to conversations about the Word of Wisdom. Teachers and students noted that my actions and language set me apart. Being an example was one of the ways I felt like a pioneer.

Sharing the gospel with others has been an adventure, bringing unexpected results. My brother, Jansen, helped a friend get a job as our building's doorman. We spoke to him about the gospel, and he was given a Book of Mormon. The missionaries soon followed. The young man is still not a member, but someone he referred to the missionaries was baptized.

My sister, Jesse, shared the Book of Mormon with one of her friends, James Martin Mulligan. He read the entire book, took the discussions and was baptized. Now James has a full scholarship to run track at Fordham University and plans to give it up after a year, if necessary, to serve a mission. New York City has given my family many opportunities to plant small gospel seeds in the hearts of friends and watch them grow.

Being one of eight children I cherished my time with family members. I also enjoyed time with members in the ward, the missionaries, and missionary couples. I looked forward to church on Sunday and weekday youth activities. These opportunities built my faith and strengthened my spiritual armor.

Years ago the *Daily News* wished to write an article on how a family of seven is raised in the city. The article featured my mom and dad. Unfortunately, there was no sequel for the additional three children that followed. Since other Latter-day Saint youth were scarce outside of our own family, we learned to love and get along with each other. To this day, we all speak to each other weekly and love each other's company.

It is nothing short of miraculous how the Church has grown since my family moved to New York. Today Manhattan is its own stake. In June 2004, we dedicated a temple where people once played racquetball, tennis and ate at Long John Silver's. I think the purpose of the building today is much more noble than in days past.

# SINGLE IN THE CITY

The writer E. B. White once described the city as containing three types of people: those who are born here, the weekday commuter and the person who was born elsewhere and came to New York in quest of something. "Commuters give the city its tidal restlessness; natives give it solidity and continuity; but the settlers give it passion." The same can be said about the single members of The Church of Jesus Christ of Latter-day Saints in New York City. Following are some of their own insights and observations about their experiences here.

### ON MOVING TO NEW YORK

I came 10 years ago with a Masters degree in medieval literature and a plan to stay for one year. There isn't much market for medieval literature scholars so my back-up career of editing has become my primary career. Now I own real estate and an automobile. I'm here for the duration. DAWN ROSQUIST INWOOD FIRST WARD FINANCIAL COPY EDITOR

I came as a nanny eight years ago to work for only one year. I've had a variety of experiences in the corporate world and have begun graduate studies. JOANNA LEGERSKI MANHATTAN THIRD WARD RESEARCHER, CHILD PSYCHIATRY, COLUMBIA UNIVERSITY

I came in 1986 in a mid-life career move after graduating from Brigham Young University law school. I meant to stay about three years. I have called New York City my home for quite a while now. JOANNE ROWLAND UNION SQUARE FIRST WARD ATTORNEY

I came because I needed a place where I could be anonymous and figure things out and I feel like a lot of people are doing that and so I'm not alone in my struggle. LAURA SUMMERHAYS MANHATTAN EIGHTH WARD PUBLISHING

### ON SINGLES WARDS

There was opposition to the idea of creating the first singles ward. I was stubborn against [the opposition] because I saw all of these wonderful single people and I felt so strongly that they needed to be together for their optimum growth. I had worked in singles programs in Salt Lake City and had seen how well they work when approached in the right way. Focusing directly on trying to get people married never works. The focus has to be on two things: on service and on spiritual development. **ELIOT BRINTON FORMER NEW YORK NEW YORK STAKE PRESIDENT WHO OVERSAW THE FORMATION OF THE FIRST SINGLES WARD IN NEW YORK CITY**

In the beginning, I was one who was against the idea of the singles wards being established. I have completely changed my view. I believe very strongly that because of the establishment of the singles wards the Manhattan stake was formed. And because of the singles wards—the people who came and stayed—the stake grew and the temple was built largely because of that population being here. **PATRICK PERKINS, FORMER BISHOP OF THE MANHATTAN THIRD WARD** ENTERTAINMENT ATTORNEY

When [the three singles wards were combined to meet during the construction of the temple], I was first counselor in the elders quorum. There was a lot of discussion about losing of identity, and a fear of losing track of members was the constant focus of the quorum. On Sunday, we would have a really hard time getting the quorum together just because there were huge groups of people moving in the halls. It became like fighting traffic and so a lot of people would just stay outside in the hall talking and socializing. The Sunday School classes would be delayed and therefore priesthood and Relief Society meetings would be pushed back as well. **DAVID FERNANDEZ MANHATTAN THIRD WARD** RESEARCH ASSISTANT, CHILD PSYCHIATRY, COLUMBIA UNIVERSITY

[One] phenomenal thing to come out of the "megaward" was the music.[1] There was this huge talent pool of concert pianists trained at Juilliard and singers of opera and Broadway along with a whole variety of different musicians with different specialties. As we sang, there was so much joy and exuberance in our worshiping and praising God. **WARREN WINEGAR MANHATTAN THIRD WARD BISHOPRIC** ART DEALER

## ON DATING

I love being in the singles ward here. There are so many opportunities to meet people. When friends of mine visit from other parts of the country, they always express something like jealousy about attending church here because of the dating opportunities. **KEVIN SHELLEY MANHATTAN THIRD WARD** ENTREPENEUR

My wife is an investment banker. When she was attending the third ward, she told her dates that she was either a hair stylist or an airline stewardess. She felt that her profession was a dating liability. **TAYLOR PETREY FORMER MEMBER OF MANHATTAN EIGHTH WARD** GRADUATE STUDENT, HARVARD DIVINITY SCHOOL

## ON SERVICE

I was a student at New York University when I joined the Church. Shortly after my baptism, I returned home to California where my parents were not supportive of my decision and I did not attend church regularly. When I returned to school in the fall, I continued in my inactive mode. However, my visiting teacher kept in touch. At Thanksgiving time, I had an emergency and was in a position of having to move at the same time that I was supposed to go away for Thanksgiving. As I sat wondering how I could do the move, my visiting teacher called and asked how I was doing. I told her the problem and she said, "Don't worry, we'll take care of it." Then she called the home teachers and they came and did the move for me. Later, I injured myself rollerblading and again my visiting teacher was there to assist in getting groceries and other things. But, also, we began to read the Book of Mormon together. By the time we got to King Benjamin's speech, I had a bright live testimony and I again became an active member. **KRISTINA HARRIS UNION SQUARE THIRD WARD** STUDENT, MUSICAL THEATER AND PRE-MED, NEW YORK UNIVERSITY

# MARRYING IN THE CITY

Latter-day Saint people converge on New York City for many reasons, but usually for education or a career. Following the organization of a singles ward in 1991, the number of single members coming to the city increased rapidly. Soon thereafter two additional singles wards were formed. New York has always been a target city for many ambitious young people. For some, it is a place to meet a spouse too. Here are some of their stories.

ANDREW AND CHRISTINE (BRINTON) SANDGREN Christine came to New York City to study law at New York University. Andrew, a third-year student there himself, was assigned to be Christine's mentor through the LDS Law Student Association. They became friends and occasionally had lunch. At the time, they were both members of the eighth ward. Christine recalls being overwhelmed by the size of the ward. She felt more comfortable when the ward was divided and she became a member of the sixth ward. Andrew was called to serve as stake financial clerk and, having turned 27, moved into the Manhattan Third Ward. Following Andrew's graduation, he and Christine continued having lunch. After Christine graduated and both were working in the city, they were still lunching. In March 2003 lunch evolved into serious dating. They became engaged in August and married in March 2004.

*After a brief residence in the Union Square First Ward, Andrew and Christine moved to Moscow to pursue career opportunities.*

KAH LEONG AND ANNIE (BENAC) POON When Annie came from Dallas to New York City to study art, Kah Leong was already living and working here as a photographer. After her first day at church, Annie boarded the A train with other members. Kah Leong saw her and, knowing the friends she was with, came to talk to her and ask her if she would consider participating in a photo shoot. They became casual friends. After two years Annie accepted a mission call to Croatia. When she returned from her mission, she was living with her sister in Brooklyn but decided to come into the city to watch general conference at the stake center. She came fasting about meeting the right person to marry. As it turned out, Kah Leong also came to the conference fasting for the same thing. When the lights came on, they discovered they were sitting next to each other and both had a fleeting thought that their prayers might have been answered. By the third date, they were talking about where they would go on their honeymoon. Six months later at Easter they were engaged. They married the following August in the Dallas temple and then went to Singapore for a Chinese wedding with Kah Leong's parents.

*Kah Leong and Annie are members of the Union Square First Ward where he serves as gospel essentials teacher and she as family history specialist.*

TAYLOR AND STACEY (BALL) PETREY Taylor came to New York City from South Jordan, Utah, in 1994 as a freshman at Pace University on a debate scholarship. At that time there was only one other Latter-day Saint undergraduate living in Manhattan (a student at Columbia University). After one year at Pace, Taylor left from his South Jordan ward to serve a mission in Italy. He returned to New York to continue his undergraduate studies in 1998, by which time there were two singles wards and many more undergraduates. Taylor claims he only had six dates in four years and that the reason for his limited dating life was simple dating economics. He was a poor undergraduate; the women preferred to date men who were more financially viable. Stacey Ball, for example, who was herself an investment banker, initially, crossed him off her list.

In 1998, Stacey was living in New Jersey working for Credit Suisse First Boston. She accepted the encouragement of a friend to move into Manhattan and attend the eighth ward. Stacey's move was in part a search for a spiritual renewal, as she had not been attending church for some time. In the singles ward she found an intellectual and spiritual vibrancy and began to attend regularly. She also began to date; she was one of the few women in the ward who had five dates a week.

During Taylor's last semester at Pace, Stacey had an extra opera ticket and invited Taylor to go—thus beginning a short, intense courtship. Six weeks after the opera, Taylor asked Stacey if she would consider moving to Boston where he had been accepted for graduate studies at Harvard University. She said she could not make such a big move without a ring. Taylor gave her the ring, and they were married before Taylor's Harvard studies began.

JONATHAN AND SHANNON (OAR) HILL Jonathan came to New York City for a job in investment banking. He was in the eighth ward and then the third ward, where he attended for four years. Shannon came to the city for an arts management job that quickly went away after September 11, 2001. Determined to stay in the city, she worked several part time jobs until eventually securing a job with Christophe Landon Rare Violins on the Upper West Side in the spring of 2002.

Soon after moving to New York, Jonathan's focus as a young single adult shifted from strenuous searching for the one to just relaxing and enjoying going out with many different women. A mutual friend recruited both Jonathan, a violinist, and Shannon, a cellist, to play in a string quartet that had been organized for the third ward Easter program. After meeting, they became close friends and began dating right away. With similar backgrounds (both from small college towns and both musicians with other similar interests) and complementary personalities, it didn't take long to know that they were made for each other. They became engaged near the end of May 2002 and married in October 2002. Even after becoming engaged, Shannon was apprehensive about entering this new phase of life. On the wedding day the sealer was 40 minutes late. While they were waiting in the celestial room, Jonathan said, "Let's be sure to pray and read scriptures together every day and to have family home evening each week." That was the answer to all of Shannon's prayers and they were married and lived happily ever after.

*Jonathan and Shannon left New York in summer 2004 to pursue career opportunities in Utah.*

DARREN AND NICOLE (MATTHEWS) BERRY Darren had been living and working in New York City for a number of years when Nicole arrived. He had been through periods of avid dating and infrequent dating. He first saw Nicole at the stake Christmas concert in 1999. He arranged with friends to be seated near her during the cultural hall portion of the evening and then to be invited to the same party the next day. After these informal, "coincidental" events, he felt it was safe to ask Nicole out. He recognized early on that she was "the one" he had been looking for. Nicole, on the other hand, wasn't looking or waiting for anybody. She had just arrived, and had professional goals and things to see and do before getting serious.

In fact, she was a little tired of relationships where the men were interested in how she would fit into their lives, rather than in how they might fit into hers. That's where Darren was different. He was a driven, goal-oriented man, but he showed interest in the achievement of her goals. They talked at length of their ardent belief that individual strengths only make a greater union. Nicole felt the courtship was quick, but when Darren told her, "I'm not going anywhere, when you're ready, let me know," she melted and agreed to marry him. They became engaged July 11, 2000, and married October 14, 2000.

*Darren and Nicole are members of the Union Square First Ward, where he serves as second counselor in the bishopric, and she as president of the Young Women. Their daughter, Rachel, has begun attending the Primary nursery and they are expecting their second child in November 2004.*

BRANDON AND AMYLU JAMESON AmyLu and Brandon met at a linger longer or a roof party or an outing to the beach. They talked at church, saw each other at singles conferences, hung out with the same group of people, went to the movies in large groups, participated in dinner clubs, saw each other at ward council meetings and even "graduated" from the younger to the older singles ward together. They did this for four years, becoming reasonably good friends along the way. Finally some strangely magical night, Brandon realized that he *liked* AmyLu in an entirely different way and started scheming ways to ask her out. She helped by asking him over for dinner and a walk in the park. Suddenly, "hanging out" felt just like knowing each other—beyond the false fronts erected for the singles ward. They found mutual admiration, respect, affection and love. They were married December 27, 2002.

*Brandon and AmyLu are members of the Inwood First Ward, where Brandon serves as first counselor in the elders quorum presidency and AmyLu serves as first counselor in the stake Young Women presidency.*

# A WOMAN'S VIEW

## REFLECTIONS: A STUDENT WIFE AND MOTHER IN NEW YORK DELIA JOHNSON

### NEW IN NEW YORK

The first week we moved in, I wanted to mail a letter to my parents. A giant green mailbox stood outside our apartment building, and I thought how nice to have one so close, even if it was a funny color. But after looking around it several times, I could not find an opening for the letter. Our superintendent laughed and told me the mailbox was on the corner. It took several months to figure out that the green mailboxes were for mail storage.

### THE DOUBLE STROLLER

We had been living in New York for just over six months when I started to earn extra money by babysitting. To help with an added child, I was considering a purchase of double stroller, since Ivan was only seven months old. Then by sheer coincidence, my sister offered me hers. Several weeks later it came, a nice big inline stroller. It held one child in front and another in the back, but a few times while babysitting I would have four others hanging on the sides. I'll always relish the second, third and sometimes fourth looks I would get.

As time went by, I realized the stroller worked as an all-purpose cart. The dirty laundry would go in it as I headed to the basement or even out to the laundromat. It hauled groceries home from the store. We took it with us when we went to midtown to purchase a window air-conditioning unit our first summer in New York. It also hauled my sewing machine to 14th Street to be repaired. In preparation for a farewell party Woodrow and I threw for about 30 friends our last summer, we took all the food, games and party supplies up to the Columbia campus in that stroller. I could have bought a cart, but the stroller worked just as well.

### "OH, WHO ARE THE PEOPLE IN YOUR NEIGHBORHOOD?"

In New York I learned that getting to know your neighbors might take time. I sometimes wonder, though, if it isn't easier to talk in New York because there are fewer cars and roads to separate you. Here is are some people I still think of fondly from 113th Street.

We had a little play garden on our street. The neighbors got together and really put time and effort into it. Not only did we get to know the families on 113th, we also did some gardening. A regular street person slept on the corner of 113th and Broadway. Woodrow learned his name—Eddie—from reading an article about him in Columbia University's student newspaper.

Osman, the doorman for the apartment complex at Morningside Avenue and 113th, became a nice friend. We even went out for lunch a few times. I would sometimes stop in and say hello if I hadn't seen him for a while.

My daughter Sarah Naomi would get off the school bus on 113th and Broadway where a bookseller named Steve plied his wares. I struck up a friendship, and he gave the kids a few books.

Our UPS deliveryman was named Henry. He was a great, friendly guy. Outside the city, the UPS man puts your package on the doorstep, rings the bell and walks away. You don't even get a chance to say hello.

After my morning walk, I would often stop at the Westside Market for bread or milk. The "Entenmann's Guy" was a friendly, talkative person. I never got to know his name, but I spent quite a lot of time listening to his stories. He had the perfect New York accent like the ones I had heard in the movies.

When Columbia was building their new student housing/public library on 113th and Broadway I would stop for 10 or 15 minutes so Ivan and Sarah could watch. One of the construction workers, Johnny Graham, would visit with them, and even gave them a construction helmet. They've had several comments about having a "real" hard hat. The funny thing was that the following summer, some ward friends and I took our kids down to Hudson River Park one week, and we ran into Johnny working on a site. I think it impressed—or shocked—our friends that I knew construction guys that far from home.

I never got to know the firemen at Engine 47 firehouse, but the kids always waved at them as they headed out to a call.

### SIGHTS AND SOUNDS OF NEW YORK CITY

Soon after we moved to the city, I checked out a guide book about New York, and it mentioned a couple of "ghost stations" on the subway lines. One of them was on the 1/9 line. Every time we rode, I would tell the kids to watch for the ghost station. It kept them quiet for at least two stops.

I loved walking over the Brooklyn Bridge. I finally walked across the George Washington Bridge the week before we moved.

In Central Park, I loved wandering the gardens in the northeast corner, taking swimming lessons with the kids at Lasker Pool and inline skating at the loop.

On a boring summer day, it only cost subway fare for a ferry ride to Staten Island and back—that was always entertaining for the kids.

Shopping in New York seemed such a hassle. The lines were long, and the aisles crowded. It seemed that the people behind the counters never had any answers. It was the same at the grocery store, the electronics store, to get your MetroCard, or even when visiting the emergency room (which I did at least four times with Ivan, and two times with Sarah Naomi).

Whenever we had family visit, we signed up for a trip to the Federal Reserve vault. Where else can you see piles of gold bullion? Woodrow asked on one trip if anyone had ever tried to break in and steal the gold. The answer was, "only in Die Hard."

## THINGS YOU NOTICE WHEN YOU'RE GONE

There are four immediate differences I noticed after we left New York City to Oregon.

First, out here when drivers hear a siren, they pull off to the side of the road and stop.

Second, it never bothered me to have to go to the basement to do my laundry, or even out to the laundromat. So I was really surprised at how much I thrilled in the luxury of doing laundry in the comfort of my very own home.

Third, I've complained about shopping in New York, the crowds, the small aisles. On one of my first visits to the giant grocery store after moving, I just needed to get a gallon of milk. We walked inside, and I got a feeling of *too much space.* I had to walk *all* the way to the back of this *giant* store for one measly gallon of milk! I knew then that I had really acclimated to New York in our five years there.

One last story to explain difference number four. During a Relief Society lesson before we moved to New York, the teacher asked everyone to tell something unique and special about themselves. One person, finding it hard to think of something, mentioned she didn't have a dishwasher. More than several people told her to try again, they too had to suffer as she did. Several stories later, a sister commented that not only did she wash her dishes by hand, she did it with a one-bowl sink. She got moans of sympathy.

After we moved to New York, I chuckled when I remembered this Relief Society lesson. In most Columbia University apartments, there were no dishwashers, and only single-bowl sinks. I lived with it for five years, and felt lucky to have a nice kitchen. However, it doesn't stop me from enjoying my new double-bowl sink and dishwasher out here.

## REFLECTIONS: A MOTHER AND A CAREER IN NEW YORK
CHRYSULA WINEGAR

My time in New York City has been a time of huge change. I arrived here as a newlywed with no job, no furniture and no home. I am now a mother, a partner in my husband's fledgling business and an international business manager for a multinational cosmetics company. So many things to juggle—the eternal lament of all mothers.

Being a mother for the first time enhanced all of the city's challenges, and my relationship with this city remains one of both love and hate. My husband, Warren, and I are on a Church assignment in a singles ward, which has been wonderful: amazing people in an intellectually and spiritually stimulating environment. And yet as a young married woman with children, I am occasionally lonely as there is no one else with whom to share my stage of life.

Now more than ever I have realized that I am responsible for my own spiritual nourishment, as it is impossible to hear or feel much on a Sunday with 2 busy little girls squirming in my arms. At a time when I should be relying on the Lord more deeply than ever, it's harder to hear him and I have less time in which to ask.

Yet I find the Church in New York to be full of spiritual and intellectual richness. The Church here has a stimulating quality to it without losing a strong service culture. Whilst we don't make each other Jell-o salad or funeral potatoes, there is a sense of community within the wards I've been part of. There is a lot of love, and an incredible amount of creativity and energy. The same things that drive people to New York City cross over into Church life: ambition, passion and commitment. Being an actor, opera singer or corporate banker in the world's most competitive city is quite something.

My hope for the stake in Manhattan is that some of us imports stay, not just a few years, but to raise families, perhaps even grandchildren and great-grandchildren. I'm not sure if I can be one of these as it is such a challenging place to be.

Every time I tell my husband, "We have to go, I can't stand it anymore," I think about the Church here—its vibrancy, its intelligence and its sheer tenacity. It makes it easier to view myself on assignment to build the kingdom in a difficult land, like President Young has sent me to a harsh desert or swampland. The challenges are different, of course, but I envy those who feel at home here because that has not been my experience. Yet I love the city and I certainly have been blessed to experience it in a very rich way.

## CONVERSATIONS: SINGLE WOMEN ON CHURCH, SCHOOL AND WORK

EXCERPTS FROM A ROUNDTABLE DISCUSSION WITH SIX FEMALE SINGLE LATTER-DAY SAINT NEW YORKERS, SPEAKING ABOUT LIFE IN NEW YORK CITY.

JOANNE ROWLAND came to New York to stay in 1986 after graduating from Brigham Young University law school. She practices law in New York. She has not attended any singles wards in New York because when she first moved to the city they were not yet created. She is Relief Society president in the Union Square First Ward.

DAWN ROSQUIST arrived 10 years ago, planning to stay only a year after graduating with her Masters in medieval literature. In New York her "back-up career," editing, became her primary career. She is a vice president and supervisory analyst at JP Morgan where she is associate managing editor for the New York region. Dawn attended the Manhattan Third Ward until 2001, when she began attending the Inwood First Ward.

BRITTA JENSEN came to New York City in August 1999 to attend Fordham University in the acting performance and directing program. She currently works at Columbia University and attends Columbia's Teacher's College in the English education program, focusing on creative writing. She attends the Manhattan Eighth Ward.

RONNIE GRAUMAN has family in New Jersey. She moved to New York City in 1996 and began working as an archivist for Sony Classical. She is now an inspector for the Bureau of Alcohol, Tobacco and Firearms, and attends the Manhattan Third Ward.

JOANNA LEGERSKI came to New York in 1996 from Utah State University. She initially came to work as a nanny for only a year but stayed because she loved New York. Joanna attended the Manhattan Third Ward before it split in 1996, then moved to the Manhattan Eighth Ward for a year, and then "graduated" back into the third ward. Last year she began attending the Inwood First Ward. Joanna left New York in August 2004 to pursue graduate studies in psychology.

LAURA SUMMERHAYS has been in New York City since February 2001, when she came to work in publishing. She now works for a literary agency in the foreign rights department and is enrolled in a Master's program in international affairs at New School. She is in the Manhattan Eighth Ward, but spends a lot of time in the Harlem First Branch, where she works in the Primary.

### SOCIALIZING WITH "MARRIEDS"

JOANNE Are you invited socially by families who are married with children to go to parties? And dinner and movies, etc?

BRITTA Married people recognize that it might be uncomfortable to invite a single person along and feel that they have to set them up with someone else. I've found that that is not always the case because we tend to stretch the boundaries.

DAWN I've really gone out of my way to call women in the ward and say, "Can you make plans with your husband to take care of the kids, because we are going out." I don't think a lot of women with young children will take that opportunity on their own and say, "I really need this," but if there is someone saying, "come with me," it gives them a little bit more of an impetus. . . I figured I would provide that and, of course, I like to hang out with the kids and I have a great posse of the "under-three's."

## BEING SINGLE

JOANNA I came to New York City when I was 26, as a nanny. This was at a period of time when there were still [LDS] nannies in New York, where there really aren't anymore, but you felt like a second-class citizen. You were looked on as being very stupid. Particularly there was a group of men that felt we were husband chasers—that as a nanny our purpose was to come to New York to get a husband. Which was really irritating because I really wanted to run around and say, "I have a degree and I am going on to graduate school. This is just an experience." But, of course, you really can't run around saying those kinds of things.

DAWN I think it is culturally expected for people to assume that if you have the components of father and a mother and children that you've got the ideal family. Well, [I think] that there are other components like loyalty, honesty, diligence, spiritual maturity and the reality is, yeah, I don't have the male component of my family, but I do have the loyalty, the respect, the spirituality and these are things that I work on as a single person.

## "FAMILY WARDS" AND "SINGLES WARDS"

RONNIE I like meeting with a group of people over 30 because I feel that we are at the same point in our lives and we don't have people coming in and out because of internships and changing schools that they have in the [younger wards].

LAURA One nice thing I like about the singles ward [in New York] is that people tend to be a little bit more honest about working through their difficulties. I remember going to church at BYU and nobody would ever talk about, "Oh, I had this struggle and I overcame." It was always, "This is true and I love keeping the commandments," which is nice but it didn't really do anything for me because I was going through so many crises of faith. It left me so flat. The nice thing about here is that I feel like New York is kind of a refuge in a way.

There was a time I only went to the family ward, but that was only for a couple months or so and in some ways it was wonderful but I felt like I was becoming a hermit almost I think because I don't live in Harlem, so I wasn't interacting as part of a community. I live in Washington Heights so I wasn't socializing with Harlem people that much. I just felt like I was in limbo and went back to the singles ward and had a completely different attitude about it. Instead of feeling guilty that I went there to have a social interaction with people, I decided that was fine. I also go to church to worship and that happened at Harlem, but I needed to see other people who are my friends, you know.

RONNIE There is an endless list of singles who have served outside of their wards. Maria Stahl was the Primary president in Harlem for a least a year and I remember that by the time she got to church she'd be exhausted already and then she'd go to our ward and have choir practice and then a fireside or whatever else at night. Instead of focusing on ourselves who have moved here from other parts of the country because we wanted to be in New York, let's look at the youth that grew up here and see them as the future leaders of the stake and how can we help them grow into that? Because it is their stake, not ours.

# VARIATIONS IN THE CITY

**REFLECTIONS: JOSEPH SMITH LETTER TO EMMA SMITH[1]**
FROM NEW YORK CITY, OCOBER 13, 1832

Oct. 13 1832
Pearl Street House
NY City

My Dear Wife,

This day I have been walking through the most splendid part of the city of New Y[ork] - the buildings are truly great and wonderful to the astonishing of eve[r]y beholder and the language of my heart is like this can the great God of all the earth maker of all thing[s] magnificent and splendid be displeased with man for all these great inventions saught out by them my answer is no it can not be seeing these works are calculated to mak[e] men comfortable wise and happy therefore not for the works can the Lord be displeased only against man is the anger of the Lord Kindled because they Give him not the Glory therefore their iniquities shall be visited upon their heads and their works shall be burned up with unquenchable fire the inequity of the people is printed in every countinance and nothing but the dress of the people makes them look fair and butiful all is deformity there is something in every countinance that is disagreeable with few exceptions Oh how long Oh Lord Shall this order of things exist and darkness cover the Earth and gross darkness cover the people after beholding all that I had any desire to behold I returned to my room to meditate and calm my mind and behold the thaughts of home of Emma and Julia rushes upon my mind like a flood and I could wish for [a] moment to be with them my breast is filld with all the feelings and tenderness of a parent and a Husband and could I be with you I would tell you many things yet when I reflect upon this great city like Ninevah not desearning their right hand from their left yea more than two hundred thousand souls my bowels is filled with compassion towards them and I am determined to lift up my voice in this City and leave the Event with God who holdeth all things in his hands and will not suffer an hair of our heads unnoticed to fall to the ground there is but few Cases of the cholra in this City now and if you should see the people you would not know that they had ever heard of the cholra I hope you will excuse me for writting this letter so soon after w[r]iting for I feel as if I wanted to say something to you to comfort you in your beculier triel and present affliction I hope God will give you strength that you may not faint I pray God to soften the hearts of those arou[n] you to be kind to you and take the burdon of[f] your shoulders as much as posable and not afflict you I feel for you for I know you[r] state and that others do not but you must cumfort yourself knowing that God is your friend in heaven and that you have[e] one true and living friend on Earth your Husband.

Joseph Smith Jr

## REFLECTIONS: EARLY SPANISH-SPEAKING CHURCH MEMBERS SARIAH TORONTO, SARA ANDERSON AND JOANNA LEGERSKI

The two Spanish-speaking wards in the stake are among the most effective in attracting new members. The growth and turnover are also great; consequently, the stories of many early converts are in danger of being forgotten. Following is a sampling of these stories.

RÓMULO MACÍAS On a rainy day in 1982, Rómulo Macías' father was taking a New York City bus home from work when he decided to get off the bus at 65th street. He took shelter from the weather at what turned out to be the local Latter-day Saint church building. Two missionaries invited him to a baptism that was then taking place. After the baptism, the missionaries invited him to learn more about the gospel. He declined the invitation, but asked them to "please teach his 24-year-old son, Rómulo."

Rómulo began meeting with the missionaries. When they challenged him to read the Book of Mormon, he finished it in one night. He attended church meetings faithfully for nearly six months, but had difficulty in committing to baptism. Finally, the missionaries gave up on him. In the summer of 1982 one of the missionaries, Elder Ismael Mayans, asked God for a baptism as a birthday present. Shortly after the elder's prayer, Rómulo announced out of the blue that he wanted to be baptized on August 11th, which happened to be Elder Mayans' birthday.

The baptism was held on a Saturday and the next day Rómulo went to Church. Bishop Mir handed Rómulo the manual for the youth Sunday School class and asked him to teach it. There was no looking back. Later that day, Rómulo was called as a youth Sunday School teacher.

Rómulo's father was baptized in 1988. He initially agreed to become a member of the Church but only if a missionary from Africa baptized him. Six months before Rómulo's father died, he was baptized by an elder from

Nigeria who was on a Spanish-speaking mission in New York.

*Former Manhattan Fifth Branch president, Rómulo Macías now attends the Inwood First Ward with his wife Arleen and their children.*

ANDRÉS NIETO INTERVIEWED BY GENNY GÁMEZ At age seven, I came to this country and immediately started to attend the Spanish branch (meeting on 81st Street). My father had arrived in 1965, and I went every Sunday with him. The branch was small and the feeling during this time was very special. Being in the Church and with people of Hispanic cultures, I felt surrounded by a family and could hide a little bit of the sadness I felt from leaving my country where my family had stayed.

The branch continued to grow and later became a ward. I had the opportunity of being in the young men and in Boy Scouts, and to share with people from different places, including South America, Central America, and the Caribbean. I enjoyed the activities very much since there was a large number of youth. The youth were a strong engine in that time. Many completed missions and came back leaders of the Church. These people had families, and their children grew up within the Church.

I think that the Spanish wards are important since there are many immigrants who arrive in this country seeking to feel at home with people of their same culture. I have had the opportunity to see how these people grow spiritually. They are strengthened and enjoy everything that the gospel brings. I think that if the Church had not had the vision of organizing the Spanish wards, many of us perhaps would not be here.

*Andrés Nieto, son of New York City's first Spanish ward bishop, Manuel Nieto, now lives in New Jersey.*

VIRGINIA CASELLAS I grew up with the gospel in my life in Argentina. My family descends from early Argentinean Latter-day Saint pioneers. Soon after I came to New York, I joined the third ward on their trip to the Kirtland temple and had the most amazing experience. I had developed a great admiration towards the Prophet Joseph Smith during my mission, and so being able to visit some of the historical sites where he spent his last years as a prophet reinforced my testimony. I cried when I contemplated the house where Joseph Smith and his family lived for a short time. It was there where his two newborn twins died as a direct result of the persecution he suffered.

It was hard to imagine how the School of the Prophets took place in such small quarters. I thought to myself: "It is here in this small room where Joseph Smith received revelations for the last dispensation!" I saw a profound symbolism in the prophet's life: terrible persecutions, sufferings, no place to live—in contrast with a tremendous occurrence: The Church of Jesus Christ was established once again upon the earth.

I believe that a temple in New York City will be an instrument for fundamental change in the lives of members and nonmembers. The gospel has helped me in every aspect of my life. I consider that the Lord has many ways to teach us, but the most powerful is when he teaches us through personal experiences and trials. I've learned that important choices can be made every single day, which bring eternal happiness and joy. The gospel has helped me to distinguish good from evil and also good from better.

I firmly believe that diversity in our stake is a great blessing! I would like to encourage each member of the stake to catch the vision of working together as a single culture—the gospel culture.

*Virginia is a member of the Manhattan Fourth Ward.*

LUÍS ANTONIO ROJAS RODRIGUEZ **INTERVIEWED BY AL GÁMEZ** In June 1974, a month after we were baptized, I traveled to the United States. I came to New Jersey by myself. The branch president in Bogotá counseled me to look for the Church when I arrived in the United States, because many Mormon families go inactive and fall away when they come from another country. I did exactly what my branch president counseled me to do and only once did I miss a sacrament meeting in the fifteen years that I spent in New York.

When I arrived I went to Queens, and that very week I found the Church in Manhattan. When I went to live in New Jersey, I could not find a Spanish-speaking branch, so I came into Manhattan for church. I went to 81st Street on the west side every Sunday. The first people I met were Brother Garces, who was the branch president and Brother Nieto. Brother Garces' wisdom and Brother Nieto's diligence were very valuable to my growth in the Church.

I received my first calling the Sunday after attending the branch for the first time. Brother Nieto asked me to help in Sunday School. I thought he wanted me to move a desk or something like that, but then he gave me a manual and asked me to give the next lesson. I was barely familiar with the Bible and the Book of Mormon, and felt I did not know anything about the gospel.

Brother Nieto told me that I had the best teacher, the Holy Spirit. He told me to read the lesson, fast and pray, and on Sunday I would give the lesson as a Sunday School teacher. I became absolutely convinced of the power of the Holy Spirit, as that Sunday I noticed its effect on me. It was at that time that I began to learn the gospel, and to understand that the Holy Spirit was what helped me to search for the truth in the first place.

Since I worked and lived in New Jersey, it was difficult for me to attend Church activities, but when I had to do my home teaching, I would come from work in New Jersey by bus, then train, then another bus, to meet up with my teaching companion, who had a shoe store in Queens. Sometimes I would get there, and it would be too late to visit people who lived in Brooklyn, the Bronx, and Manhattan.

I began to learn how the Church functions when I was called to the high council. That helped me to see the way Americans manage Church affairs. Then I was called as a counselor in the stake presidency, which turned out to be difficult, as I did not know how to speak English. Meetings were hard, for I did not want somebody to have to translate for me. But Brother Raymond Rivera, who was so dear and such a good worker, offered to translate. He was executive secretary of the Spanish-speaking ward and a great man.

If I hadn't been introduced to the gospel, my life would have been frustrated like the lives of my parents. Instead my children are the great people that they are. All my children have served missions, and we are all sealed in the temple. Even my wife and I have served as missionaries. If I had not been introduced to the gospel, perhaps I wouldn't have had a family. I could have lost it upon coming alone to the United States if I hadn't followed the counsel of my branch president in Colombia.

## REFLECTIONS: CONVERSATIONS IN HARLEM
INTERVIEWS WITH HARLEM FIRST BRANCH MEMBERS
BY SARAH ARCHER-BECK, MATTHEW ARCHER-BECK AND ANNE KNIGHT

"When I was baptized, I liked the idea of being downtown [for church meetings]. I enjoyed the diversity. My idea was never to leave. Then, after about five years in the Manhattan Second Ward, the announcement was made that some of us were going back to Harlem. I was upset and thought, 'Nobody asked me if I wanted to go.' That was my attitude. Then to top it off, we were going to a restaurant [Sylvia's]....The thought, "Where the Lord wanted me, I would go," was in my head—but it was not in my heart. Going to a restaurant just did not appeal to me. The night before our first meeting, I prayed about it and was told that I was meant to be in the new branch. So I went. I was called as Relief Society president, which was a shock."
POLLY ANN DICKEY **BAPTIZED IN JUNE 1992**

"Whenever a new unit is formed, there's naturally a resistance to change....[In Harlem] most of the people think of the church as a location, a building and that's their church. They don't think so much of the larger, worldwide, global organization that is the Church. For some people it was kind of hard, you know, 'Lincoln Center is my church and now you want me to go to a different church.'" RONALD ANDERSON **FIRST HARLEM BRANCH PRESIDENT**

"At Sylvia's...it was not always easy to feel the Spirit at the beginning. I think we lost a lot of members, first of all when they found out we were coming to Harlem and then the situation did not appeal to some members. One sister, Josephine Walker, never came. We talked about it on the telephone one night and I said, 'This was the sort of thing the pioneers went through.' But for her

Sylvia's was a place of parties. Her husband [a professional jazz musician] had played the trumpet there. And she even saw someone die there one night. She could not imagine feeling the spirit at Sylvia's—so she stayed downtown in the second ward." POLLY ANN DICKEY **FIRST HARLEM RELIEF SOCIETY PRESIDENT**

"In 1999, I happened to be on a bus and there were two sister missionaries. And I had heard about the Mormons, but not really having enough information. But there was always something about the elders, the missionaries, when I would see them in the streets that would just make me want to ask, 'Who are you? What are you doing?' My curiosity was so piqued on the day I was on the bus. I had a little difficult time getting up out of my seat to go over to approach the sister missionaries. But somehow I said 'If I don't, they're going to get off the bus and this is my chance.' So I did. And I told them I was interested in learning more about the Mormon faith."
GLORIA LYNCH **RELIEF SOCIETY PRESIDENCY**

"The days [as a Harlem missionary in spring 1999] were packed with appointments, usually about seven and nine appointments a day. Most of the times, of course, we didn't eat lunch. We didn't have time to do that. But it was fun work...we baptized two or three brothers and sisters each week within a district of six [missionaries]. It was just the hottest part of the mission."
AARON SATTLER **RETURNED MISSIONARY**

"In the second year [1999] we had about 60 baptisms. The problem was that we had 60 baptisms at the same time that we were just starting to get a Sunday School organized for the first time. And we were still struggling with getting people trained and ready. And so all of these people were coming in and we really didn't have the infrastructure in place to support them. So it was a very challenging time that way." RONALD ANDERSON **FIRST BRANCH PRESIDENT**

"[Before joining the Church] I was complaining, feeling sorry for myself. My daughter was trying to encourage me.... We lived on the top floor in a railroad apartment with three doors. While I was in the back room...it was about two o'clock, there was a knock on the door. No one ever knocked on that door, but used the first one with a bell. I opened it without asking who was there. Two missionaries were standing there. I said to my daughter, 'See what I mean. Things are getting worse and worse. Now I've got two lawyers at the door.'" POLLY ANN DICKEY **FIRST HARLEM BRANCH RELIEF SOCIETY PRESIDENT**

"Coming to the branch here [after moving to the former Jehovah's Witness Hall on West 129th Street] is really great. They were having it at Sylvia's. I didn't like it there. Not because of the Church or anything, it was the environment; the setting—it was like a club. I mean, we could feel the Spirit because it was about us, but here it's totally different. This building itself...it's our building. We're not sharing it...We've really got some great sisters here. They really bring back a lot of what we used to feel at 65th Street. The sisterhood and all." AGNES MARTINEZ **VISITING TEACHING COORDINATOR**

"65th Street. Yeah, I remember going down there. I mean [we] didn't go every Sunday but I remember going every once in a while [at age four and five]...But then when Sylvia's came, that is when we started going. To Sylvia's Café, and we used to have church meetings down there. And we used to have classes by the kitchen and all. And then we were trying to find a building and we got this place [Jehovah's Witness Hall in December 1999]....Before, all the missionaries had to do the sacrament—and now it's all the boys. I've seen a lot of changes in people, too—the way they act and what they do. Things like that. A lot of changes in me, too—from 65th to Sylvia's, to here." CHRISTOPHER CACERES **PRIEST'S QUORUM** AGE 16

"You can see instant impact...very minute efforts see great big fruit. So it just goes to show if you really thrust in your sickle, you're really making a difference. That is one thing that has been amazing—you get to see a branch, in this case, from the very embryonic stages blossom into something unbelievable." MAURICE MATSUMORI **FIRST COUNSELOR YOUNG MEN PRESIDENCY**

"It's not been easy. But it's been good and very rewarding: to see people gain testimonies, to see people reaching out to each other. And helping one another with the problems they're facing in their lives, the difficulties that we each have." LISA ANDERSON **PRIMARY PRESIDENT**

"Life is very hard for a lot of people around here [in Harlem] and as they prioritize, the church in not always the first thing on their mind. It will take time to create a culture. Not a church culture, because Harlem has a church culture. But an LDS Church culture—one that requires consistent commitment." AMINI KAJUNJU **FIRST COUNSELOR, YOUNG WOMEN PRESIDENCY**

"This is indeed a small branch. This is a branch in a place where a branch would not be expected to exist. It does have its problems. We do have our trials. But, in the end, this branch will persevere. In the end. Because the members that are still members constantly strengthen each other." MARK RODRIGUEZ **CONVERT OF TWO YEARS** AGE 17

## THE HARLEM GARDEN RAQUEL COOK

Three years ago when the Church purchased the 129th Street building that now serves as the Harlem chapel, the neighboring lot was a wasteland of weeds, rubble, and broken glass. Like most vacant lots in New York City, garbage piled mercilessly against the fence and graffiti stained the walls. But in the summer of 2001, Church members in Harlem turned the 125' x 25' lot into a beautiful garden space, creating a source of neighborhood pride and a valuable missionary tool for the Church.

Harlem members pushed forward the idea to clean up the vacant lot when physical facilities funds were made available for the landscaping. Because professional services could not be hired, the entire branch participated in the development process. Members traveled to New Jersey where they purchased plants and, in a single Saturday, planted flowers and laid the sod.

On the day of the planting, a passing resident provided sodas from the local grocery and dozens of neighborhood children battled for turns with rakes and seeds.

"They thought it was their summer garden camp," reported Christian Jacobs, a counselor in the branch presidency. "They're now very protective of the space."

Over 30 types of flowers, roses, impatiens, petunias, pampas grass, and rhododendrons, to name a few, line the perimeter of the garden; and half a dozen evergreens promise future shade. From the vines, gardeners hand tomatoes to passers-by.

Much of the novelty of the garden came in rearranging existing rubble, rather than hauling it away, in order to portray the creative energy of the people who live and worship there. Stray bricks were laid to create the path between the grass and the vegetable plot, large stones were stacked into a wall along the south border, and dozens of colorfully painted smaller stones—origin unknown—decorate the western fence. The tip of a lone, spare tire peeks out of the earth near a tomato plant.

Many Church members in Harlem believe the garden has united their branch and opened dialogue between members and 129th Street residents. The patch of green is a slice of beauty in an otherwise land of concrete.

### VISITING THE DEAF BRANCH PRIMARY PROGRAM
JOANNE ROWLAND **STAKE PRIMARY PRESIDENT**

April Worthington, the newly called president, had only begun the Primary in the deaf branch a few months before this Sunday program. The Primary consisted of approximately seven children, some hearing, some deaf, all different ages and in all stages of intellectual and spiritual development.

Although most of the Primary are hearing children with deaf parents, they are not necessarily skillful in sign language. Sister Worthington had the daunting task of teaching these children to sing and sign the Primary songs so that they could hear them and their parents could see them. She also helped them learn short speeches on the subject of following the prophets. She made them costumes out of vests and dishtowels to represent the ancient prophets they were talking about.

The children in the deaf community do not have the habit of conventional reverence. They said aloud whatever was on their minds. Most of the congregation were not aware of a complaining child's voice saying, "What now?" or "Not another song!" Then, having voiced their objections, they went ahead and performed beautifully.

The best part of the deaf branch Primary program was how enthusiastically it was received. The parents and other adult deaf members were visibly and audibly gleeful seeing their little ones up there speaking and singing. They were themselves not at all traditionally reverent. They giggled and pointed and clapped their hands together and made other enthusiastic noises to express their pleasure with the sacrament meeting. It seemed to me a most generous welcoming of their children into the community of the Saints.

## FROM THE FAR CORNERS OF THE EARTH: THE CANAL STREET (CHINESE) BRANCH JENNIFER REEDER

When Elder W. Craig Zwick of the Seventy visited the Chinese members of the Manhattan Second Ward in February 2002, he was impressed with their sincerity. He promised that in the near future they would be organized into a branch and would be involved in temple work nearby and missionary work in their native lands. His words have marked the growth of Asian members in Chinatown.

Organized in March 2002 under the direction of Stake President Brent Belnap with Ned Butikofer as branch president, the Canal Street (Chinese) Branch has experienced significant growth. The idea of the branch began with Mission President Ronald Rasband in May 1999. Through the hard work of devoted missionaries, whose activities include street contacting and providing English classes, the branch has gathered Asian converts together in Manhattan.

The Canal Street Branch is a vibrant group. With a majority of members from Fuzhou, China, and other Asian locations, the branch often experiences frequent transition as immigrants move on.

Siewli (Wendy) Lee, age 19, met the missionaries in 2001, shortly after her family moved to Manhattan from Malaysia. After joining the Church, Siewli's two brothers and parents soon followed. While it is difficult for the family to attend due to employment commitments, Siewli recognizes her opportunities as a member of the Church. "I am so lucky," she said. "Many people struggle to know the truth. I can't say I know everything, but I have faith to believe, especially in Christ."

Kai Hwong, from mainland China, was baptized in May 2004. After four years in New York, he met the missionaries. He was touched by the Church's emphasis on family and the plan of happiness. While learning about

Christianity, Brother Hwong recognized the love his Heavenly Father has for him and for the Asian people. When his wife arrived from China three months after his baptism, she saw a new love and joy in her husband's life, and is now investigating the Church.

The branch's renovated meeting space on Elizabeth Street attests to the unit's growth. In the dedicatory prayer, President Belnap said, "We look forward to the day when this rented space will be too small to house all who desire to worship here. We pray that this branch will continue to grow and strengthen, that it will be filled with faithful Saints who will serve thee in thy temple, who will increase in testimony of the restored gospel of Jesus Christ, who will send their sons and daughters as missionaries to the far corners of the earth, including to the People's Republic of China and to other nations, and who will strengthen this community and bless their fellowmen through acts of service."

The branch draws mainly from members of established wards to fill leadership positions. Many of whom served Chinese-speaking missions. Elders quorum president Jerry Hsiech, born in Taiwan and raised in California, feels drawn to his calling. "The Lord needs me here to help build the kingdom."

Jenny Hsu completed a mission in New York and after returning for graduate school and attending the eighth ward, now serves as Relief Society president. "We train the members to lead themselves," she said.

Carter and Sarah Chow act as branch clerk and family history leader. While neither speaks Chinese, they are aided by missionaries and Eleanor Chin, a Malaysian member who often translates from Mandarin to English and Cantonese. President Butikofer, who served a Cantonese-speaking mission to Hong Kong, studies Mandarin on the subway and at lunch in order to better serve. All feel a unique call to serve the people of Chinatown.

## NYC IN UTAH: STAKE YOUNG WOMEN SHARE THEIR CITY
JOANNA LEGERSKI INTERVIEWS MELISSA PUENTE, MANHATTAN FIRST WARD YOUNG WOMEN PRESIDENT

Two young Hispanic women from the Manhattan First Ward, Deleenys Andino and Olga Cacho, went to Brigham Young University's Especially For Youth (EFY) in summer 2002. They had such a good experience that Jennifer Stanworth of the Manhattan First Ward Young Women presidency had the idea of getting a bigger group to go in 2003.

Twenty-four girls attended, most from the Manhattan Fourth Ward, as well as some from Inwood second, Manhattan fifth (now Union Square first), and a Spanish language ward in Brooklyn. Private donations were obtained, and EFY waived the girls' tuition. Melissa Puente, Nicole Berry (Manhattan Fifth Ward) and Melanie Yorgason (Manhattan First Ward) went along as leaders.

The girls were happy to be there. They loved Utah and kept saying how clean it was and how nice the people were. In particular, they were stunned by a candy store in Crossroads Mall, which had large open buckets of candy, freely accessible to potential shoplifters. When they attended the Mormon Tabernacle Choir program "Music and the Spoken Word" in the Salt Lake Tabernacle, the announcer welcomed the girls from New York City. A highlight of their trip was the opportunity to sit on the stand behind the prophet in his home ward sacrament meeting.

At EFY, some of the girls said they had a difficult time at first. As is usual at EFY, the girls were divided up and joined groups of youth from other areas. They felt very different from everyone else. Their transition eased when youth in their groups started asking the girls to teach them Spanish. Throughout the week the New York girls formed new friendships. One young woman from the Manhattan Fourth Ward didn't have scriptures. However, when the kids in her group noticed, they bought leather scriptures as a gift.

All the girls from the Manhattan Fourth Ward tried out for the talent show in the BYU DeJong Concert hall. Vanessa Gutierrez led the effort to teach them all a Latin dance. They were huge hit. The girls all wore I LOVE NY t-shirts, and the audience went crazy.

During one dance, EFY leaders asked the group to come up to the stage and show everyone how to salsa. At the beginning of the conference, one of the EFY leaders greeted them and said they had been waiting for them all summer. They knew about the group because they had made an exception to let all twenty-four kids attend together. Usually, they don't let large groups from one stake come together.

By the end of the conference, not one of the girls wanted to return home. They were all in tears, following some powerful spiritual experiences from bearing their testimonies and from sharing their culture.

## WAITING AT THE BAR THE CONVERSION STORY OF JESSICA LOPEZ
SARA ANDERSON

Jessica Lopez has lived in New York all her life, but it was the Manhattan New York Temple that finally made her really "feel alive."

Born in Manhattan into a Catholic family, she remembers going to the Catholic Church with her grandmother. When she was three years old, her family became Jehovah's Witnesses. At age 18, Jessica moved out and studied at Lehman College, earning degrees in business administration, theater, and eventually political science.

She fell out of close contact with most of her immediate family, but she maintained a happy life in the city. She worked with troubled youth in the Bronx, teaching them theater and the arts, and helping them stay off the streets. She says she felt genuine satisfaction when she saw the kids she worked with rejecting crime, drugs and alcohol. Chasing a childhood dream of becoming a singer, she sang in a band that recorded a hit Latin dance single with Tito Puente in the late 1980s.

Jessica remained extremely close with her brother Alexander, who had diabetes, and they planned for him to move into her apartment. Then, in 1999, her brother's diabetes confined him to the hospital. Although Jessica was often with him, one day she was at home when he slipped into a coma and died. The sorrow and guilt she felt at being away when he was in his final moments bothered her for years.

She turned to drugs and alcohol for relief; she occasionally stayed out drinking at clubs all night and sometimes missed work. Even drunk, though, she talked about God with anyone who would listen. One night at an after-hours club as she sat drinking and preaching, someone started preaching back to her. A woman told her to "forgive herself and find the light." She told her to stop blaming God for her difficulties, be baptized, and obtain forgiveness.

Jessica put her drink down, went home, sat down, and made a list of things to change in her life. She stopped blaming God for past trials and committed to praying more frequently. At a new job, her boss Carmen Andrade also helped her get her life together. The Jehovah's Witnesses resurfaced in her life, coming to teach her at work. But on the weekends, Jessica still went out drinking with friends.

Then on Friday night, May 7, 2004, she had plans to go out with them as usual, but her boss confronted her. "You've been searching for God," she told Jessica. "I know a place where you can get tours of a temple, and after a while, they are going to close it to visitors." She invited Jessica to go on a tour of the temple with her family that night. The temple invitation was so compelling that she accepted and called her friends to tell them she would be late.

As they went into the temple, Jessica found comfort and peace in the idea that she was in the house of God, but a more personal spiritual message was waiting for her in the baptismal font area. As she looked at the font and started up the stairs she burst into tears, she became weak in the knees, and had to be helped up the stairs as she gripped the handrail. She was overwhelmed with the feeling that she had a work to do–to get herself baptized and then to be baptized for her brother in that room.

Continuing through the temple, Jessica says she continued to feel spiritual promptings. She felt happiness and joy, but also sadness and remorse for the people she had hurt. In the celestial room and in the sealing room, she saw a bit of her future in a flash–a future that including getting "married Mormon."

When they came down to the cultural hall after the tour, she asked someone, "How can I join this church?" She says she felt like she had found something that made her feel alive and she wanted to be a part of it. Her cell phone was ringing and she knew it was her friends. But she was not interested in the bar or her girlfriends. She went out to 65th Street but didn't want to be out of the temple. So she went back up.

In the next month, Jessica started going to church and studying with the missionaries in preparation for baptism. She visited the temple frequently, enjoying the feeling she found there. She spent hours volunteering to clean in preparation for the dedication and was able to clean the chair where the prophet would sit.

She found it difficult to stop smoking and drinking coffee. But on June 12, her birthday, Jessica was baptized, fulfilling one of the promptings she felt at the temple five weeks earlier.

The following morning Jessica returned to the temple for its dedication. She sat in the baptismal font area and watched President Hinckley put mortar around the cornerstone. For the dedication she had a new white handkerchief embroidered by Rebecca and Alice Lord from the Manhattan Third Ward.

Jessica says she is shocked by how much her life has changed since the first time she went to the temple in Manhattan. She comments, "I left my friends waiting at the bar, and they are still waiting." Then she adds, "They are going to be waiting a long time."

**WASHING AND DRYING IN THE CITY** PAT AND STEVE HODSON TAKE ON MANHATTAN ALLISON CLARK

Since moving to New York City in 1990 and 1991, Steve and Pat Hodson have met, married, changed careers, had four children, and been part of two new wards and now the stake presidency. Their experiences in the city offer an interesting glimpse into the ever-changing church in New York City.

Steve came to New York in 1990 to study cello at the Juilliard School of Music soon after completing his mission. Pat arrived a year later to act and work in musical theater, already having a degree in acting and theater history. While the passion for music and theater remained strong, both turned within a few years to professions that provided greater financial stability.

After meeting so many individuals in the Church in New York involved in the fields of finance and business, Steve decided that in addition to music, he had an interest in pursuing a career in investment management. He earned an MBA from Columbia University and has since worked for several financial companies in the city.

Although still pursuing ad hoc film and theater work, Pat worked for a financial printing company for several years up until the day she went into labor with her first child. Although Pat initially intended to continue working, she and Steve decided it made the most sense for her to be home while their children were young. But even as the children came, she still did occasional film work for the Church, including a series of Church history videos for seminary.

Steve and Pat both described the joy of being a part of the creation of new wards in the city and personally experiencing the Church's growth. Soon after each of them moved to the city, the first singles ward was created. Although Pat was hesitant, Steve joined the ward soon after it was founded. Pat eventually attended the new ward and there they met through their respective callings coordinating family home evening. After marrying in 1994, they lived together in Washington Heights where Pat was already living. Two years later a branch was formed in Washington Heights that eventually became the Inwood First Ward.

For most Church members in New York, seeking balance between family, work, and Church service is a constant negotiation. For a period of time, Steve served in the bishopric and Pat in the Relief Society presidency in the Inwood First Ward. Pat described this experience as an opportunity for them to learn how to support each other and take turns focusing on family and church service.

Every week had different church meetings and family obligations. More recently, Steve has spent even more time in church service working on the high council, and now in the stake presidency. Pat explained that for the six months leading up to the temple dedication the focus of the whole family was on the temple and supporting Steve in his direct responsibilities related to the dedication.

For Pat this meant that her focus was on running the house and keeping the family together, knowing that he could not be involved in the day-to-day events of the family. She said supporting him was their way of also supporting the temple.

On the day Pat had an inkling of Steve's eventual calling to the stake presidency, she revealed that she wanted to cry in frustration. At that time, her family of four children and wheelchair-bound mother, recently arrived, were living in a two-bedroom apartment. Problems appeared to be looming at the local public school where her older children attended. And, in a challenge perhaps only urbanites can understand, a young baby in the home made trips to the local laundromat ever stressful and more frequent. Pat and Steve both felt that their family was "being driven out of the city."

Despite the problems of space and schooling, they accepted the calling and with it the commitment to remain in Manhattan. Pat explained that when her husband was set apart they were promised that their concerns would be taken care of. Within a few months they were able to move into a four-bedroom apartment, the problems at the local school disappeared, and they got a washer and dryer—no small feat in an urban environment.

Today, the Hodsons have seen the Church grow in Manhattan from nine units and one church building to 23 units spread across two stakes (Manhattan and Westchester) with seven buildings and one temple.

Pat and Steve believe the church experiences in New York City are exceptional due to the drive and diversity of so many members living here. The couple seems to relish the opportunity to be in such a diverse and vibrant place.

### SOUL-AND-VIRTUAL-OFFICE MATES: BEN AND JULIE MCADAMS
JULIE MCADAMS

In August 2000, my husband, Ben, and I drove across the George Washington Bridge in our Ryder moving van to begin what we expected to be a few years in New York for law school. Ben was beginning his first year of law school and I was starting my second year, having transferred to Columbia University after completing my first year of law school at Brigham Young University. We arrived at our new place early in the morning, but we couldn't get the keys to our 350-square-foot studio apartment until the Columbia Housing Office opened at nine o'clock.

Thanks to a highly organized elders quorum, several Latter-day Saint students came to our apartment to help us move in—even though many of them had not finished unpacking themselves. Some new Latter-day Saint friends showed us around our new neighborhood and helped us to find the cheapest grocery stores, barber shop, hair salon (not so cheap!) and navigate the many highs and lows of living in New York. We began to feel at home quite quickly.

Since so many of our Latter-day Saint friends helped to ease our transition to the city, we wanted to do the same for others considering a move to New York. Ben established an open door (and couch, and floor) policy at our apartment by inviting friends, family and prospective law students to come and visit during every conversation. Overall, we housed more than 70 different people during our 18 months in out first New York City apartment. When Ben's brother and sister came with their fellow interns who were working in D.C. for the summer, we think they set the record for house gusts at the same time: 13 persons side-by-side across the floor of our studio apartment!

Maybe it was due to the time we spent hyping New York City as amateur tour guides shortly after arriving in our new home town, but it didn't take very long before I started thinking that I would like to stay in New York after law school and Ben was easily persuaded. We loved the energy of the city, and started to investigate the possibility of staying in New York long-term. My church calling working with the young women gave us an opportunity to observe some of the advantages and also challenges of growing up in New York. We were both a little jealous of the opportunities, experiences and diversity that surrounded the youth we came to know. We decided we were willing to consider starting our careers and having children in the city.

After graduating in 2002 and 2003 we decided to buy an apartment, taking a gamble both on our decision to stay in the city and on the New York real estate market. Ben regularly searched the online listings in the *New York Times* inserting internet search terms such as "dump", "needs TLC", or "wreck", insisting that he could turn anything into a palace. I was doubtful. We finally found the perfect fixer-upper on East 84th Street.

After three years in the first ward and on the west side, we joke that the transition from the west side to the east side was more difficult than the transition from Utah to New York. Although our 450-square-foot walk-up still isn't the Trump Tower, Ben proved his construction ability and I became the learned apprentice. (After countless visits to buy required supplies, I even managed to convince the local hardware store to give me a contractor's discount.)

We currently work at New York City law firms while concocting "exit strategies." The hours are long and the work is either challenging or insanely boring—rarely anything in between. A typical day begins around 9:30 a.m. and doesn't end until 7:00 or 8:00 p.m., and sometimes goes into the wee hours of the morning. We don't work at the same firm but our offices are only a few blocks apart, so we try to meet often for lunch and dinner. We always email each other and talk on the phone several times a day. And if we're both working late at night, we leave each other on speakerphone and become virtual officemates.

**THE JUGGLING ACT:** JOHN AND AMY WARNER SARIAH TORONTO

The day after their wedding in 1997, John and Amy Warner moved to Manhattan so John could begin a career in investment banking. After living in Boston, John may have had an idea of what living in a large city was like, but Amy was in for some surprises. Very newly married, she was moving from Utah to New York City and would find herself coming home to a dirty, dingy walk-up apartment with a homeless person making his nightly bed in the vestibule. And her new husband worked at the office from dawn until far past dusk.

Seven years later, John and Amy have had two children (Johnny and Samantha), a job change for John, added Church responsibilities (John was called as bishop of the Manhattan First Ward), improved housing, and the Warners finally feel they have found their place in New York. That place demands a constant juggle of professional, church and family responsibilities.

Like most members of the Church who are professionals in Manhattan,

John finds that his religion distinguishes him. "Everyone knows you are Mormon," he says. John explains that the ramifications of having such a conspicuous identity have been only positive. He says a number of members of the Church have paved the way in the world of finance and have created the expectation that if you are Mormon, you are sharp and do good work.

While John has found his work environment to be positive, it is difficult to speak as glowingly of the work hours. A career in financial services in New York City dictates early mornings and late nights, day in and day out, leaving precious little time for outside interests and duties—family, hobbies, and in John's case, church responsibilities. Because of his work schedule, everything else for the most part "happens at night." Weekly bishopric meetings tend to begin around 9:30 p.m. and run until midnight or one a.m. Interviews also occur at similar times, usually at John's office at JPMorgan or at the Warners' apartment, due to time limitations and the logistics of getting around the city. On most days, John also spends a couple of hours during the day tending to the affairs of his ward, whose members' emotional, spiritual and physical needs are amplified by the difficulties of living in the city.

The ongoing balancing act between professional, church and family responsibilities means Amy and the children see John for a few hours during the week and only a little more on the weekend. In their free time together, the Warners enjoy visiting museums, taking Johnny to skate at the skateboard park, playing baseball, and spending time with members of their ward.

They believe their ward community is one of the great blessings that have come as a by-product of juggling responsibilities, in this place where the level of intensity in professional and church life is great. The community means that there are people around who are available and willing to help, and who are empathetic—for more often than not, they find themselves in similar life situations. The Warners believe an equally great blessing of being Latter-day Saints in New York havs been the opportunity to serve in the Church—being both needed and required to serve in ways that neither John nor Amy did in their native Utah. While the requirements are great and the juggle of time and resources ongoing, the Warners feel they have had exceptional opportunities and that they are rewarded for their sacrifices in ways that create a unique experience they could have only in New York

## LIVING IN THE CHURCH TOM AND MEGUMI VOGELMANN
SARA ANDERSON

In a city full of people who stay for a season and move on, Megumi and Tom Vogelmann are an anomaly. Currently members of the Union Square First Ward, they were baptized together in New York City in 1971. They stayed in Manhattan to raise three children, making them a part of a small group of city Saints to do so. And as the custodial supervisor for the stake center for almost 30 years, Tom's experience with the Church has been particularly unique. But it all started with the most typical of New York stories–young performers coming to the city.

The Vogelmanns moved to New York as a young married couple in 1968 to study music–voice at Juilliard for Megumi, and piano for Tom at the Manhattan School of Music and later New York University. Megumi's mother had converted to Christianity from Buddhism before World War II, and had raised Megumi as a Protestant, a rarity in Japan. Tom, also a Protestant, was the son of a minister from Wisconsin.

As the young couple settled into their life in New York, they started to ask themselves if there wasn't something more to find. At about this same time, Tom's sister and her husband accepted a visit from the missionaries and were quickly baptized. As they talked to Tom about their conversion, Tom was hesitant and decided to study everything he could about the Church to convince them of their mistake. Instead, he went to Megumi and told her that he thought the Church was true. Megumi, however, was reluctant.

Following the conversion of Tom's mother and another sister that fall, Megumi decided to start reading the Book of Mormon. As she did she had a deeply spiritual experience. On April 10, 1971, Tom and Megumi were baptized together in the old synagogue on 81st Street where the Church then met. The baptismal font was a concrete vault sunken in the middle of the podium in the main meeting room and it had only a cold-water faucet that delivered rust-colored water.

They committed themselves to attending church each week and Tom was quickly called to be executive secretary for Bishop Al Woodhouse. Megumi served as the Primary chorister. She remembers that in those early years, when Relief Society was held during the week, Jean Woodhouse drove around the city in her station wagon gathering sisters to take them all to Relief Society. The happy experiences she had in Relief Society gave her an opportunity to grow; she says she was a "dry sponge" soaking up all she could learn.

In the old building on 81st Street, there was a bell tower with a small living space, and a graduate student couple from the ward lived there and did custodial work in the church. Tom and Megumi were living in Spanish Harlem on East 95th Street at the time, and when the college couple moved out of the 81st Street bell tower, Bishop Woodhouse asked the Vogelmanns if they would like to take that position. They accepted the job and moved in above the church.

Soon after, construction began on the new stake center. Tom and Megumi stayed in the 81st Street building until it was eventually sold. At the same time the new building needed a custodial supervisor. Tom filled that position with the understanding that when things were settled, he would resign and begin his career as a pianist.

Tom regretted not being able to serve a mission, and now in the new stake center he poured all his energy and enthusiasm into working in the building. He worked 18 or 19 hours a day, hardly sleeping. On holidays, he gave the other four custodians a vacation and did the whole job himself. He was tired, but felt satisfied and pleased to be able to do the work. It was a big job since the building housed not only a chapel, but also a visitors' center, which had to be maintained and cleaned daily. Tom accepted more and more responsibility during the transition to the new building, and eventually, the position became permanent.

Two years after their baptism, Tom and Megumi had their first child, Winona. Their two sons Jeremy and Kevin came in quick succession, and Megumi took on the day-to-day work of raising three children, each one year apart. She says she constantly prayed for her children. Once when her boys were small, she had dropped them off at a library in the Village. Driving off before seeing that they made it inside, she drove about a mile down the road when she felt prompted to go back. She turned around and found the two boys outside the library, which turned out to be closed that day. They had been praying that their mother would return for them.

Since Tom worked at the stake center it was possible for his children to spend time with him there during the week, despite his time-consuming work. Winona, Jeremy, and Kevin sometimes watched videos at the visitors' center. In later years, Megumi would send Tom to work with lunch and after-school-snacks for the kids who would come over after school or music lessons. They would eat together and then go practice while Tom continued his work. At the end of the day Megumi picked up the whole family to go home.

Tom and Megumi are proud of the life they have had as members of the Church in Manhattan and content when they think about raising their three children here. Although they never got to really pursue their music careers, they both continue to enjoy playing and singing at church services and concerts. Their children are grown and they now have two grandchildren. They have no regrets as they recall the activities and friends that filled a unique life here in New York City.

Clifford Mannings, Ron Anderson, Van Woods and Polly Dickey on the branch's last week at Sylvia's Restaurant, November 29, 1998. Photo courtesy of Lisa Anderson.

This Kingdom Hall of the Jehovah's Witnesses and the adjoining empty lot would become the meeting place of the Harlem branch, with a beautiful garden next door. Photo courtesy of Lisa Anderson.

# ARTISTS IN THE CITY

### A PORTRAIT OF LATTER-DAY SAINT ART  GLEN NELSON

The story of pioneers moving to the West it is a familiar one. A less well-known chapter in Church history relates how some pioneers made a reverse trek. They came from the West to New York City, and, armed with training they received here, returned to edify the entire Church. This is particularly evident in the realm of visual arts.¹ Paris was, initially, the ideal training ground, but many LDS artists would soon venture to one of the western world's newest artistic capitals—New York City.

### THE ARTIST-MISSIONARIES – 1890-1917

On June 3, 1890, three young men were set apart as missionaries in Salt Lake City, Utah. At a time when hundreds of missionaries for the Church left on missions overseas, the departure of three more elders would be a rather unremarkable event—except that these three young men received callings, not to preach the gospel to the French, but to study painting at the Academie Julian in Paris.²

By 1890, Church leaders realized that in order to decorate the Salt Lake Temple as they wished, artists needed to study with the world's best teachers. The three pioneering artists sent to France in the summer of 1890 were John Hafen, Lorus Pratt, and John B. Fairbanks. They arrived in Paris on July 24, 1890—a holiday celebrated in Utah as Pioneer Day.³

The lessons learned in Paris—either by training or by association—were the teachings of the Avant-garde. Upon their return, the missionaries were engaged to paint large-scale murals for the Salt Lake Temple. These were paintings of religious events re-envisioned in a modern, French spirit.

For the next 20 years, these artists and others who followed (Lee Richards, Alma Wright, Mahonri Young, and Louise Richards⁴) created murals, easel paintings, friezes, and sculptures for the temples of Hawaii, Alberta, and Arizona, and for local chapels and tabernacles. Today, these are some of the most popular images in the visual consciousness of the Church.

## THE LEGACY OF NEW YORK CITY IN LDS ART AND SCULPTURE—1917-1964

As significant as the work of these pioneer artist-missionaries was, the next generation of LDS painters contributed even more to the creation of a Mormon art. With the outbreak of World War I, the LDS student painters shifted their studies from Paris to New York City. John Hafen and the others who taught young painters in Utah encouraged those with talent to study in the East, even though the financial sacrifices were great. Mahonri Young worked as a portrait artist at the *Salt Lake Tribune* for $5 a week for four years until he could save the $400 required to study at the Art Students League in New York for a single year.[5]

For Utah artists desiring exposure to a new world of art, they could not have timed it better. In 1917, the infamous Armory Show brought the latest paintings from Europe to New York City, shocking the locals. Here were works several steps beyond Impressionism. Picasso, Duchamp, Matisse and many other innovators literally stopped American painters in their tracks. Mahonri Young was on the committee that organized the exhibition.[6]

The Church members who studied in New York between the World Wars and witnessed this revolution have become the most revered of the Church's artists. Their influence over the succeeding generations of artists whom they taught in burgeoning academies in Salt Lake and Provo is unmistakably connected to their experiences in New York.

A stroll through Temple Square and the Museum of Church History and Art in Salt Lake City today is nothing short of a retrospective of New York influence. Think of the "Miracle of the Gulls" monument and the life-size sculptures of Joseph and Hyrum Smith by Mahonri Young, who studied at the Art Students League in New York and taught classes there intermittently from 1916 to 1943;[7] "The Handcart Monument" by Torlief Knaphus, a Norwegian sculptor who studied at the Art Students League upon his immigration to the United States in 1906; three monuments by Avard Fairbanks, an artistic child prodigy who was awarded a scholarship to the Art Students League at the age of 14, as well as his "Monument to the Three Witness of the Book of Mormon" and monuments depicting the restoration of the Aaronic Priesthood and the centennial of the Relief Society which are on display in the Temple Square Visitors Center. Inside the temple, there are murals retouched by Mabel Frazer who studied at the Art Students League around 1915.[8]

In the Museum collection across the street from the temple, there are paintings by Louise Richards Farnsworth, Minerva Kohlhepp Teichert, Calvin Fletcher, LeConte Stewart, Lynn Fausett and George Dibble, all of whom studied in New York City. In the first two decades of the 20th century, these artists studied at Columbia University, the Pratt Institute, but principally at the Art Students League at the League's current home on West 57th Street.[9]

To understand the New York-induced metamorphosis of LDS art, it is necessary to grasp the influence of the Art Students League in the development of American art. Founded in 1875, the League was organized by students who craved instruction in modern painting, an education not available elsewhere. That LDS artists in Utah gravitated to such an institution, instead of more traditional painting schools, is evidence of their openness to new and exciting developments in the arts.

The League's list of instructors and students includes the A-list of the nation's artists: William Merritt Chase, Thomas Eakins, Childe Hassam, John Sloan, Winslow Homer, Paul Manship, Stuart Davis, Georgia O'Keeffe, Rockwell Kent, Thomas Hart Benton, Reginald Marsh, Norman Rockwell, Jackson Pollack, Hans Hoffmann, Mark Rothko, Louise Nevelson, Barnett Newman, Roy Lichtenstein, Philip Guston, Louise Bourgeois, Eva Hesse, Robert Rauchenberg, Alice Neel, Milton Avery, John Marin, James Rosenquist, Isabel Bishop, Ben Shahn, Robert Henri, David Smith, Alexander Calder, among many others.[10] The League's influence, reaching into every fine arts museum in the country, shaped LDS art as well.

The Mormon artists who came to New York in the early 20th century soaked up modern art, and upon their return to the West, the Church put them to work. Although only the early painters were set apart as art student missionaries, the majority of the artists who studied in New York received commissions for public buildings, memorials, church houses, temples, and Church art collections. If one keeps in mind their New York training, one can see the works of these early 20th century LDS artists in a new light. In a LeConte Stewart painting of Utah farms, the viewer senses the psychological loneliness of Edward Hopper. The Angel Moroni of Cyrus E. Dallin would feel stylistically welcome in Rockefeller Center. Expressionist Wasatch landscapes of Louise Richards Farnsworth echo the daring color choices of modern German masters. A Minerva Teichert pioneer woman is attired in a dress whose complex pattern is worthy a Matisse portrait, with a faint exoticism of a Gaugin Tahitian beauty. The watercolor sketches of Temple Square by George Dibble reveal an embrace of Cubism and a vibrant love of color reminiscent of the American modernist John Marin.[11]

As technology for color reproductions emerged, regional museums grew up, and quality art instruction developed in universities, painters had less need to journey east. But in the early 20th century, there was no substitute for study in an art capital. Mahonri Young wrote of his ten years in New York, Paris and again in New York: "The last two years abroad were the most valuable. During them, something of the ten years of struggle and study began to take form and fairly definite conclusions were reached."[12]

A few of the artists settled in New York City rather than in the West. Mahonri Young, the last grandchild of Brigham Young, made his entire career in the New York area, teaching at the Art Students League for nearly 30 years. His friend, painter Waldo Midgley from Utah, also remained in New York. Lynn Fausett, whose murals hang at the "This Is the Place Monument," served as the president of the Art Students League from 1933-36. Another LDS artist, Louise Farnsworth, spent the majority of her adult life in New York City although her subject matter remained the landscape of her Utah childhood.

For over a hundred years, the Church in New York City has enjoyed the presence of LDS artists who have come to New York seeking training or their fortunes in the world of art. These men and women are taking up the challenge issued by Elder Spencer W. Kimball in 1967: "The story of Mormonism has never yet been written nor painted nor sculpted nor spoken. It remains for inspired hearts and talented fingers yet to reveal themselves. [The artists] must be faithful, inspired, active Church members to give life and feeling and true perspective to a worthy subject."[13] In many ways, little has changed since 1890. Young, ambitious and talented students still yearn to prove themselves and to serve the Church as LDS artists.

## MANHATTAN LDS ARTISTS INTO THE 21ST CENTURY

At the end of 1999 an informal survey identified 128 members of the Manhattan stake who are active artists out of nearly 2,000 active stake members. The survey counted people who were either professional artists (art is their primary source of income) or full-time students majoring in one of the arts.

Many additional members were not counted who have strong artistic backgrounds and interests, but who are not at this time in the professional and/or student categories. The survey identified 96 professionals and 32 students, most of whom were accounted for in the following categories.

|              | Professionals | Students | Total |
|--------------|---------------|----------|-------|
| Musicians    | 28            | 16       | 44    |
| Theater/Film | 21            | 9        | 30    |
| Dancers      | 9             | 1        | 10    |
| Writers      | 10            | 2        | 12    |

## CONVERSATIONS: MORMON ARTISTS SPEAK THEIR MINDS
JOANNE ROWLAND AND TODD FLYR

During the 20th century in particularl, Church congregations in New York have included an astonishing number of professional artists at various stages in their careers. Are these Latter-day Saint artists in any way distinguishable from the thousands of other artists who flock to the city looking for instruction and opportunity? Does their religion make a difference to artists, and do their artistic pursuits reflect on their religion?

To answer these questions, we interviewed a random sample of artists working in a wide range of disciplines and media. Here, they discuss the Church, their work, and life in New York City.

The plan was that if I could find an apartment in two weeks, we would move [from LA to New York]. It's difficult to rent an apartment in New York City if you don't already have a job in the city and difficult to find a job if you don't already live here. When the two weeks were just about over, I managed to rent a studio apartment in Hell's Kitchen. I returned to Los Angeles; we sold our car, bought plane tickets with the money and made our move to New York City. KENT CHRISTENSEN, **PAINTER/ILLUSTRATOR**

When I planned to come, it was not my intention to stay; I had a grant to study jazz for two weeks. But when I came to the city, I had such a strong feeling that every question I've ever had could be answered here—that the answers I needed for my soul to be free were here. When I called to tell my father that I wouldn't be coming home in two weeks as I had planned, he said, "Oh honey, I knew that." LISA DESPAIN **JAZZ PIANIST**

The decision to come to New York City was a result of prayer—we were considering Seattle at the same time. I'm not sure why we were directed to come to New York. My acting career has not been what I hoped for. Maybe our being here was for the education and opportunities it has provided for our children. Ansel studied at the School of American Ballet and has danced the role of Fritz in New York City Ballet's "Nutcracker." Norma has sung in the New York City Opera Children's Choir Opera and at St. John the Divine. Another reason might have been to be bishop. NED BUTIKOFER **ACTOR & BISHOP/BRANCH PRESIDENT**

Following the opening night performance of "The Dead," the opera Murray Boren composed to my libretto on the short story by James Joyce, I walked home from the theater. Opening night was great and I was on a real artistic high. It was after midnight and as I walked from the theater to our West 57th Street apartment, I was yelling, "This is my city! There's my Empire State Building! There's my Chrysler Building! That's my garbage can!" I was a little out of control, but that's how it feels to open a show in New York City. GLEN NELSON **LIBRETTIST**

I can still remember the day that I was playing for a rehearsal in the Minskoff Theater for a Tony Award-winning choreographer and a renowned actor and looking out the window where great big snowflakes were coming down in front of Sardi's and I thought, "Look at me! Look at where I am!" ROYCE TWITCHELL **ACCOMPANIST & MUSICAL DIRECTOR**

I believed that the Church expected me to choose a career that would be more secure in order to provide for a family, etc. But then when I tried to say exactly who had told me that, I had to admit, only I had told myself that; I couldn't think of anyone who had ever actually said it. I like that my being active in the Church requires people to shift the paradigm a little bit; you know, an "unruly" musician who does really good home teaching. CHRISTIAAN CRANS **OPERA COACH/VOCAL ACCOMPANIST**

At the Ford Modeling Agency, when they pull my chart up on the computer, it says, "no smoking, no alcohol, no lingerie." I've recently been called as the stake Young Women president, a calling that comes at a time when I do feel a balance in my life. My children and my husband are my first priority; my Church callings and my career demands come second. MARILEE MOE **FASHION MODEL**

Before I joined the church, I would have taken any role, regardless of its moral presentation, because I would have considered it part of the enlightening aspect of art. Now, I feel that I have a responsibility to nurture and care spiritually for myself and for others. Accepting a role is often a subject of prayer. JENNY WELCH-BABIDGE **OPERA PERFORMER**

I might be willing to play a murderer and kill someone if the role showed the negative aspects of the action. There have been times when I have felt punched in the stomach; awful and dark as I have read for roles that have been offered to me that were not appropriate. The only way I know which roles to take is to discern by the Spirit. ALLISON STANDER **ACTOR**

Spiritual experiences and artistic experiences come from the same place. I tend to have big transcendent experiences within an orchestra community. I've also had very spiritual experiences at times when I am performing as a soloist and I feel a connection with the audience. APRIL CLAYTON **FLUTIST**

Sometimes, right when the curtain goes up, you feel something from the audience, the energy is tangible almost like a breeze on a hot summer day. On other occasions, it grows throughout the performance. Everyone thinks "Wow, something is happening" and there is a moment that transcends this world. It is a spiritual experience when all hearts are tuned to a moment in time that is not of this world; it is something purer. KIPLING HOUSTON **BALLET & BROADWAY PERFORMER**

In New York we have a whole generation of artists and media professionals who are succeeding in their work on a local and on a national level. The atmosphere fosters creativity and encourages us to try new things—to be different, to be bold in our ambitions. SCOTT TIFFANY **DOCUMENTARY FILMMAKER**

I guess having so many artists makes [Church] a little quirky. A community needs artists to be a healthy community. But a community of only artists is not healthy. We need a good mix. MARK GRAHAM **PAINTER/ILLUSTRATOR**

**AN ECUMENICAL SONG FEST** THE MORMONS AND MARTIN LUTHER KING
JOANNE ROWLAND

In January 1995 I was invited by Francois Clemmons, director of the American Negro Spiritual Research Foundation, to attend an annual Martin Luther King musical celebration and vigil. I was told I wasn't required to sit for the full five hours but was free to wander in and out of the Upper West Side church where it was held. As it turned out, I did sit for the full five hours spellbound by the variety of singing: opera singers sang the simple spirituals with full operatic passion quite startling at such close range. Musicologists brought pots and pans and wooden spoons they passed out among the congregants to bang on while they sang their renditions of the traditional songs.

It occurred to me more than once during the evening of listening to songs with texts about the trials of this life and the hope of a better afterlife, that the text, "and should we die before our journey's through, happy day all is well" would fit right in. At the end of the evening I asked Mr. Clemmons what he thought about including a Mormon choir the next year. He said, "Let's talk." The following fall he called to ask what I had in mind. I told him about the hymn written while crossing the plains in a time of discouragement and death and reminded him of the Mormon Tabernacle Choir as assurance that Mormon's could sing. He said, "Please, come. Sing your hymn and then sing two of ours. And do you think you could get Ariel Bybee to sing too?"

Stake President John Stone gave his blessing to the project and stake music director, Cynthia Pannell, agreed to form a choir. She conducted "Come, Come, Ye Saints" and David Skouson conducted "Every Time I Feel the Spirit" and "Don't be Weary Traveler."

During the 1996 vigil, ours was the only racially integrated choir, thanks, in part, to Lisa Anderson who on her own initiative taught the music to two recently baptized African-American sisters. Several other black and mixed race members also learned the music to perform along with the fine contingent of blond performers.

Although our participation was listed in the middle of the program, it was well after 11:00 p.m. before Mr. Clemmons announced us. Ariel Bybee sang first and filled St. Michael's Episcopal Church with an absolutely stunning rendition of David Fletcher's "Weepin' Mary." We were very well received and were invited to sing every year thereafter until the vigil program was phased out several years later.

In 1997, we suffered from poor rehearsal attendance but somehow managed to again give a rather stirring performance under David Skouson's skillful direction. We sang as our Mormon contribution Skouson's arrangement of "The Spirit of God."

In 1998, Lisa DeSpain took the baton bringing with her a large and helpful contingent from the single wards. Ariel Bybee again sang "Weepin' Mary" and again brought the house down.

In 1999, plans for a spring concert at Carnegie Hall overshadowed all other musical endeavors. However, at the last minute, Christiaan Crans cheerfully agreed to get a group of his friends together and provide a Latter-day Saint contribution to the vigil. With two rehearsals, the eleven professional, young white singers prepared the most polished performance of the 1999 vigil.

Thus ended our participation in the Harlem Spiritual Ensemble-sponsored Martin Luther King ecumenical singing vigil. While it lasted, it was a great community participation opportunity and the way things work out in New York City, it stands to reason that we should expect another similar opportunity to present itself before long.

### ONLY IN NEW YORK GLEN NELSON

When residents of the nation's largest city hear the phrase, "Only in New York," they smile. A nod of recognition follows, and the New Yorker will repeat, knowingly, "Only in New York."

The phrase refers to the paradoxical, the bizarre, and, in our city, the commonplace occurrences that remind us of our singular New York life: the Mexican restaurant run by a Chinese family; the sight of blue-haired matrons on the bus chatting with purple-haired teenagers; the traffic sign that says, "Don't even think about parking here!"

The Church has its set of "Only in New York" moments, too. To my mind, the special events of our church community speak loudly about the place's character. Special events highlight the singularity of our religious community and illustrate why they could take place only in New York.

New York stake events frequently have an element of showmanship. If New York is the center of the performing arts in America, it is logical that members of the Church from all over the country would come here either to study or perform in the worlds of fine art, opera, Broadway, and dance. During their stays, these performing artist-members have organized and enabled large-scale events that congregations elsewhere would be hard-pressed to muster.

Yet, it seems to me that we take these things for granted. We fail to see how unusual it is to have composers at the ready to write new music and arrangements for our meetings, to have so many musicians that an orchestra can be amassed to perform difficult music expertly. There are so many singers here, that any of a few dozen could step in on short notice and give a beautiful recital.

It would be impossible to catalog all of the events of our stake during the last seventy years, or even the last seven years—but following is a sampling of events that I have witnessed or heard about in our stake.

Music performance of a high caliber has long been a hallmark of the Church here. Reid Nibley and Grant Johannesen tell of talent nights in the 1940s. At one of them, featuring both pianists (fresh from national tours and local recitals) on the Church's baby grand piano, someone had polished the piano (including the keys!) immediately before the performance. The keyboard was so slippery that their fingers kept falling off. It was one of many talent evenings that included musicians and painters who had arrived from the West to study and pursue careers in New York.

When the Lincoln Square stake center was about to be dedicated in 1975, local leaders requested a large concert-sized piano for the chapel, feeling it was needed for the many fine musicians who played in church. They were turned down. Undeterred, the leaders raised the money themselves. They organized a concert at Avery Fisher Hall, diagonally across the street from the church. Pianist Grant Johannesen gave a benefit recital which generated sufficient funds to purchase the Steinway grand piano that has graced the chapel ever since.

For the decades that Metropolitan Opera soprano Ariel Bybee lived in New York, it was common to have special vocal musical events. A production of the Christmas opera, *Amahl and the Night Visitors* was mounted one year, for example. I recall an especially memorable ward Christmas party in which Sister Bybee arranged to borrow a live donkey from the opera house to carry Mary through the streets of Bethlehem (our gymnasium). For the Easter sacrament meeting in 1991, the ward choir along with Sister Bybee and other opera soloists sang a newly commissioned cantata by ward member Murray Boren. Only in New York.

An annual performance of *The Messiah* with orchestra and soloists is a continuing tradition in the New Jersey stakes. When Manhattan followed suit in 2002, the stake had so many gifted soloists that the four solo parts (soprano, alto, tenor, and bass) were divided between a dozen singers to give each one an aria.

The city's large halls have been host to various church conferences and events, including Radio City Music Hall, Carnegie Hall, Avery Fisher Hall, and Madison Square Garden. In each, elaborate choirs were organized with original music composed for the occasion. There is an expectation that when visiting authorities attend conferences in New York, the music will be superior. Part of the fun of going to conferences is to see the shocked look on visitors' faces: this is great music!

On April 8, 1999, the New York New York Stake and the surrounding stakes joined for an evening celebration in Carnegie Hall. David Fletcher conducted a large choir of over 100 voices drawn from congregations in the area and soloists who had once lived in New York or were still here. The event, produced by Claudia Bushman, took place simply because a few people thought it sounded like a worthwhile endeavor. Frank McAllister raised the money to make the concert free to the public.

Special events have taken many forms. In 2000 and 2001, Adam Russell organized a stake arts festival that filled two floors of the chapel with art displays, film screenings, lectures, performances, readings, and panel discussions on religion and the arts. Simultaneously, there were presentations of fine photograph techniques, piano recitals, children's art workshops, visual art exhibitions and vocal master classes. The events were like a three-ring circus of art.

At Christmas time in the early 1990s until 2002, a living nativity was mounted in the lobby of the stake center. In the evenings and after church on Sunday, parents with infants dressed in costume sat peacefully in a theatrical set designed and constructed by professional set designer Doug Ellis. Pedestrians bustling past the large windows of the lobby would stop to look and smile. It was an informal presentation. The families didn't really look much like Mary and Joseph. And the infants were of such varying sizes, colors and even numbers (over the years three sets of twins were laid in Jesus' manger) that the entire scene had a friendly, folksy feel. Speaking English was not a requirement, nor was speaking at all. I spent one afternoon with a young deaf couple whose first child had just been born. Unlike hearing families who often took a few minutes to adjust to the notion of sitting still and quiet, the deaf couple immediately radiated warmth and peace.

Church friends in New York City are always moving away, a consequence of the city's vitality. But when it comes to events, turnover is an advantage. It brings new energy, a delight in discovery, and a freshness that are found only in New York. Leaders move away, others take their places, and develop different activities—equally interesting and equally appropriate for that moment.

For the long-time resident, this sometimes-painful pattern guarantees a sense of wonder and adventure. We want to participate in activities because we can rightly ask, "Will this ever happen again?" Perhaps not, but members of the Church in New York City take solace in knowing that if that perfect activity doesn't recur, something great will replace it.

Macías family nativity – may be a place for this at the end Members of the stake formed a living nativity scene in the lobby of the stake center during Christmas seasons in the late 1990s. Rómulo, Arleen, Adam, Christopher and Raquel (baby) Macías pose in December 1995. Photo courtesy of América Cruz. America Cruz

Erik Orton, elders quorum president in the Inwood First Ward, wrote and produced a musical, "Berlin," in fall 2003, featuring a cast of twenty-one performers, four of whom were members of the New York New York Stake. The show is currently in development with two Broadway producers for a hopeful return to New York City. Image courtesy of Erik Orton.

One of many singers in the stake, Sandra Turley, Inwood First Ward, sang Cosette in Les Miserables on Broadway for three years. Photo courtesy of Sandra Turley.

IT'S A WONDERFUL TOWN

# PART 4: THE CHURCH IN MANHATTAN AND THE METRO AREA

# 1997-2004 NEW YORK NEW YORK STAKE
# AUXILIARIES ANNE KNIGHT AND SARIAH TORONTO

*Following are summaries of highlights and insights from the New York New York Stake's Relief Society, youth, Sunday School and Primary programs over the last seven years.*

## RELIEF SOCIETY: FINDING THE COMMON DENOMINATOR

Marilyn Higbee Walker was called as the first stake Relief Society president of the New York New York Stake when it was organized in November 1997. Like many of the leaders of the new stake, Marilyn was young—just 29 years old—and she felt keenly her inexperience at the time of her call.[1] When Susan Woodcock Robison was called to take Marilyn's place in April 2000, she likewise felt inexperienced, not in terms of age or Church experience, but in terms of knowing New York and what it meant to be a Relief Society sister in Manhattan.[2]

Aided by the Spirit, these women drew together counselors who rounded out their own abilities and experience, and enabled them to ably lead the women of the stake through the first seven years of the stake's existence.[3]

Two substantive Church-wide changes to the Relief Society program occurred during these seven years. In 1998 the Church changed the Relief Society and priesthood curriculum so that twice a month both men and women had lessons on the teachings of one latter-day prophet for the entire year. Local priesthood and Relief Society leaders chose lesson topics for the first Sunday of the month, while material for the fourth Sunday was drawn from articles on a certain principle by various General Authorities.[4]

Another change came in 2000, when monthly Homemaking meetings were changed to Home, Family and Personal Enrichment Meetings, with the goal of bringing a more spiritual focus to activities planned around the application of gospel teachings.[5]

One of the stake's traditional yearly Relief Society events was a chili supper before the general women's broadcast in the fall.[6] Another yearly event was the Women's Conference in March to celebrate the Relief Society's anniversary. The Women's Conference usually entailed a light meal and a presentation. Conference themes and speakers from a few recent years included "Eve in the Big Apple" with Doris Cottam (2001), "Service Through Our Talents" with Linda Mamone (2002), "Make It Personal" with Claudia Bushman, Sydne Parker and Kelly Marshall (2003) and "Sacred Spaces" with Sheri Dew and Sharon Larsen (2004).[7]

After the attacks of September 11, 2001, people from around the world rightly perceived that the stake was deeply affected by the incident. As Stake Relief Society president, Susan was well aware of the outreach to the members of the stake.

"We received phone calls, letters and quilts. People came from Washington State with hundreds of teddy bears. We distributed the bears and the quilts through government agencies. We also received a lot of letters, which we put up around the cultural hall at November stake conference so our stake members would know that people were thinking about them."[8]

Six months after September 11th, President Hinckley visited Manhattan and announced that there would be a temple in the New York City metro region within two years. Members of the New York New York Stake participated in the edification of the temple; some sisters volunteered for everything from cleaning to addressing invitations for the Open House. The stake Relief Society also organized sisters from the stake to make altar cloths and shawls for use in the temple.[9]

Over the course of the seven years from 1997 to 2004, one of the New York New York Stake Relief Society's primary goals was to promote unity among the sisters in the stake and within each ward and branch.[10] As with the stake's population at large, the make-up of the Relief Society was rather diverse. Marilyn reflected, "Everyone can think of categories—older, younger, single, married, economic, linguistic, geographic, length of membership in the Church—which are potentially alienating but in reality can add wonderful diversity and strength to a group."[11]

In an effort to foster unity, the Relief Society leaders planned events around themes relating to a common culture in Christ.[12] Commenting on the diversity of the women in the stake, Susan said, "One of the opportunities we have is to learn and understand that women walk in different paths. We can learn to respect those women and the different paths they have chosen or are pursuing. More important than the diversity and the differences, we can focus on the things that unite us. We are similar because we are women, because we are sisters in the Church and because we have the gospel as a common denominator."[13]

## COMBINED YOUTH ACTIVITIES 1997-2004

In the seven years beginning with the organization of the New York New York Stake in 1997, the stake youth program evolved rather dramatically—

both in terms of the overall focus of the program and in terms of the events that leaders organized for the youth.

At the beginning of this period, after the dust of the stake's beginnings had settled, Jennifer Buckner and David Buckner, the stake Young Women and Young Men presidents, realized that no one had a good sense for who the youth were—where they lived, what their names were, what their family situations happened to be. There were a couple hundred youth living in Manhattan according to the Church's records, but many of those records were not up to date, and roughly two-thirds of the youth were the only members of the Church in their homes, and/or they lived in a home without a priesthood holder.[14]

Tracking down each individual youth in the stake became the youth leaders' top priority, and beginning in summer 1998 the ward Young Men and Young Women presidents set out to meet with every young man and young woman in his or her home. In addition to finding and meeting each youth, the leaders' objective was to determine how they could provide the youth with the resources they needed, as Jennifer put it, "to make their gospel life whole."[15]

Concurrent with this emphasis on finding each individual young man and woman, the youth leaders made fundamental changes in the stake's approach to youth conference. Before 1997, the youth had attended two youth conferences every year: a spring conference and a two-day winter conference at Frost Valley, a YMCA camp in upstate New York. As more than three quarters of the youth budget was going toward the Frost Valley activity, and since it excluded 12- and 13-year-olds because they could not sleep over at the camp, the new stake's youth leaders decided to no longer take the youth to Frost Valley.[16]

David and Jennifer Buckner envisaged holding a number of mini-youth conferences along the lines of the Especially for Youth (EFY) program.[17] In 1998, in place of the winter conference, the youth attended a one and a half-day mini-youth conference at the stake center in Manhattan.[18] The mini-youth conference tradition was brief; however, the spring youth conference became the main youth event in the stake. Beginning in 1998, the annual conference was held in a National Park Service forest in Catoctin, Maryland, next to Camp David.[19] (In 2002, the youth conference took place at a campground in Pennsylvania; in 2003, it was at Camp Liahona, the Church-owned camp in New York's Hudson Valley; and in 2004 it convened in Manhattan.[20])

Another tradition was born when stake presidency counselor Josh Yamada suggested holding a Mini-Missionary Training Center (MTC) Day. Meredith Higbee, first counselor in the stake Young Women presidency, organized the first daylong Mini-MTC in 2000.[21] The youth received calls to foreign-speaking missions and were assigned companions.[22] They knocked on doors and sometimes had those doors slammed in their faces, and they participated in culture and language classes. By the end of the day, some could even share their testimonies in their country's language. The Mini-MTC is now a bi-annual event, after having been a yearly activity for a few years.

Perhaps the most difficult stake youth activity followed directly on the heels of the events of September 11, 2001. The stake had planned a Young Men and Young Women back-to-school social at the beach for Saturday, September 15, 2001. Following the tragedies, parents and stake and ward leaders had many discussions about whether to cancel the activity because the city was in so much chaos. But for that very reason, the stake went ahead with its plan. Debbie Bingham, a nurse and Young Women leader in the Inwood First Ward recalled, "More than ever, our city-locked youth needed this trip out of Manhattan for a day. They needed to be away from the TV, from the images of pain and from the smell of destruction."[23] In hindsight it seemed everyone agreed that not canceling the event was the right decision.

The following year, another successful on-going activity was born: the auction fundraiser. Based on the success of an auction to benefit the youth programs of the Manhattan First Ward in 2002, stake youth leaders first organized a stake-wide auction in 2003. Members of the stake donated goods (cakes, concert tickets, a Park City condo) and services (babysitting, voice lessons, personal training sessions), then on auction night stake members bid on those donations in both silent and live auctions.

The 2003 event was so successful that in 2004, stake youth leaders decided to make the auction their sole fundraising event. At the 2004 auction, in one night, the youth raised over $10,000 to defray the costs of girls camp, Scout camp and youth conference.

In addition, a stake-wide mentoring program is now in place, proving a boon to both the youth and single adults who become their tutors, advisors, and confidants.[24]

Finally, as a culminating event of the last seven years of activities, the New York New York Stake Youth prepared the Harlem dance segment for the Manhattan temple Jubilee, where they performed for President Gordon B. Hinckley at Radio City Music Hall the night before the temple was dedicated.[25]

The many activities and opportunities available to the youth in Manhattan in 2004, seven years after their stake's organization, owed much to strong support from the stake's leaders. Two members of the stake presidency, Brent Belnap and Josh Yamada, and the stake Young Women's president, Marilee Moe, were raising their families in the city and had or would soon have children in the youth program. These leaders had a vested interest in vibrant, successful Young Men and Young Women programs. As Marilee stated, "We and others are choosing to raise our families here. We want the lives of our children and their friends—as a group—to be rich in wholesome experience and moral social opportunities."[26]

## YOUNG WOMEN: URBAN TESTIMONIES

When the New York New York Stake was created in November 1997, much of the stake's leadership was rather young—late 20's and early 30's—by typical Church standards. Jennifer Jackson Buckner, the new stake Young Women president, was just 28.[27] For Jennifer, as for the other stake leaders, however, youth and inexperience did not stand in the way of effective leadership.

As Jennifer stated, "It's all about the process of learning, and just doing your best."[28] When Jennifer was released in January 1999, one of her young but capable counselors, Marilee Jacobson Moe, was called as the stake Young Women president.

For these young leaders in Manhattan from 1997 to 2004, girls camp was the biggest yearly event in terms of planning and organization. The first year, 1998, the new stake took its girls to Camp Liahona, the Church-owned camp in New York's Hudson Valley. Only 10 girls came, in large part because the unit leaders were responsible for transportation—but, as is typical in Manhattan, hardly any of them had cars.[29]

The following year, 1999, Young Women leaders realized that to get more girls to camp, the stake had to make it easier for the girls to get there. That year 43 girls attended camp, thanks in great part to fundraisers the stake organized.[30] In addition to transportation, another girls camp challenge for Young Women leaders in the stake was having adequate camping gear. People in Manhattan in general do not have tents, sleeping bags and other camping gear, partly because storage space is scarce, partly because camping is not an easily accessible activity.

As such, the stake made a concerted effort to acquire enough camping gear for all the girls who want to attend girls camp. By fall 2003, Marilee indicated, "we now have a big stove, enough tents for all the girls, and where we're short on sleeping bags, we borrow from the scouts."[31]

In addition to girls camp, the stake hosted a yearly event for the young women in conjunction with the annual Young Women broadcast from Salt Lake City. The girls assembled for pre-broadcast activities such as mother-daughter cake decorating and mother-daughter massages and manicures, and then watched the broadcast together.

The Young Women organization during this time in Manhattan was made up of a wide-ranging, diverse set of girls.[32] "The variety of girls was so exciting," as Jennifer stated.[33] Many young women hailed from Spanish-speaking countries, including Puerto Rico, the Dominican Republic and several Central and

South American countries.³⁴ Some girls were deaf, some were Chinese. A few young women had been in the Church their whole lives, while others were converts, sometimes the only members of the Church in their families.

One stake Young Women leader recalled her experience working with these urban youth. "They are smart, sassy and on fire. Many come from single-mom families, with dads who don't exist, or who are in jail...they deal with mental illness, abuse, alcohol, drugs and death. [Yet] they have a testimony of a loving Heavenly Father—with few or no role models of how men are supposed to treat women."³⁵

The Young Women program, with events like girls camp and youth conference, and caring leaders and mentors, gave Manhattan's young women the opportunity to find a home in the gospel.

## YOUNG MEN: MANHATTAN AND THE GREAT OUTDOORS

Thomas Epting was one of the stake Young Men presidents (1998 to 2003) who specifically focused on developing the scouting program. He worked closely with Malcolm Draper, high council adviser to the youth, and Wayne Collier, scouting specialist and a driving force in planning and training.³⁶

At summer camp in 1999, five boys from the stake joined a Jewish group at the Ten-Mile River scout reservation (southwest of Monticello, New York, near the Pennsylvania border). Within three years, the camp was developed into an all-LDS summer camp at Ten Mile River, drawing in roughly 125 boys from Church units in the five city boroughs.³⁷

At winter camp, scouts slept in tents on a frozen lake and participated in a high adventure three-day trek. They also played hockey on the lake as well as hiked and snowshoed into the Catskill Mountains.³⁸ This is no small feat for young men growing up in a city of eight million people.

Leaders who moved to New York City—having grown up in wide open spaces—were sometimes reminded that the scouting program was begun, in part, to provide learning opportunities for city boys in 1907 London.³⁹

Through a number of efforts, including those of stake presidency counselor Josh Yamada, a close working relationship was established with the New York Council of the Boy Scouts of America. Additional support for scoutmasters and their boys in merit badge work, record keeping and fundraising was available through a stake scouting committee.

Meanwhile, one of the stake Young Men presidents, Justin Rucker, prepared a manual for leaders (who changed fairly frequently) to guide their boys–whether entering the Young Men program as 12-year-olds or as new converts between the ages of 12 and 18–to advance to the scouting rank of First Class in one calendar year, while fulfilling their respective quorum and Duty to God responsibilities.⁴⁰

A program called Aaronic Priesthood: Fulfilling Our Duty to God, introduced in 2001 by the First Presidency,[41] correlated with scouting but highlighted and promoted personal goals, as well as family and quorum activities that help boys prepare specifically for the Melchizedek Priesthood. Along with a strong seminary program, this played an important role in the lives of the stake's young men.

Challenges continue, certainly in the lives of the youth. But their leaders today, as before, accept the larger challenge "of the Aaronic Priesthood program...to train up boys to be men of God, willing and able to lead their families and the Church in righteousness" with the ability to "organize self-sustaining families, congregations, and communities."[42]

### SUNDAY SCHOOL: A REPORT CARD

Stake Sunday School president Thomas Vogelman [2000 to 2002] drew up a checklist of 25 criteria to help evaluate teaching in Sunday School classes and visited units in the stake, where he found the instruction better than expected but somewhat uneven.

He felt that the stake could support local units through training sessions with bishops for a discussion of what makes a good teacher and the value of calling Sunday School class presidents to arrange for prayers and set a reverent tone before beginning the class. He recommended at least quarterly meetings with each unit Sunday School presidency and sees a role for the stake in handling administrative details like ordering manuals for the coming year in July or August and ensuring that scriptures along with other useful materials are available in meetinghouse libraries.[43]

Noboru (Bob) Takahasi accepted a call as stake Sunday School president in November 2002, and began to emphasize in ward conferences and visits to Sunday School classes the importance of preparation by the students. This could be encouraged by providing information on the ward websites and in sacrament meeting programs. He saw the need to round out local Sunday School presidencies, especially as they now oversee training for all teachers in their unit and assist librarians in how to best manage the meetinghouse libraries. Brother Takahasi noted, too, the value of class presidents in preparing the room and challenging students to read lesson material in advance.[44]

### PRIMARY: A CREATIVE AND DIVERSIFIED FLOCK

Three things might set the Primaries found in New York City apart from Primaries in other places throughout the LDS Church. First, the cultural diversity, second the continual changes as people move in and out of the city and third, the use made by the Primaries of the rich artistic community available in New York City.

As to the cultural diversity, of the twelve units in the New York New York Stake in spring 2004, eight of them had Primary organizations. The children of the Union Square First Ward and Second Branch met together. The three singles wards did not have Primaries and at the time of this writing, there were no children in the Canal Street (Chinese-speaking) Branch.

Virtually all of the children in the stake's two Spanish-speaking wards were bilingual. Many of their leaders spoke Spanish only. The Sunday lessons and songs were taught in Spanish. In the past, the deaf branch maintained a separate Primary where the children were taught in both English and American Sign Language.

For approximately one year, while the Union Square building was being prepared, the fifth (English-speaking) and fourth (Spanish-speaking) ward Primaries met together doing everything in both English and Spanish. The fall primary program in 2002 featured all of the children singing, first in one language and then in the other. Subsequent to the program, however, because so much of the valuable teaching time had been devoted to language, it was decided to separate the Primaries so that the focus would be again on teaching the gospel.

The problem of the ever-changing population of the city's wards could discourage leaders who had to continually ask their bishops to issue new callings, as colleagues they had grown to love moved on. Of course, while talented people were forever leaving the city, more talented people continued to come and there was almost always a rich pool of members to draw upon.

Summertime, however, always presented staffing problems. With many families leaving the city on vacation, and many college students away for the summer, Primary leaders were frequently left to host vacationing children visiting from around the world.

Even though New York Primary leaders could not count on using the summer months to get ready for their fall primary sacrament meeting programs, the programs, year after year, in both the large and the small units were of an unusually high quality. Which brings us to the blessing of the big arts community.

In New York City, it is possible to staff many of the Primaries with at least one or two professional or student musicians, dancers, singers, or actors. Trained in the performing arts, those leaders help create and rehearse Primary programs that will satisfy all of the children who perform and more than satisfy all of the adults who attend.

In spring 1997, Diana Murphy and her counselors instituted the first annual stake Primary book fair.[45] It was held on a Saturday afternoon at the stake center and was attended by Primary children and their parents. The elaborately decorated cultural hall created a carnival-like atmosphere in which children were assisted in making puppets, listening to stories and participating in creative dancing of stories. Parents were invited to learn about library cards and children's literature. The children were all given a new book to take home at the end of the activity. The books had been collected earlier by asking for donations from all of the members of the stake.

The success of the book fair inspired Joanne Rowland, a member of a committee formed to create a stake arts festival, to suggest a children's art fair be part of the larger festival. For both years of the festival, in March 2000 and in March 2001, arts activities for children were included. The 2001 festival included a children's concert featuring the eight cello composition *Bachianas Brasilieras* by Villa Lobos and Aaron Copland's *Old American Songs*.

In May 2003, the ideas of book fair and art fair were merged when Grant Johannessen agreed to perform a children's concert as part of the book fair, featuring three children's books with narration. Gene Pack, Utah radio announcer, came to New York City to perform with Johannessen, who is a member of the stake.

From 1997, the book fair continued annually until 2004, when the temple dedication took precedence over any stake-sponsored activities.

In the fall of 2001, everything in New York City changed for a time following the September 11th attacks on the World Trade Center. The boundaries of the Manhattan Fifth Ward (now the Union Square First Ward) encompassed Ground Zero. The fifth ward's primary president, Deborah Gaebler, and her second counselor, Louise Wallburger, lived near enough to Ground Zero that both their families understandably decided to move out of Manhattan, leaving the fifth ward Primary bereft.

While we struggled in New York City proper, Church members throughout the nation were also grieving and wanting to help in some way. Many, many outside Primary presidencies conducted sharing time activities to comfort any potentially grieving New York City children.

They wrote and mailed volumes of cards, letters and posters—enough to cover the cultural hall walls once for general conference in October and a second time for stake conference in November.[46] There were enough stuffed animals sent to the stake Primary to provide gifts for the Harlem branch Christmas party, and to replenish the four nurseries then in the stake. The missionaries were the recipients of numerous cookie and candy donations. Fortunately, no lives of New York New York Stake members were lost, but there were hardships. The outpouring of this spontaneous love and support was overwhelming.

Stake youth at youth conference in the Catoctin Mountains, April 2001. Photo courtesy of Sariah Toronto.

Stake youth at a trip to Robert Moses State Park, September 15, 2001. Photo courtesy of Sariah Toronto.

Young men from the stake with Bishop Jim Green at Ten Mile River Scout Camp, February 1999. Photo courtesy of the New York New York Stake.

# UNIT HISTORICAL OVERVIEWS

*Following are personal recollections and overviews of the New York New York Stake units' histories, focusing on the years since the current stake's organization in 1997.*

## WHERE LAWYERS AND MUSICIANS MEET: MANHATTAN FIRST WARD, 1997-2004 SUMER THURSTON EVANS

The Manhattan First Ward is an English-speaking standard geographically defined ward located on the west side of Manhattan. Its borders run from West 59th Street to 125th Street, bounded by Central Park on the east and Riverside Park on the west. Its chapel is located across the street from Lincoln Center at 125 Columbus Avenue. The new Manhattan New York Temple is in the same building.

The current bishop is John Warner and before him was Scott Huntsman (1995-2000). An informal poll of active members shows that 73% of the members are married, 22% are single or widowed and 5% are divorced and not remarried. Of those members who are married, 44% have children living at home and 15% have grown children.

The first ward has been characterized by several major events, commencing shortly before the division of the stake in November 1997. In October 1997, the ward was divided between the Upper West Side/Morningside Heights and Harlem. In addition to losing members to Harlem, a few people still inside our modified ward boundary were asked to attend the Harlem branch to offer support. Of course, many were unhappy to lose a number of our most prized members and to see racial and cultural diversity reduced. Today our ward is approximately 78% Caucasian, 10% African-American, 7% Hispanic, 4% Asian, and 1% other.

Around 2000, in a second major event affecting the ward, youth programs were added. For many years all of the youth programs in the stake were administered through the second ward on the east side where a larger number of youth resided. Families with teenage children were automatically assigned to the second ward. The first young woman in our independent program was Alexandra Moe. Youth programs give the ward more depth by adding older children, and strengthen ties to their families since they can now be long-time members. The ward's youth program is thriving, with eight young women and six young men, and more are on the way: our senior Primary has 22 children (ages 8-11 years), our junior Primary has 20 (ages 3-7 years), and our nursery has 17 (ages 18 months to 3 years).

Affecting all of us personally—as well as the rest of the world—was the third major event in our recent history, the terrorist attacks on the World Trade Center on September 11, 2001. Several ward members worked in and around the World Trade Center. Immediately after the tragedy struck we began calling members of the ward to make sure they were all right and to see if anyone needed assistance. Bishop Warner expressed relief as he hung up after each call. None of our ward members were injured. He recalls that on a day of despair one bright light shone through. Each person he spoke with asked him what he or she could do to help others.

Currently, our ward has almost 140 active families. Since this is such a large number, the stake presidency often calls our members to serve in stake leadership positions. Around 15-20 of our members serve in other wards or in stake callings. Additionally, our ward has been instrumental in organizing several stake activities.

The Manhattan First Ward is well known for its musical talent. In addition to professional musicians, we frequently have several students studying at the Juilliard and Manhattan Schools of Music. The musical numbers in sacrament meeting can rival the quality of performances at Lincoln Center across the street. Frequently we hear music composed by our own members. Additionally, the ward is home to professional ballet dancers, models, television/movie actors and producers. The Church Public Affairs missionary representatives attend our ward. Currently, Sharon and Ralph Larsen serve in this capacity, having recently replaced Pat and LaVell Edwards. Until the temple construction, we were the home to the family history missionaries, and now that the temple has arrived we are home to eight temple missionary couples.

The ward membership is a diverse and highly educated group. About 46% of our ward has attended or is currently attending some sort of graduate school, with a total of roughly 88% of ward members having attended college. Almost 20% of the ward members are students. The majority of the students attend Columbia University or its affiliates. Each September we expect 15-20 new families–with almost the same number leaving each summer. A substantial number come for summer internships and leave before September. Most students study law and business, but we also have PhD candidates, students of real estate and medicine, and a handful of undergraduates. Several college professors attend the ward.

Even with all the comings and goings, our ward feels like a large extended family. One of our goals has been to "Count Every Sheep," that is, for each of us to be responsible for the welfare of others in the ward. This nicely fits in with another of our goals: excellence in home teaching and visiting teaching. Many in this ward have extremely time-intensive professions, and they take special care to assure that work obligations do not overcome church responsibilities. We have a regular rotating assignment to assist in cleaning the church building. We often see members who work long hours in high-paying jobs vacuuming the halls on a Saturday morning.

The year 2004 has been an amazing year with the temple being built right over our heads. At times our chapel felt like a construction site; sometimes we arrived home from church covered in dust. It was a sad day when they dismantled our beautiful original pipe organ, but it has truly been a blessing to witness this temple construction. We feel especially fortunate and grateful to have a temple within our boundaries and look forward to attending regularly.

## MANHATTAN FIRST WARD TIMELINE

**1837** Church meetings in Manhatan begin in 1837 under Elder Parley P. Pratt and continue until the exodus to the West. Services are then held intermittently until the 1890s, when regular branch meetings resume.

**1934** The Manhattan Branch becomes a ward when the New York Stake is created. Goreon Affleck is sustained as the first bishop.

**1964** The World's Fair is held in New York City. As a result of the Church's exposure there, many people are baptized, and the Manhattan First Ward grows quickly, adding a Spanish-speaking group. The ward meets in a former Jewish synagogue on West 81st Street.

**1966** A Spanish-speaking branch is formed in Manhattan, drawing on Spanish-speaking members of the first ward.

**MID 1960'S** The Manhattan Second Ward is created for members living on the east side and downtown.

**1975** The new building is dedicated at Lincoln Square. It houses a visitors' center as well as a chapel and mission offices.

**1997** The Manhattan Ninth Branch (later renamed the Harlem First Branch) splits off from the first ward.

**1999** A youth program is started in the ward. During the 1980s and 1990s, all families in the stake with teenage children were assigned to the Manhattan Second Ward.

**2000** John Warner is sustained as bishop.

Subway stop at Columbia University on the 1/9 train.

Women in the Manhattan First Ward at play group in October 2001. Jo Lambert (with Eleanor), Bobbie Sandberg (with Tanner), Sara Anderson (with Adam), Ashley Moffat (with Kimball), Vanessa Schaumann (with Ethan), Kelly Paulson (with Joseph) and Jana Greer (with Alex and Ellie). Photo courtesy of Jana Greer.

The Manhattan First Ward, meeting in the gym of the stake center during temple renovations. One ward member joked during a talk that he had never before had church in Home Depot. Photo courtesy of Maria Hunter.

D. Fletcher and Ariel Bybee take a break from dancing at the Black and White Ball, a joint deaf branch, Manhattan First and Second Ward activity, March 14, 1998. Photo courtesy of Kent Christensen.

## EAST SIDE STORY: THE MANHATTAN SECOND WARD
KENT CHRISTENSEN

To understand what the Manhattan Second Ward looked like in 1997 and the tremendous changes that it has undergone since that time, you have to look to the late 1980s. At that time the second ward was the ward people attended with teenagers, since it was the only ward in Manhattan with a youth program. The second ward was thought of as the family ward. Prior to the existence of a singles ward in New York City (created in June 1991), all of the members who lived south of 59th Street and did not have Primary or youth-aged children attended the "old" Manhattan Third Ward. In June 1991, while Andrew Winkler was bishop, the third ward was folded into Manhattan second. One week we were in the smallest ward in the stake, and the next week we were in a huge family ward with people from the east side and Lower Manhattan. Paul Gunther was called as bishop of the enlarged second ward, replacing Tony Fennimore.

The end of the 1980s brought an economic recession, followed by an unprecedented economic and real estate boom in the 1990s, which affected the growth of the Church in Manhattan, including the second ward. The very factor that had so burdened the old third ward (skyrocketing housing costs south of 59th Street and on the west side) caused a northward shift in member population as people sought more affordable places to live. The Upper East Side became the population center of the ward. It became routine to see other members of the ward out in the neighborhood during the week, where in previous years one would generally only see other Latter-day Saints at church on Sunday.

In October 1995, Mark Peterson was called as bishop of the second ward. Our unit was still the largest in size, both in terms of geography and population in Manhattan. Its boundaries included everything south of 59th Street from the East River to the Hudson and everything east of Fifth Avenue all the way up the island, not to mention families with teenage children who lived elsewhere. At one point, there were well over 2,000 membership records. Verifying and sorting out of all these records was like swimming upstream. If you stopped for a week, a new wave of records would overwhelm you and put you that far back.

During the terms of Bishops Gunther and Peterson, the second ward was more diverse and complex than it had ever been or may ever be again. Those of us who thrived on this kind of diversity thought it was wonderful. Some newcomers weren't quite sure what to think of a ward that included, in fairly equal proportions, artists, bankers and business people, attorneys and law students, doctors and medical students, military families (until the closing of the Coast Guard facility on Governor's Island), recent immigrants, deaf people, and academic/intellectual types. The ward included some of the richest and poorest zip codes in the United States, which happened to be right next to each other.

Looking back, however, I think everyone who was there and involved in the second ward during these years remembers them with fondness. There are many touching, troubling, and funny stories that come from these years. For the most part, we all got along famously and made fast friendships with people we otherwise might never have had reason to know.

In September 1997, James Green was called as bishop. The last few years of the 1990s were amazing times in the second ward. We had huge, lively ward parties and benefited from having so much talent. To become better acquainted with the Manhattan First Ward, we had a combined party each year for four or five years. Some of our most memorable and successful ward activities took place in Central Park—ward picnics and games, and the annual Primary party at the carousel. Speaking of Central Park, there is a tradition of walking home from church through the park, one of the things we will miss once the new building on the Upper East Side is completed.

With the creation of the Harlem First Branch, the makeup of the ward changed. Just as when the deaf group began to meet independently, we became less ethnically and economically diverse. This trend reached its apex with the creation of the Manhattan Fifth Ward (later the Union Square First Ward) in December 2000 for members living south of West 59th Street from the Hudson River to Fifth Avenue, and below East 50th Street from Fifth Avenue to the East River. In just a few years, the second ward went from being the largest and most diverse in the stake to being one of the smallest, geographically as well as in number of members, and probably the least ethnically and economically diverse. In 2002, Joseph Jensen was called to be bishop, a calling he continues to serve in at the end of 2004. The second ward has continued to grow and is now a strong neighborhood ward.

**MANHATTAN SECOND WARD TIMELINE**

**MID 1960S** The Manhattan Ward, Manhattan's only ward for many years, is split to create the Manhattan First and Second Wards. Al Woodhouse is sustained as bishop of the second ward. Both wards meet in the former Jewish synagogue the Church owns on West 81st Street.

**1975** The new stake center on West 65th Street is dedicated.

**1991** Ward boundaries now include the Upper East Side and all of Manhattan south of 59th Street, as well as all families in Manhattan with teenage children.

**1994** Manhattan Seventh (deaf) Branch is formed from group that met in the second ward.

**1997** Manhattan Ninth Branch (later renamed Harlem First Branch) is created, taking some members from the second ward.

**1997** James C. Green is sustained as bishop.

**2000** Manhattan Fifth Ward is created for downtown members, including Chinese speakers in the Chinese group.

**2001** James Green is called as second counselor in the stake presidency; Joseph C. Jensen is sustained as bishop.

Carolee, John and James Scowcroft dance together at the Black and White Ball, a joint deaf branch, Manhattan First and Second Wards activity, March 14, 1998. Photo courtesy of Kent Christensen.

Kent, Janet, Anne and Jane Christensen with Larry and Audrey Weitzman (all from the Manhattan Second Ward) at a stake Pioneer Day activity in Central Park, 1997. The Christensens came to New York in 1988 from Los Angeles after Kent graduated from Art Center College of Design. Several of his teachers had encouraged him to move here, so they thought they'd give it "a couple of years" - which have turned into 16, so far. Photo courtesy of Kent Christensen.

The former Manhattan Third Ward consisted of members living below 59th Street without children, but it was folded into the Manhattan Second Ward. Here, members of the former third ward at a last gathering at Kent and Janet Christensen's apartment on East 50th Street in 1989. Left to right, back row: Karen Deem, Glade Jacobsen, Bishop Andy Winkler, Jeff Hagen, Tom Miner, Quentin Reed, Victoria Barker, Stephen Bennett, Rick Rabe, Jason Southerland, Jim Elmer, Janet Christensen, Kent Christensen. Middle row: Julia Miner, David Reese, Kim Reese, Alise Orlandi, Graceann Irvine, Leslie Benfell, Lori Richards, Tim Inman. Front row: Kay Anderson, Heather Turner, Wendy Turner, Colleen Pratt, Mary Jane Price, Taft Price. Photo courtesy of Kent Christensen.

The Manhattan Second Ward meeting in the gym during temple-related renovations on the chapel. Photo courtesy of Maria Hunter.

## THE FIRST SINGLES: STORY OF THE MANHATTAN THIRD WARD ADAM RUSSELL

The Manhattan Third Ward offers its members an opportunity to rub shoulders with lots of great people. Many of us come to the city hoping to do big things, bringing our skills and talents with us. We are looking for a different culture and church experience in New York, and we find it here.

The original Manhattan Third Ward was a standard geographically defined ward that was formed in 1980. Four bishops served in this ward: Mark Graham, Robert Pinkerton, Stephen Quinn, and Andrew Winkler.

In June 1991, less than one month after the stake's boundaries were realigned to include southern Westchester County, and the New York East Stake was dissolved, the Manhattan Third Ward was reorganized by stake president Eliot Brinton as the stake's first singles ward. Almost immediately after its creation, an under-31 age limit was lifted so as to include all singles living within the stake who wanted to attend. Mark Bench, head of Church-owned WNSR (later WMXV) Radio in Manhattan, was called to be the first bishop.

In February 1993, Brent Belnap, a former of member of the ward, was called as the second bishop after a year and a half of marriage. He was able to reach all kinds of people and nurtured the Saints by bringing in "the one and the ninety-nine." Many members recall fondly many well attended and lively ward activities, temple trips, and other events, including the opening socials held each September on Governor's Island and later Roosevelt Island.

On October 27, 1996, the singles ward was divided into two wards according to age—an "older" singles ward and a "younger" singles ward—along an age division of 27 rather than the common age of 31 often used in the Church. Transitioning to the newly constituted third ("older") ward was initially unsettling for some, but the ward gradually regained its spirit of friendship.

A little over one year later, in November 1997, Bishop Belnap was called to be president of the New York New York Stake. He was followed as bishop of the third ward by Keith Allred, who served for just nine months. Many benefited from his short term of service and remember him fondly. Patrick Perkins was called as the next bishop. As Bishop Allred's counselor, Bishop Perkins had a head start getting to know the ward. As bishop, he organized an event that has been a highlight ever since. We rented two buses and visited Church history sites in Kirtland, Ohio. We had the privilege of holding sacrament meeting in the Kirtland Temple.

In 2000 the ward moved upstairs to the newly completed fifth floor chapel. The new quarters were smaller than those on the third floor and lacked the wider spaces for mingling. John Scowcroft, who had been serving as our high council representative, was called to lead the ward in 2001. He brought an admirable set of skills to the table. Broad-minded and compassionate, Bishop Scowcroft reached ward members who might otherwise have been lost.

Working with the stake leadership, Bishop Scowcroft enlisted ward members to serve outside the ward in newer or struggling units of the stake. They were called to staff vacant leadership positions and help with various priesthood and auxiliary organizations.

Due to the shortage of space caused by the temple construction that commenced in September 2002, the third ward joined that August with the two Young Single Adult wards for a combined sacrament meeting while holding priesthood and auxiliary meetings separately. For many, this was what they'd been waiting for: a singles' Mecca. Some visitors to combined sacrament meetings were thrilled to see the chapel and gym filled to capacity with single members of the Church, although others were overwhelmed by the sheer numbers. Some of those who were overwhelmed used this as the incentive they needed to join traditional wards. Although the "megaward" sacrament meeting attendance swelled, attendance in Sunday School, priesthood, and Relief Society tapered off.

On July 6, 2003, several months before the separation of the "megaward," David Passey was called to be bishop. Bishop Passey brings something special to the position. He is loving and temperate and has an inclination to direct our attention to the new temple.

When we were reunited again as the third ward, we were anxious to see what the group would be like. We started small, but people began to reappear. As we face additional changes following the dedication of the temple, we hope to maintain and augment the quality of our meetings and the standard of service in what we've come to know and love as the Manhattan Third Ward.

### MANHATTAN THIRD WARD TIMELINE

**1980** Manhattan Third Ward is created as a standard geographically defined ward.

**1991** Manhattan Third Ward is redesignated as a singles ward, and the families previously attending the third ward are assigned to the Manhattan First and Second Wards. E. Markham Bench is sustained as New York City's first singles ward bishop.

**1993** Brent J. Belnap is sustained as bishop.

**1996** Manhattan Third Ward is divided by age to create the Manhattan Eighth Ward; Brent J. Belnap continues as bishop of the Manhattan Third Ward.

**1997** Stake is divided; Brent J. Belnap is released as bishop and called as stake president. The new bishop of the Manhattan Third Ward is Keith Allred.

**1999** Patrick T. Perkins is sustained as bishop.

**2000** Both stake singles wards are moved up to the new fifth floor chapel in the stake center.

**2001** John Scowcroft is sustained as bishop.

**2002** Manhattan New York Temple is announced. Manhattan Third, Sixth, and Eighth Wards begin meeting together for sacrament meeting as the "megaward."

**2003** David Passey is sustained as bishop while three singles wards still meet together.

**2003** "Megaward" dissolves and Manhattan Third Ward begins meeting separately again in stake center.

Members of the Manhattan Third Ward participate in a sports competition at 109th Street on the east side of Central Park, summer 2004. Photo courtesy of Kim Hales.

The Manhattan Third Ward, meeting in the gym during temple-related chapel renovations. Photo courtesy of Maria Hunter.

Manhattan Third Ward luau party in the stake center cultural hall, fall 2003. Semi-finals of hula-hoop contest. Photo courtesy of Kim Hales.

Manhattan Third Ward luau party in the stake center cultural hall, fall 2003. Photo courtesy of Kim Hales.

## NYC'S FIRST SPANISH WARD: MANHATTAN FOURTH
SARA ANDERSON

The Manhattan Fourth Ward was originally created as the Spanish-American Branch in 1966, after the baptisms of an influx of new members following the 1964 World's Fair in Queens. Originally the only Spanish-speaking unit in the New York City metropolitan area, its members came from New Jersey and all the boroughs of New York City. It grew from a small branch into a large, strong, and culturally diverse ward by the late 1970s and 1980s, with many different Latin American nationalities represented in the congregation.

As Spanish-speaking wards and branches were created outside of Manhattan, members of the Spanish Ward (as it became known in 1977) were called to be leaders in the New York Stake and in other Spanish language wards in the area. The most recent division of the ward in about 1993 gave the ward its current boundaries, which include Manhattan south of 155th Street.

Through the years, one of the ward's most constant characteristics has been devoted temple worship. One of its greatest blessings and difficulties currently is the high rate of convert baptisms.

In 1997, Felix Pichardo was the bishop of the fourth ward. The years with Bishop Pichardo were particularly productive for temple work, both living ordinances and work for the dead. Arturo Tapia and Manuel Vera took a group of 20-25 people to the stake genealogy library nearly every Sunday to research family history.

As they had for years, the ward regularly went to the Washington Temple together, filling a bus nearly once a month. They would spend all day Saturday at the temple, arriving around 5:00 a.m. and leaving late in the afternoon. Investigators and new members who could not attend the temple sessions spent their time at the visitors' center or walking around the grounds. Youth did baptisms for the dead. Arturo Tapia estimates that of the endowed members currently attending the Manhattan Fourth Ward, the majority went to the temple for the first time during this era.

In December 1999, Kurt Wickham from the Manhattan First Ward was called as bishop of the fourth ward. The ward had not been led by a non-Latino since the 1960s. President Belnap counseled Bishop Wickham to take care of the youth and promised that if he did, their parents would support him and he wouldn't have problem being perceived as a "gringo bishop". Following this counsel, Bishop Wickham focused on the kids and eventually the activity levels of the youth improved dramatically. He says some of the the things that impressed him most about the ward members were their "humility, financial sacrifices, baptisms, priesthood advancement, youth attendance, Primary attendance, home teaching, temple attendance, personal warmth, and 'ward family' feeling."[1]

For the past four years, the ward has enjoyed tremendous growth, with sometimes as many as 10-15 baptisms in a single month. The many new members in the ward make the job of fellowshipping a sizable one. Under the leadership of the current elders quorum president, Ignacio Medel, the fourth ward began what Bishop Wickham calls "home teaching blitzes" to make sure all the members were looked after. Priesthood members "would meet every week on a certain night and blitz a neighborhood doing home teaching visits," recalls Bishop Wickham. "Many members were reactivated, and the brothers who participated had really neat experiences. It was really an amazing effort by the priesthood holders."

Strong temple attendance has always been a hallmark of the ward. "Before Manuel Vera passed away," Bishop Wickham recalls, "I got to witness the sealing of Manuel and Nilda in the Salt Lake City temple. Nilda's children from her prior marriage were also sealed to them. Her children are all active in the church and those that are married are sealed to their spouses. Their sealing was one of best and sweetest memories I have."

Bishop Wickham was released when he moved to San Diego in February 2003, and David Skouson, from the Inwood First Ward, was called as bishop. At the time of his call, the fourth ward had been meeting with the fifth ward (an English-speaking ward covering lower Manhattan) for sacrament meeting because of the temple construction at the stake center. The wards alternated holding sacrament meeting in Spanish and English with headset translation for those members who were not bilingual.

While meeting jointly, members of the two wards developed a cameraderie and reached out to one another as never before. Sometimes the two Primaries met together on Sundays, and the youth from the two wards combined for weeknight activities. Recently, two young people from the ward have left on missions. Juan Luis Peguero returned in December 2003 from Oakland, California (Spanish-speaking), and in November 2004 Mónica Paulino returned from serving in the Temple Square Mission in Salt Lake City.

One of the greatest challenges for the ward today is managing its tremendous growth. In the current congregation, the majority of members are first generation converts, and as those numbers continue to increase, teaching new members about living the gospel day-to-day becomes an increasingly large task.

Bishop Skouson felt that the dedication of the temple in Manhattan would help in this effort. He noted that new members who visit the temple grounds within two months after baptism are far more likely to remain active in the long term. Consequently, the fourth ward members worked to make sure that newly baptized members got to the temple to do baptisms or just walk around the grounds. With a temple in our city, its influence will be within easy reach for everyone.

Only two weeks after the temple dedication, Scott Higbee of the Manhattan First Ward was called to serve as bishop, replacing Bishop Skouson who moved to Las Vegas. Al Gámez and Geraldo Nieves, also of the Manhattan First Ward, were called as his counselors. As always, the fourth ward now looks forward to a new phase of change and development.

## MANHATTAN FOURTH WARD TIMELINE

**1965** Spanish groups (with Spanish classes for Sunday School, Relief Society and priesthood) are formed in the Brooklyn Branch and Manhattan Ward. Soon after, the Brooklyn Spanish-speaking group is disbanded. The mission forms a Spanish-speaking branch in Manhattan, the New York Spanish Branch.

**1968** The Spanish-American Branch is organized in Manhattan under the authority of the stake rather than the mission.

**1975** The Spanish-American Branch, along with two other units in Manhattan, moves to the new building on West 65th Street.

**1977** The Manhattan Spanish Ward is created with Manuel Nieto as the first bishop. As the only Spanish-language unit in the area, Spanish-speaking members from all over the New York metro area attend this ward.

**1978** Elder Robert Hales reorganizes the stake. The stake president of the New York New York Stake is Frank Miller, with counselors Al Woodhouse and Spanish ward Bishop Manuel Nieto. Gilberto Perea is sustained as the new bishop.

**1982** Jaime Mir is sustained as the bishop.

**1984** Luis Gallegos is sustained as bishop, a calling he keeps for nine years until called to serve in the stake presidency. During this time, the ward enjoys frequent ward activities, including ward culture nights for Columbus Day (Día de la Raza), trips to Lake Liahona and bus trips to the Washington, D.C. temple.

**1993** The Manhattan Spanish Ward becomes the Manhattan Fourth Ward, with Albis Gómez as bishop. The Manhattan Fifth Branch is created for Spanish-speaking saints in Washington Heights and Inwood.

**1994** Amadeo Durante is sustained as bishop.

**1997** Felix Pichardo is sustained as bishop. Around 40 families who had been attending the Manhattan Fifth Branch uptown become part of the Manhattan Fourth Ward again for three years.

**1999** Kurt Wickham, member of the Manhattan First Ward, is sustained as bishop.

**2002** The fourth ward begins meeting jointly with the Manhattan Fifth Ward for meetings due to construction of the future temple.

**2003** J. David Skouson, member of the Inwood First Ward, is sustained as bishop.

**2004** D. Scott Higbee, member of the Manhattan First Ward, is sustained as bishop..

The Manhattan Fourth Ward, meeting in the gym during temple-related chapel renovations. Photo courtesy of Maria Hunter.

Manhattan Fourth Ward Relief Society activity to celebrate Pioneer Day, 1984. Photo courtesy of América Cruz.

## A HAUNTED HOUSE: INWOOD SECOND WARD HISTORY
SARA ANDERSON

In September 1993, the stake split the Spanish-speaking ward and created the Manhattan Fifth Branch for Spanish-speaking members of the Church who lived north of 155th Street. For a while some members say they felt a little like castaways, especially since they had no meeting place until several months later. During the subsequent years of meeting in a rented school building, however, the branch strengthened in unity and size. By the time a permanent chapel was constructed in Inwood, the fifth branch had grown in numbers, developed its own identity, and was ready to become the Inwood Second Ward.

The branch was formed before it had a home. It first held Sunday services in the 65th Street building while leaders looked for a meeting place uptown. Antonio Cruz served as president during this time. In February 1994, the Church rented the Herbert L. Birch Manhattan Early Childhood Center at 554 Fort Washington Avenue, but the building was not ready to be occupied.

Rómulo Macías, who became branch president after President Cruz moved, remembers that it "looked like a haunted house." Members of the branch worked hard to clean up the mess and the cobwebs, and eventually contractors came in to finish the job of making it usable. However, the workers worked all week, including Sundays, and the noise and dust were a serious distraction during services. It was so bad that the branch suspended Sunday School and held only sacrament meeting and followed by only Relief Society, priesthood, and Primary meetings. After three months, President Macías insisted that the construction work stop on Sundays, and the branch resumed its normal meeting schedule.

Meeting in the school was a mixed blessing. While it was much closer to branch members' homes, it was very uncomfortable. The one narrow stairway between the five floors had to be climbed several times during the course of Sunday services. Sacrament meeting was three flights down from street level; Primary was two floors up. The bathrooms were on the top floor; chairs needed to be set up and taken down; and there was no heat or air conditioning. Fans in the summer blew so loudly that people sitting near them (and most preferred this cool spot) often couldn't hear the speaker.

Despite the difficulties, the branch flourished during those years and started to see itself not as a splinter group, but as its own unit. The number of those consistently attending Sunday meetings grew from 120 to more than 200; the Relief Society had to split into two groups for classes. The elders quorum, Primary, and youth programs enlarged considerably and were cramped in the small spaces at the school. Sofía Soriano gives some of the credit for this growth to President Macías' hard work, friendliness, and enthusiasm for missionary work and the gospel. David Jones suggests that the growth may also have had something to do with rising immigration rates from the Dominican Republic, where the Church is increasingly well known and respected. Rómulo Macías points to the 16 full-time missionaries serving in the unit, and the branch's determined efforts to search out people ready for the gospel.

To manage the needs of all the members, President Macías depended heavily on the Relief Society presidents with whom he served: first, Sister Sofía Soriano, and then Sister Teófila Marte. He describes them as having been his "right hand." Sister Soriano recalls working closely with César Riofrío (the elders quorum president) to solve whatever problems arose, and then taking their solutions to President Macías.

President Macías focused intensely on the teenagers, and the branch's youth programs were some of the largest in the stake, which at that time included Westchester County. Nearly 50 youth enthusiastically performed in road shows, and many prepared for missions. They went on frequent temple trips, as did the adults, continuing the tradition started in the Spanish-speaking ward downtown.

Every month they would rent a bus, leave at midnight on Friday, arrive in Washington, D.C. around 5 a.m., spend all day Saturday at the temple, and come home exhausted late Saturday afternoon. During the summers, instead of going to the temple, the ward took a trip to the Hill Cumorah Pageant in Palmyra and visited the nearby church sites and Niagara Falls. The branch's frequent activities gave members opportunities to grow together and share a sense of belonging.

To the great excitement of the fifth branch, the stake broke ground on a new chapel to be built at 1815 Riverside Drive in Inwood in June 1997. Members were thrilled that soon they would be leaving the school and have a place of their own. Six months after the construction started, President Macías was released; Francisco Sandoval, one of President Macías' counselors and a convert of almost three years, was called to be the new branch president.

President Sandoval worked to activate members who had stopped coming to meetings and encouraged the youth to attend seminary. He also nurtured relationships with the neighborhood by encouraging community service. Sofía Soriano, who at the time was Primary president, organized an annual project for the older primary children to sew sleeping bags for the homeless with a local organization called the Fresh Youth Initiative.

As the branch came together around the prospect of a new chapel, it dealt with one more division during the three-year period while the chapel was constructed. In December 1997, due to severe capacity constraints on the rental facility and conflicts with the proprietors of the Herbert Birch School, the stake was forced to split the branch and send 40 families living between 155th and 173rd Streets to meet with the Manhattan Fourth Ward in the 65th Street building. It was hard for those who now had to travel to Lincoln Square to no longer be able to walk to church when their neighbors were enjoying the proximity of the branch. However, when the Inwood chapel was dedicated in June 2000 and the branch became the Inwood Second Ward, the families who had been meeting further downtown with the Manhattan Fourth Ward returned to become a part of the new ward.

The opening of the new building "transformed the ward," recalls David Jones, currently the executive secretary for the ward, giving members a place to call their own. Now new members could be baptized in the same building where they would attend church. They could more easily have parties and use this neighborhood church for wedding receptions and other occasions, which had been difficult to schedule in the very busy stake center on 65th Street. Members felt a connection to the chapel and ward that they did not feel in the school and even in the Lincoln Square building. Finally, the ward had its own home. In August 2001, Bishop Sandoval was released; Matthew Day from the Inwood First Ward was sustained as the new bishop.

Missionary work has thrived recently as ward members invite their friends to church and fellowship new members. During 2003, 32 new members were baptized, around 80% of whom are still active. While fellowshipping so many new converts and teaching leadership and administrative skills is a challenge, the new members are excited about the gospel. Many are preparing to go to the temple, attending the temple preparation class in Sunday School, and doing baptisms for the dead on frequent ward temple trips.

One recent convert, Argelis Peñaló, is serving a mission in Anaheim, California. In April 2004, long-time ward member Edward Félix left on his mission to Las Vegas, Nevada. Bishop Day sees the tremendous potential of ward members. He says their deep spirituality comes out in the prayers and testimonies. He hopes that soon the ward will be strong enough to divide again and create a second uptown Spanish-speaking ward.

### INWOOD SECOND WARD TIMELINE

**1993** Manhattan Fifth Branch is created for Spanish speakers living north of 155th Street. Initially the branch meets at the stake center. First branch president is Antonio Cruz.

**1994** The branch moves to the Herbert Birch School in Washington Heights.

**1997** A new meetinghouse in Inwood is announced.

**1997** Due to overcrowding at the Herbert Birch School, a portion of the

Manhattan Fifth Branch (members residing between 155th and 173rd Streets) return to the Manhattan Fourth Ward. Francisco Sandoval is sustained as branch president.

2000 The new chapel at Riverside Drive in Inwood is dedicated.

2000 Manhattan Fifth Branch becomes Inwood Second Ward. President Sandoval is sustained as first bishop.

2001 Matthew B. Day, member of the Inwood First Ward, is sustained as bishop.

Members of the Manhattan Fifth Branch made this covered wagon for a stake Pioneer Day activity in Central Park, 1997. Photo courtesy of América Cruz.

The Inwood Second Ward in early 2004. Photo courtesy of Maria Hunter.

## DREAMING IN UPPER MANHATTAN: INWOOD FIRST WARD HISTORY   CINDY BUTIKOFER

The Manhattan Sixth Branch was formed out of part of the Manhattan First Ward in February 1996, with boundaries running from 155th Street to the top of the island. Michael DeLange was called as the first branch president, with John Corrigan and David Skouson as his counselors and Jaque Bell Poulson as Relief Society president. Along with a Spanish-speaking unit, the Manhattan Fifth Branch, it met in the Herbert L. Birch Manhattan Early Childhood Center at 554 Fort Washington Avenue.

There had always been a spirit of camaraderie among the members in upper Manhattan (Inwood and Washington Heights), due in part to our geographic separation from other members of the Manhattan First Ward. We had Sunday dinners and picnics together. Still, when the branch was created, it was wrenching for the long-time members to leave friends and the security of the Manhattan First Ward. Though small at first, the branch had warmth and friendliness. People were willing to work. They were accepting of one and all who walked through the door: investigator, long-absent member, or new arrival to the city. There was a genuine, down-to-earth feeling.

There were fears that the population would not prove stable enough to keep a branch growing in the area. However, as affordable housing became scarce in other parts of Manhattan, the branch grew and was organized into the Inwood First Ward in November 1999. John Corrigan, who had been serving as branch president following the DeLanges' move to California in 1998, was called to be the first bishop. His counselors were Thomas Hughes and Stephen Hodson. While he was bishop, the meetinghouse at 1815 Riverside Drive was completed after many years of planning and work. This was the first meetinghouse to be built in Manhattan since 1975. It was dedicated in March 2000 by Bishop Richard C. Edgley of the Presiding Bishopric, and members of the Inwood First and Inwood Second Wards gratefully moved into the beautiful space.

The Inwood First Ward is made up mainly of young couples and families who have come to the city to follow dreams. These are dreams of a better life as they emigrate from other countries, dreams of artistic careers, and dreams of further education. A good case in point is Mark Johnson, who was called to be the bishop in June 2000, after the Corrigans moved to Connecticut. He came to New York to go to film school. His first two counselors were Scott Holden, a concert pianist working on a PhD, and Adam Wilcox, who was here to get a PhD in hospital management.

Talent abounds in this ward. Activities are creative, ranging from Shakespeare plays and nights of vocal and instrumental concerts to a roller derby in the unopened parking garage and lessons in Dominican cooking.

More importantly, the spirit of service, love, and acceptance that was evident in the beginning of the branch still exists, passed on from those who are leaving to those newly arriving. All who have passed through have made invaluable contributions to the lives of the members in the ward.

Now, with a temple in Manhattan, we feel very blessed and humbled. We pray to be worthy of the blessings that can be ours because of its presence. On a personal note, having lived here almost 20 years, I find it nothing short of a miracle that I will be able to get on the subway and be at the temple. The Church was so little when we first arrived. I am so grateful for this temple. It will truly be mine. My children, who were born and raised here, will be able to take out their endowments and be sealed in their own hometown temple.

### INWOOD FIRST WARD TIMELINE

**1996** Manhattan Sixth Branch is created from the Manhattan First Ward. Michael DeLange is sustained as branch president. Branch boundaries from 155th Street to the top of the island. The branch meets in a school on Fort Washington Avenue.

**1997** A new meetinghouse in Inwood is announced.

**1998** The sixth branch's first counselor John Corrigan is sustained as branch president.

**1999** Manhattan Sixth Branch organized as the Inwood First Ward, with John Corrigan as the first bishop.

**2000** The new chapel at Riverside Drive in Inwood is dedicated.

**2000** Mark Johnson is sustained as bishop.

**2004** Nathan Jones is sustained as bishop.

The elaborate shows performed in the Hodson's backyard in the summers were a much-loved Inwood First Ward tradition. Here, Curtis Brien and Will Swenson perform in *Comedy of Errors* in summer 2001. Photo courtesy of Matthew Day.

Inwood First Ward congregation. Photo courtesy of Maria Hunter.

## GROWTH SIGNS: THE UNION SQUARE SECOND BRANCH
DELIA JOHNSON, JOANNE DONVITO AND CHAD DONVITO

The Manhattan Seventh Branch for the deaf was formed in April 1994 after several years of missionary work in sign language and deaf members meeting as a dependent group within the Manhattan Second Ward.

A significant turning point in the growth of the deaf members from a group to a branch came with the baptism of Mary Cheese. Brother Marion Gorka and one other deaf member were participating in the Manhattan Second Ward's deaf group when the missionaries met and baptized Sister Cheese. Mary had lost her hearing when she was about 16-years old in an accident. In 1990, at age 65, she met the missionaries after she heard a voice tell her in a dream that she should be baptized "the same way as Jesus was baptized." Soon after the dream, two signing missionaries knocked on her door.

Mary was baptized by immersion into the Church on February 3, 1991, and later introduced the missionaries to many of her friends. During the next year, the deaf group grew significantly in both strength and numbers due, in large part, to Mary's influence. Mary was endowed a year after her baptism but passed away shortly afterwards.

During the period when the deaf group met with the Manhattan Second Ward, hearing ward members Cindy Spencer and Marcia Nelson, along with the sister missionaries, provided translation in sacrament meetings. They also helped to teach classes in Sunday School, Relief Society, and priesthood meetings. In order to learn sign language, Bishop Paul Gunther hired a teacher and invited several members of the second ward to take a class in American Sign Language along with him.

To bring the ward and the deaf group closer, Marcia Nelson taught the entire second ward congregation a few hymns in sign language. Marcia recalls, "I can't tell you how wonderful it was to look out over the congregation and see 200 people signing a hymn together. The deaf members would be in tears as would many of the hearing members. It was incredibly beautiful."

From the time of its organization in April 1994 until June 1998, the Manhattan Seventh Branch was led by five branch presidents. Pablo Nievas, a hard-of-hearing member who had been serving in the elders quorum of the Manhattan First Ward, was called to be the first branch president. President Nievas served for approximately 10 months and then moved to Utah. He was followed by a string of deaf program missionaries: Elder Maldonado, Elder Garcia, Elder Fierstein (a senior missionary serving in the branch with his wife) and Elder Bonnell, also a senior missionary serving with his wife.

Bart Worthington, a young, single, hearing man with extensive experience as a sign language interpreter, served as counselor to President Nievas. In

June 1998, still single, Bart Worthington was called as branch president. In 2004, married with children, he continues to serve in that position.

Judging by attendance, social activities and group trips are as enjoyable for deaf members as Sunday worship. Several long-time members recall a Manhattan First Ward party where square dancing was the activity. A professional dance caller was hired to guide the activity. She seemed bewildered by the disorderly way squares were formed, with adults and children, hearing and deaf, and nobody taking it too seriously. The members remember the fun of participating together.

While the deaf group met with the Manhattan Second Ward, they also met separately Friday evenings for social gatherings. A similar tradition continues now that the group is an independent branch, with parties taking place about every other month. The parties begin Saturday afternoon with members bringing potluck dishes. The deaf branch Christmas parties have been memorable partly because of gifts for the children provided by branch members.

Over the years, the group has had consistent baptisms, but the average sacrament meeting attendance has hovered around 45 to 55. Until recently, members held sacrament meeting in the Relief Society room at the Lincoln Square building. Attendance improved in November 2003, when Sunday services were moved to a new meetinghouse near Union Square. This building has more room and a chapel for meetings.

In 2004, the branch has seen some of its less-active members return to church. With their return and a series of baptisms, sacrament attendance hovers around 60 people per Sunday. Many of the branch's members come from the Bronx to attend church. More and more members are preparing themselves to receive their patriarchal blessings, pay their tithing, get married in the temple, and do endowments for themselves and others. These strides are in large part due to the focus and attention members are giving to the new temple in Manhattan.

## UNION SQUARE SECOND BRANCH TIMELINE

**1980s** Deaf members of the Church meet with the Manhattan Second Ward with translation in sacrament meeting and separate classes.

**1994** Manhattan Seventh Branch is formed, with Pablo Nievas as first branch president.

**1998** Bart Worthington is sustained as branch president.

**2003** Manhattan Seventh Branch moves to the new Union Square building and becomes the Union Square Second Branch.

## FILM, OPERA, AND THE MANHATTAN EIGHTH WARD TARA BENCH

The Manhattan Eighth Ward is composed of talented, ambitious, energetic young single adults from all over the world. This amazing group of people worships and socializes together and brings their unique strengths, love, and knowledge to form one of the most influential wards on the East Coast.

The Manhattan Eighth Ward was formed October 27, 1996. At that time the only singles ward in Manhattan, the Manhattan Third Ward, was divided by age, with ages 18 through 26 forming the eighth ward and ages 27 and older remaining in the third ward. The first bishop was Douglas R. Jackson, who resided in Scarsdale. Bishop Jackson was known for his loving hugs and endless capacity to counsel with members in need.

In November 1997, the New York New York Stake was divided and Bishop Jackson was called as the new stake president of the new Westchester New York Stake. Bishop Belnap of the Manhattan Third Ward was called as the new stake president of the New York New York Stake. Roger Johnson, who had been serving as a counselor to Bishop Jackson, was called as the new bishop of the eighth ward. With his tender heart and brilliant mind, Bishop Johnson was a guide and loving strength to the young ward. At that time the ward was still relatively small. Everyone knew one another. Members recognized newcomers and quickly drew them in.

Marilyn Higbee, the first Relief Society president, set the standard for relating to the women of the ward, helping them meet the challenges single women faced in New York City. Lisa Farr took her place, and continued the attitude of welcoming each new member. She strengthened the new member committee and kept impeccable records so that no one was lost. The first elders quorum president was Layne Bracy, after which David Byrd served as president for several years. Subsequent Relief Society and elders quorum presidents strive to continue their work.

During the early years, ward activities included overnight excursions to Camp Liahona, fall opening socials on Roosevelt Island, Christmas dinners, and football, softball, soccer, and picnics in Central Park. Everyone participated because the ward family included your closest circle of friends. Smaller groups would take trips to the Hill Cumorah Pageant and Niagara Falls, beach excursions to Cape Cod, or long weekends to Duck Beach.

David Buckner was called to be bishop in February 2001, following a move by Bishop Johnson and his family to Massachusetts. Bishop Buckner brought energy and motivation to the ward just in time for a surge in population. He worked with the ever-growing ward to set goals for spiritual and personal growth. In 2001, growth in the eighth ward required that it be split. The Manhattan Sixth Ward (later renamed the Union Square Third Ward) was assigned the Upper East Side and downtown Manhattan.

The Manhattan Eighth Ward has become younger over the last few years, with more undergraduates and students mingling with working professionals, musicians, and performers. No longer does everyone know each other on a first-name basis, and the ward must work to be sure newcomers are not lost in the shuffle. Yet the ward continues to be a place to worship where friends learn from the strongest spirits in the city.

Eighth warders influence the entire stake by serving in singles auxiliaries, in the language branches, in the Primaries and Young Men and Women programs of the stake's standard wards. The service committee, now called the community outreach committee, was created in the eighth ward several years ago to organize volunteers to help other members or contribute to the city.

Because of the talents and energy of ward members, traditions have multiplied during the eighth ward's short history. We inherited the idea of a film festival from our days in the Manhattan Third Ward. At the suggestion of Stephanie Hewlett, the Lingos Film Festival is now an annual event that brings skilled filmmakers and novices of the ward together. Other events include the Pinewood Derby race, Opera in the Park, picnics, new move-in parties at bishopric homes, book club, Norris Chappell's family home evening theme song, and the ward email, which is fast becoming famous. Singles from all over the East Coast come to New York to participate in these activities.

The eighth ward currently stretches from the top of Manhattan, taking in Columbia University and Harlem, down the West Side to Chelsea and over to Fifth Avenue. Ward members look forward to seeing what changes will come with continued growth following the dedication of the Manhattan New York Temple.

## MANHATTAN EIGHTH WARD TIMELINE

**1996** Manhattan Third (singles) Ward is divided and Manhattan Eighth Ward is created for singles ages 18 through 26. Douglas Jackson is sustained as first bishop.

**1997** Roger Johnson is sustained as bishop.

**2001** Manhattan Eighth Ward is divided and Manhattan Sixth Ward is created. David Buckner is sustained as bishop of the Manhattan Eighth Ward.

**2001** Ward members are unharmed after accident on ward trip to Boston Massachusetts Temple.

**2002** Manhattan New York Temple is announced. Manhattan Third, Sixth and Eighth Wards begin meeting together for sacrament meeting as the "megaward."

**2003** "Megaward" dissolves and Manhattan Eighth Ward begins meeting separately again in the stake center.

The Manhattan Eighth Ward, meeting in the gym during temple-related chapel renovations. Photo courtesy of Maria Hunter.

Winners at the 2004 Lingo Awards (film festival) in the Manhattan Eighth Ward. Photo courtesy of Garrett Hill.

## BUILDING A BRANCH IN HARLEM  MATTHEW AND SARAH ARCHER-BECK AND DAN HIATT

The biggest challenge facing the Church in the Harlem First Branch can be summed up in the word "retention." During the mid-1990s missionaries baptized many people in Harlem, but many of the converts fell into inactivity. Mission president Ronald A. Rasband urged President John R. Stone, New York New York Stake president at the time, to form a branch of the Church in Harlem in order to retain the converts. The new branch was formed from the Manhattan First and Second Wards.

Many in the first and second wards were disappointed to see the departure of these members, as it reduced the cultural diversity of the remaining two wards. Others questioned the ability of a new branch to meet the needs of the proposed congregation, many of whom were new to the Church and to the gospel. However, the stake presidency moved forward with plans to form the branch despite some opposition. On October 19, 1997, the Manhattan Ninth Branch of the New York Stake was organized

Ronald Anderson, who had been called to the position of stake mission president only months before, was called to be the first branch president. Beginning November 2, 1997, the branch met at the banquet hall annex of the popular Harlem restaurant, Sylvia's, on the east side of Lenox Avenue close to the corner of 126th Street. President Anderson's first counselors were Clifford Munnings and Van Woods, son of Sylvia Woods after whom Sylvia's Restaurant is named. The branch presidency, along with three sets of missionaries, formed the core of the priesthood holders.

Because most branch members were new to the Church, it was difficult to fill positions in the branch leadership and auxiliary programs. However, attendance records show that retention was enhanced by "bringing the Church to the people." The Relief Society presidency, Polly Dickey, Pat Phillips, Brenda Woods, and Caroline Jennings, lent needed support to the branch presidency during the early stages. Lisa Anderson, wife of President Ron Anderson, served in various callings in the branch, including organist, Relief Society teacher, and Primary president.

In December 1998, after meeting for more than a year at Sylvia's, the branch moved to a small one-story building, a former Kingdom Hall of the Jehovah's Witnesses, and an adjacent vacant lot on 129th Street near Lenox Avenue that had been purchased and modestly renovated by the Church, and the Harlem branch experienced a period of remarkable growth. Average weekly attendance jumped from around 30 people to over 50. In addition, there were over 60 baptisms in 12 months, compared with 9 the year before.

One program was particularly helpful in fellowshipping a large number of converts and helping the members bond as a branch. Local leaders began holding family fun night, with activities such as potluck dinners, games, talent shows and spiritual lessons.

Harlem itself has changed significantly in the past few years. After decades of decline, the neighborhood is rebounding. As New York's real estate prices soared during the economic boom of the late 1990s, Harlem, which was previously by-passed by many renters, buyers, and retailers, became increasingly popular.

As more white families move into Harlem, a demographic shift became apparent in the branch. On the other hand, according to President Anderson, many converts left Harlem for the Bronx, Queens and Brooklyn as the cost of living continued to rise. So as the Harlem community changes, the Harlem First Branch is changing as well.

On any given Sunday, one will find a mix of African-Americans, Latinos and Caucasians in attendance. In spite of its cultural differences, the Harlem First Branch has developed a strong sense of community. Those who attend the branch say they often feel the warmth of the branch family.

Agnes Martinez, a Harlem branch member said, "Someone came from [the stake center at] 65th Street not too long ago and she was in the singles ward and she said, 'It's so warm here and so kind.' And it is. It took a long time to do it. It really did. Because when you are building upon a rock its really hard because you really have to mold it out. We've gone a long way."[21]

In spring 2003, the branch leadership changed as President Anderson was released and Daniel Hiatt became the second branch president. The number of men baptized into the Church in Harlem has also increased. Part of that increase may have been due to changes in Church policy implemented by the newly called mission president, Nelson Boren, that missionaries should not teach single sisters without a male present.

As a result of more men being baptized, the branch began to move towards self-sufficiency in terms of its leadership. Several returned missionaries from Ghana, Nigeria and Jamaica joined the Harlem branch, helping to provide positive role models and strengthening their brothers and sisters with their firm testimonies and knowledge of the gospel.

In September 2003, the Church finally broke ground for a new meetinghouse at the corner of 128th Street and Lenox Avenue. Weekly attendance at sacrament meeting has continued to grow, with over 100 people attending each Sunday, and the congregation is rapidly outgrowing the available space.

Today, a class occupies every available space, including hallways and the area around the podium. When weather permits, the Primary holds classes in a garden that has been planted on the vacant lot next to the church building. The garden has grass, beautiful flowers and vegetables planted by branch members. It is a great time to be a member in Harlem. The Church continues to grow, wonderful people are being baptized, and we are increasing in strength.

## HARLEM FIRST BRANCH TIMELINE

**1997** Manhattan Ninth Branch is created. Ronald M. Anderson is sustained as branch president. The branch begins to meet at Sylvia's Restaurant on Lenox Avenue.

**1998** The branch begins its annual tradition of anniversary/Halloween parties.

**1998** The branch moves to the former Kingdom Hall of the Jehovah's Witnesses on 129th Street. The branch is renamed the Harlem First Branch.

**2001** The Church finalizes the purchase of land at the corner of 128th Street and Lenox Avenue for the construction of a multi-story meetinghouse.

**2003** Dan Hiatt is sustained as branch president.

**2003** The Church breaks ground for the new meetinghouse at 128th Street and Lenox Avenue

As the Harlem branch was formed right after Halloween, an anniversary party/Halloween activity became a branch tradition. Here, Primary children pose in 2001. Photo courtesy of Lisa Anderson.

Future site of the building to be built in Harlem, on the corner of 128th Street and Lenox Avenue. Photo courtesy of Lisa Anderson.

Marie Goldson, Avril Bonfield, Jenny Alford and Dotsie McLeod, members of the Harlem branch, play a game at a baby shower for Lisa Anderson, August 1, 1999. Photo courtesy of Lisa Anderson.

# 9/11 AND A NEW CHAPEL: UNION SQUARE FIRST WARD
LAUREL DOUGALL

On December 3, 2000, our first son, Parker Dougall, received a name and a blessing in the Manhattan Second Ward. It was a memorable day and became even more so when, during the ward business portion of sacrament meeting, it was announced that the Manhattan Second Ward would be split in the coming new year.

This seemed appropriate: the second ward was huge—full of young married couples finishing up their education or starting their careers. But when the new Manhattan Fifth Ward was created, somehow it seemed that we were left with a skeleton crew. There were a few young couples without children, a few couples with young children, and a few older families. We hardly had enough members to cover the basic callings. But despite our misgivings among a few core families, most everything that needed to get done was accomplished. It was a lot of work, but it made us grateful for what we had, and encouraged a friendly atmosphere where new members and investigators were greatly welcomed and appreciated.

Not long after our ward was formed, Church leaders announced they were looking for a new meetinghouse for us. Then the tragedy of September 11, 2001, occurred within the ward boundaries. The Relief Society and elders quorum presidencies met with the bishopric to determine how to discover and address the needs of the ward, which covered all of downtown Manhattan (below 59th Street on the west side and 50th Street below the east side). Every single person in our ward directory, both active and inactive, was contacted, and to our great relief, everyone was alive and accounted for.

In the aftermath of this terrible tragedy, a few members of our ward were temporarily displaced from their homes, and a number of them lost jobs. Soon after, several left the ward boundaries. Ironically, at this same time, when our numbers were at their lowest, we learned about the large convent on West 15th Street that would become our future meetinghouse.

As one door closed, another one opened. An influx of people moved into lower Manhattan as lower rental prices lured people into reestablishing and replenishing residential neighborhoods. A number of couples that had previously lived in New Jersey and were now able to afford to live in lower Manhattan became great additions to our previously bare-bones ward. The gourmet breakfasts periodically provided by our activities committee didn't hurt in recruiting new members.

Since September 11th, we have flourished as a ward. Every summer a new influx of law and dental students as well as recent graduates inundate the ward. Looking at the number of people who attend each week, the ward now feels much like the Manhattan Second Ward felt from which we were divided less than four years ago. There are many young couples, and the Primary, which began with just a few children, has grown to upwards of 20. We still have only a handful of teenagers and a few "die-hards" who have decided to remain in the city after raising their children or reaching retirement.

When we met jointly with the Manhattan Fourth (Spanish-speaking) Ward from fall 2002 to fall 2003 due to the construction of the temple at the stake center, we all seemed to notice the warm and friendly dynamic. Spanish-speakers came out of the woodwork to translate on alternate Sundays when the Spanish-speaking ward conducted, and many in the Spanish ward humored our attempts to speak the language. They impressed us with their bilingual abilities during sacrament meetings and occasional joint Relief Society Enrichment meetings.

Many of us were sad to leave the Lincoln Square building when the 15th Street building was finished and ready to occupy in November 2003. Although many don't miss having to fight through the crowded stake center or clamor for the last headset in order to hear translation during sacrament meeting, we do miss our old friends at the stake center.

We once wondered what we would do with a building of our own, but somehow we have ended up filling it to capacity. When the Union Square First Ward met for the first time in November 2003, we filled the chapel and other rooms to capacity and continue to do so. I am grateful to be part of this Union Square ward, which is thriving as much as my now three-year-old-son—along with his one-year-old brother, one of the ward's newest members.

**UNION SQUARE FIRST WARD TIMELINE**

2000 The Manhattan Second Ward is divided to create the Manhattan Fifth Ward. J. Glade Holman is sustained as bishop.

2002 The Chinese group, which had been a dependent group of the fifth ward, becomes the Canal Street Branch, led by Ned Butikofer, member from the Inwood First Ward.

2002 During renovations for the temple, the fifth ward begins holding joint meetings with the Manhattan Fourth (Spanish-speaking) Ward, alternating weeks for one year with sacrament meetings held in Spanish and then in English.

2003 Manhattan Fifth Ward moves to the new Union Square building and becomes the Union Square First Ward.

The meetinghouse at Union Square, which houses a family ward, a singles ward and the deaf branch. Photo courtesy of Maria Hunter.

Love Gray, Vanessa Gray and Natalie Archibald Jones from the Union Square First Ward. March 2001. Photo courtesy of Sariah Toronto.

## HOCKEY TIME: THE UNION SQUARE THIRD WARD
LAURA CHRISTOFFERSON

When the Manhattan Sixth Ward was divided from the Manhattan Eighth Ward in February 2001, both wards served singles ages 18 through 26. For the first few weeks of meeting separately, a map was printed in the sacrament meeting program showing the sixth ward boundaries: everything east of Fifth Avenue from 110th and all of downtown Manhattan.

Following the division, the eighth ward retained the bishopric, but the Manhattan Sixth Ward inherited Lisa Farr, Relief Society president, and David Byrd, elders quorum president. Bishop Ron Stratton and his counselors Richard Daines and Brad Zwahlen constituted the new bishopric. A game night at the bishop's house proved that Bishop Stratton liked to have fun and could be just as competitive as any of the ambitious singles. Richard Daines generously opened his lovely apartment practically every week for family home evenings. Brad Zwahlen made us laugh while trying diligently to get us all to date and marry.

The areas encompassed by the Manhattan Sixth Ward attracted people in finance and other professional careers. A handful of undergraduates attended New York University and an even greater number attended its law school. Initially, the sixth ward was small compared to the other singles wards (the Manhattan Eighth and Third Wards), with about 100 active members. Quickly, the ward developed its own identity, preferring smaller activities to the large, hundreds-of-people activities we were used to. You could tell by looking around sacrament meeting who was there and who was missing. New faces stuck out immediately, enabling the ward leadership, as well as the members, to welcome and befriend new members and those coming back into activity. After the stake center was remodeled in 2000, the sixth ward met on the fifth and sixth floors at the Lincoln Square building.

When Bishop Stratton moved from the city in 2001, Darcy Fairbairn became the bishop. He retained both of Bishop Stratton's counselors until Ben McAdams replaced Brad Zwahlen, who also moved from the city. Bishop Fairbairn worked long hours at his law practice and would have appointments with ward members late in the night. It is a wonder he found any time to sleep.

A comment meant to stop speculation about renovations announced in summer 2002 of the recently completed fifth and sixth floors illustrated Bishop Fairbairn's offbeat sense of humor. The announcement of the "renovations" required that the three singles wards in the stake meet together for sacrament meeting, an arrangement later referred to as the "megaward." This drastic change caused a lot of buzz. Bishop Fairbairn, a proud Canadian and avid hockey player, tried to stop it by declaring that the renovations were for "a hockey rink!" Shortly thereafter suspicions were confirmed that the Manhattan New York Temple would be built on those floors.

Once temple construction began, the Manhattan Sixth Ward became a part of the "megaward." David Marriott was sustained as bishop in early 2003, retaining Ben McAdams and calling Evan Smith as a counselor. Bishop Marriott regularly held appointments at his law office during the week and hosted conference calls for Sunday morning PEC meetings at 9:00am if he was traveling for work or vacation, even when he was on the west coast.

The sixth ward membership continued to change at the normal transient New York pace, but with the "megaward," members were no longer able to look around sacrament meeting and discern who was missing, or to quickly know all the new faces. With the November 2003 move to the new Union Square building on 15th Street, however, the Manhattan Sixth Ward, newly named the Union Square Third Ward, once again enjoys the luxury of recognizing new and familiar faces.

### UNION SQUARE THIRD WARD TIMELINE

2001 Manhattan Sixth Ward is created for singles ages 18 through 26. Ronald Stratton sustained as the first bishop.

2001 Darcy Fairbairn is sustained as bishop.

2002 Manhattan New York Temple is announced. Manhattan Third, Sixth and Eighth wards begin meeting together for sacrament meeting as the "megaward."

2003 David R. Marriott is sustained as bishop.

2003 Manhattan Sixth Ward moves to the new Union Square building and becomes the Union Square Third Ward.

## CHURCH IN CHINATOWN: CANAL STREET BRANCH HISTORY
NED BUTIKOFER

In 1998, President Brent Belnap approached Ronald Rasband, president of the New York New York North Mission, with the idea of doing missionary work within the Chinese communities of Manhattan. President Rasband liked the idea and in February 1999, the stake and mission submitted a formal proposal requesting Chinese-speaking missionaries from the missionary department. No missionaries were called, however, until September 1999, after President Noel Stoker replaced President Rasband.

At the request of President Stoker, former Stake President John Stone and Elder Alfred Lee, from San Francisco, began tracting and street contacting in Chinatown. Brother Chen Fen Song was the first person in the Chinese community to accept a meeting. Soon after, other missionaries were called and a handful of people became converts. As the missionaries' efforts bore fruit, the Chinese group began to meet as part of the Manhattan Second Ward.

Ronald T. Nelson, a member of the stake high council at the time, was asked to coordinate all matters concerning the Chinese-speaking group as its first group leader. In winter 1999, the Chinese group began to hold independent Sunday worship services at a small office suite on the 12th floor of 401 Broadway, with approximately 10 members.

In May 2000, Daniel Ferguson was called as a stake missionary and as group leader. The unit had grown enough that the Church leased a larger office suite on the 10th floor in the same building at 401 Broadway in Chinatown. In December 2000 the Chinese group became a dependent unit of the newly created Manhattan Fifth Ward.

The following month, January 2001, Ned Butikofer was called to be the group leader. Subsequently, he called Brother Kang Chen as his assistant, a member of just over a year. Others who were called included Jenny Hsu as group Relief Society leader, John Thomas Slover as group mission leader, and Tony Yang as group elders quorum leader under the direction of the Manhattan Fifth Ward. The group held picnics in Central Park, celebrated Chinese New Year, and sponsored Thanksgiving and Christmas dinners and Relief Society Enrichment meetings.

In February 2002, permission to form a branch was granted by the First Presidency and on Easter Sunday, March 31, 2002, one week following a historic visit by President Hinckley to Manhattan, the Canal Street (Chinese) Branch was organized, with Ned Butikofer as branch president, Wong Hoi Man (Kevin) and Chen Fen Song as counselors, Lee Kun Huai (Jimmy) as branch clerk, Brett Helquist as elders quorum liaison, John Thomas Slover (Xiong) as branch mission leader, Franklin Chow as Young Men president,

Lee Shui Lin as Relief Society president and Jenny Hsu Primary president. Nancy Yam was later called as the Young Women president.

In April 2002, a new property for a much-needed larger rental facility was located at 41 Elizabeth Street, and in February 2003, the Church signed a lease. Unfortunately, zoning problems delayed the actual move in.

The day of our first branch conference was June 9, 2002. At last we were a functioning branch with Relief Society, Primary, Young Men and Young Women programs, and an active priesthood quorum.

In November 2002, Jerry Hsieh, from California, was sustained as our first elders quorum president. John Slover was released as mission leader and sustained to serve as the elders quorum first counselor.

On June 22, 2002, the branch had its first temple trip to do baptisms for the dead. Fourteen members took the long trip to Boston, returning very late in the evening. This happy experience was followed by substantial challenges. The original missionaries had left, and a period of change began. At one point, there were only two elders, neither with a firm grasp of the language. The little branch faltered. By the end of 2002 attendance had dropped substantially. For a long time, the missionaries had no investigators. Baptisms were at a low point.

The bright spot in all the gloom was the faith of a few members. Weekly temple preparation classes led by Tim Davis kept the branch alive. They were held from February to August 2003. Of the five who attended, two were subsequently endowed. On July 31, 2003, Sister Tam Choi Yuet and Brother Chen Fen Song went to the Boston temple to receive their endowments.

By 2004 our situation had improved dramatically. We were now smaller and humbler, but a much more confident branch. We had great leaders who were dedicated to the growth of the branch. We began to see members we hadn't seen in a while. We were more spiritually ready to move into our new meetinghouse.

Finally, on March 12, 2004, after a wait that seemed eternal, we moved into our new home at 41 Elizabeth Street. On June 26, 2004, a dedication service was held at which President Belnap offered the dedicatory prayer. We now have a membership of 45 and tremendous support from mission president Nelson Boren. He is sending us the very best missionaries. We are confident that many of the Chinese people in New York City will accept the gospel of Jesus Christ.

## CANAL STREET BRANCH TIMELINE

**1999** President Ronald A. Rasband of the New York New York North Mission requests Chinese-speaking missionaries. The Chinese group begins to meet as a part of the Manhattan Second Ward.

**1999** Ron Nelson is called to lead the Chinese group. The Church leases a suite at 401 Broadway (just below Canal Street) where missionaries teach Chinese-speaking investigators.

**2000** The Church leases a larger suite at 401 Broadway and the Chinese group begins to meet there under the direction of Daniel Ferguson.

**2000** The Chinese group becomes a part of the Manhattan Fifth Ward when the fifth ward is created from the Manhattan Second Ward.

**2001** Ned Butikofer, member of the Inwood First Ward, is sustained as Chinese group leader.

**2002** Canal Street Branch is formed with Ned Butikofer sustained as Branch President.

**2004** Branch moves into new meeting space at 41 Elizabeth Street.

Chinese branch members at a Labor Day picnic, 2004. Front row from left to right: Chen Rong Bing with two children, Ned Butikofer (branch president), Tsang Wood Kuen (in cap); second row from left to right: Cindy Butikofer, Susan Poon, Jenny Hsu, Catherine Wang, a missionary and Li Hong (with child). Far back left: Chen Fen Song (second counselor in the branch presidency). Center back: Paul Stowell (branch mission leader). Under the tree: missionaries and Huang Kai (far right) and Li Hong (Huang Kai's wife, in front). Photo courtesy of Ned Butikofer

# NEW YORK STAKE'S ORIGINAL REGION
# SEVENTY YEARS LATER
KENT S. LARSEN II

The New York Stake, created on December 9, 1934, was the first stake organized east of Colorado since the exodus to the western United States, and only the third stake (after Los Angeles and San Francisco) to be formed outside the areas of Latter-day Saint pioneer settlement in the West.

In addition to Church members in New York City's five boroughs, the city's first stake included all of Long Island, the northern half of New Jersey and all of Westchester County, and the Connecticut panhandle. This huge area included a population approaching 10 million people, while the New York Stake population was about 2,000 members[1]. Today there are nearly 4,000 Church members in Manhattan alone. Interestingly, the Manhattan New York Temple district covers roughly the same area as the original stake—with ten stakes, four districts, four missions and Church membership of nearly 42,000.

Following are overviews of how the Church units in Manhattan's surrounding areas have developed in the last 70 years and more.

## BUILDING IN BROOKLYN

When he arrived in New York City in 1892, Job Pingree found only a few members scattered in Brooklyn, Manhattan and New Jersey[2]. He soon rented an apartment on Sands Street in Brooklyn and began holding meetings in the homes of members, alternating weekly between Brooklyn and Hempstead. By 1894 both Brooklyn and Manhattan had branches of the Church; the Brooklyn Branch met in a rented hall at 50 Concord Street.

Pingree and his missionary successors found missionary success in Brooklyn, tempered by difficulty in finding suitable places to worship. The branch went through many meetinghouses in the next 15 years, ranging from the Ampheon Theatre on Bedford Avenue between South 7th Street and South 8th Street, to a series of lodge halls generally located in undesirable locations.

"It was very hard to find a meeting-hall," wrote Branch President James S. Knecht. "The only places we found were lodge halls over saloons, bowling alleys. The stench of stale beer and tobacco some was most offensive.

Investigators were hard to get to our meetings. Once they had seen the hall, which was in keeping with the reputation of the Mormons at that time, that was enough.³"

Finally, the branch secured a meeting hall at 879-881 Gates Avenue (near Reid Avenue) that was owned by a minister. The branch had sought the hall for many years, but the minister had always refused.

Meanwhile, in 1915 the Brooklyn Branch Relief Society started a fund-raising drive to build the branch its own chapel. President Isabella Wingrave directed the campaign was under the direction of. She urged members to give one cent per day toward the Church's 50% required contribution from local members towards a new building.⁴

By 1918, the drive raised enough money to build the first Church-constructed chapel east of the Mississippi since the exodus from Nauvoo. The chapel, still located at 265-273 Gates Avenue, was dedicated February 16, 1919 by Elder Reed Smoot (a Utah senator as well as a member of the Quorum of the Twelve Apostles). More than 350 people attended the dedication, held during the branch's semi-annual conference.⁵

As the roaring 1920s began the Church in Brooklyn and the rest of New York City grew rapidly. A surge of Mormons from Utah and the southern U.S. found jobs in the city. Brooklyn was at the center of much of this growth, since the Eastern States Mission home was located next door to the new chapel. This meant that the Brooklyn Branch was often visited by General Authorities who stopped in New York City, either to visit the mission headquarters or on their way to tour missions in Europe and South America.

Through the mid-1920, attendance at the Brooklyn Branch's sacrament meetings hovered between 30 and 40, but by 1928 attendance was up to more than 100. By 1930, attendance was averaging around 200, with attendance over 300 for special occasions. A high point was a sacrament meeting held July 12, 1931, at which Church President Heber J. Grant spoke to a crowd of 475.⁶

Another significant part of this growth came from immigrant Germans.⁷ Economic refugees from Germany fled the devastation of World War I to join a 750,000-strong German community in New York City, a large portion of which lived in Brooklyn.⁸ In 1927, the Brooklyn Branch started a German program, first headed by Willy Reske. The program grew to include as many as 150 members.

The growth, of course, meant that the Brooklyn Branch had to be divided. On February 5, 1931, the Bay Ridge Branch was created, with John Peterson serving as its president. The branch met at 5302 Fifth Avenue in Brooklyn. ⁹ The first New York stake was created in 1934 and the Brooklyn Branch became a ward.

In the midst of the Great Depression, church attendance in Brooklyn, in particular, plummeted. Activity in the branch's German program, a vital part of its previous growth, declined to less than 15 members. On January 1, 1935, the program was discontinued. In subsequent years sacrament meeting attendance also declined, from an average of 125-150 before the stake was formed to less than 100 in 1939.[10]

Throughout the 1930s, though, Brooklyn remained a dynamic and vital part of the stake. The chapel was heavily used for both ward and Eastern States Mission activities. Now 15 years old, the building was refurbished by the branch in the mid-1930s, adding smaller items like new blackboards, a radio and Victrola, a pipe organ and even new hymnals.[11]

Members of the ward also made significant contributions to the Church as a whole. Willy Reske, ward member through much of the 1930s and 1940s, wrote two hymns that later appeared in the Latter-day Saint hymnal–"Thy Servants are Prepared" and "God's Daily Care." The Brooklyn Ward male chorus participated in a Warner Brother's production depicting the Mormon Trek. They donated the $100 earned to help refurbish the chapel.[12]

Despite the vitality of the Brooklyn Ward, by 1948 the loss of membership was so substantial that the Brooklyn Ward became a branch again. Another difficulty arose from the Church's purchase of a former Fifth Avenue mansion in Manhattan for the Eastern States Mission, moving the mission headquarters there from the building next to the Gates Avenue chapel in Brooklyn. It appears that at that time the mission stopped assigning missionaries to Brooklyn. The membership loss also led the stake to merge the Bay Ridge Branch into the Brooklyn Branch in 1960.[13] Then, in 1962, the Church sold the old Brooklyn chapel and mission home, originally constructed by the Church in 1918.

Yet the branch's fortunes were about to change. Just before the sale, the Eastern States Mission returned missionaries to the borough. In 1964 the Staten Island Branch, now closer to Brooklyn because of the newly constructed Verrazano Narrows Bridge, was made a dependent branch of the Brooklyn Branch. At the same time, during the beginning of the World's Fair, the branch purchased a new chapel in Midwood, Brooklyn, at 1218 Glenwood Road.[14] Renovations on the building took three years and over 5,000 hours of labor prior to the building's dedication on August 20, 1967.

As elsewhere, the World's Fair swelled membership rolls in Brooklyn. The branch started giving Sunday School classes in Spanish as early as 1965, and by 1969 had organized a Spanish-speaking group. Just three years later (1972) that group became a dependent branch, and the Brooklyn Branch again became the Brooklyn Ward. In the late 1970s the growth accelerated further, and the Brooklyn Spanish Branch became an independent unit in 1978. A

Chinese Branch was created from the Brooklyn Ward in 1979, and the Spanish Branch became a ward in 1984.

In 1985, the Brooklyn and Staten Island wards and branches were united with those in Queens (until then part of the Plainview Stake) to form the New York New York East Stake. Mark E. Butler was called as stake president. With the New York New York Stake covering Manhattan and the Bronx, these two stakes covered all of New York City itself, including about 18 different units with members speaking at least four languages.

But the New York New York East Stake proved short-lived. In addition to other complications, the stake was plagued by transportation difficulties that seemed insurmountable for the majority of its members (Queens members often had to travel through Manhattan to get to Brooklyn, and vice versa).

To solve these challenges, the Church made a radical move, by carving up the stake into many small branches in two different districts. The Brooklyn Ward and Brooklyn Spanish Ward became five branches: two in Midwood (English and Spanish), a Park Slope Branch, a Coney Island Branch and a Dyker Heights Branch. The Queens wards and branches were likewise divided, creating branches in Flushing, Jamaica, Queens Village, Rockaway, Astoria, Bushwick and Long Island City.

These branches made up initially two districts, Queens East and Queens West. A Richmond Hill District was subsequently created from those two and part of the Brooklyn District, and the Queens East District was later discontinued, with its branches going to Richmond Hill and Queens West.

In 1998, the Brooklyn District became the Brooklyn New York Stake, with wards in Bensonhurst, Park Slope, Staten Island and Midwood (English and Spanish). It also included three branches in Dyker Heights (two Spanish and one Chinese) and two on Staten Island (English and Spanish).

### LONG ISLAND: A PLACE, AND A PIECE, IN HISTORY

While the Latter-day Saint presence in New York City clearly started in Manhattan and Brooklyn, it has seen its longest-lasting presence on Long Island. Here a group of families continued the Church's existence for over 100 years—from their conversion in the 1840s through the return of the Eastern States Mission in 1895 and the founding of the Long Island Stake in 1967.

Their story starts in the early 1840s, when Eastern States Mission President John P. Greene sent missionaries out to Long Island, following the Long Island Railroad, which reached Hempstead in 1839. The missionaries found quick success with families in the Christian Hook area (now Oceanside) and in Freeport. In a short time the number of converts passed 100.

Their presence and numbers attracted visits from General Authorities early on. Brigham Young, then president of the Quorum of the Twelve, visited "Hampstead, on Long Island" (sic) in February 1840 with Reuben Hedlock and "preached at Rockaway and the neighborhood till the fourth of March, and baptized nine."[15] Apparently the experience made quite an impression on Brigham, because in the 1870s he wrote to his son asking him to visit the Saints in Hempstead.

The Saints in Christian Hook apparently also had a significant effect on the surrounding area. The place where they baptized, in Parsonage Creek near where Brower Avenue now crosses the creek, became known as "Mormon Hole" and Christian Hook itself was soon known as "Mormontown." The group held Sunday meetings on the old Parsonage Farm, which had been purchased by Jesse Pettit in 1826 before he joined the Church.

Among these Saints were the Jacob Bower family (one of the first to be baptized), the Pettit family and families named Abram, Combs, Davis, Hammond, Soper, Southard and Story. Known as the Hempstead branch, the group was represented by 44 members (out of a total of 194 attending) at a conference in New York City in late 1844.

But with the beginning of the exodus of the Saints from Nauvoo in February 4, 1846, and the sailing of the ship *Brooklyn* from New York City on the same day, some of the Hempstead branch left for the West, including members of the Pettit, Oakley, Hammond and Soper families.

The Hempstead Saints continued to worship together for many years as part of the Eastern States Mission, until the mission was closed in 1869. At that time a contingent of the branch again left for Utah, led by Francis Knapp Benedict, a physician at the local poor house in Hempstead Benedict later founded the Salt Lake City Medical Society.

The remaining Saints continued to meet despite a lack of local hierarchy. Meetings moved to the old Methodist Episcopal Church, later known as the Baldwin Debating Hall or Baldwin Hall. The daughters of Jacob Brower also held meetings in their homes, and they apparently even attempted missionary work, evidenced by an 1870 newspaper article that reported the disruption of a missionary meeting by a local crowd.

It wasn't until the 1890s that local administrative support returned to the area. In 1892 Elder Job Pingree was sent to revive Church membership in the area, and by 1895 the Eastern States Mission was reopened. Elbert Soper, grandson of Jacob and Phoebe Brower, was made Hempstead branch president in 1890. Meetings were held on the Bedell farm, near where the Oaks school now stands, in a building then referred to as "Mormon Hall."

The close-knit nature of the branch can be seen in the family ties of the first branch Relief Society presidency, established in 1892. The president was

Millie Ann Soper, the branch president's wife. Her counselors were Mary Horsefall, daughter of Ira and Mary Brower Pettit, and Susie Soper, daughter of "Aunt Nautchie Soper."

The subsequent fortunes of the branch and its members were mixed. Elbert Soper was succeeded as branch president by Richard Henry Soper, a great-grandson of Jacob Brower, who had returned from Utah after being made an elder in 1898. The rural location of the branch and its members left few, if any, converts. When the New York Stake was organized in 1934, the branch was so weak that Stake President Fred G. Taylor considered abandoning it, but instead made the branch a dependent unit of the Queens Ward.[16]

At that time President Taylor asked O. Preston Robinson to move to the area to become the branch president, and the unit began growing. Six years later, migrants from the West and from outside the United States bolstered attendance enough to give the branch independent status, on June 30, 1940.

The branch continued to grow throughout the 1940s, mainly under the leadership of David D. Paine, later a counselor in the New York Stake presidency. By 1949, 127 members were regularly attending meetings and the new branch president, Walter M. Soper (son of former branch president Richard Henry Soper and a descendent of 1840s branch member Jacob Brower), was convinced the branch needed a building.

He attended a tax auction in Mineola with the hope of securing a particular property. "About a dozen hands went up on the first bid. Immediately I asked to be heard and explained who I was and what I wanted the property for. On the second bid my hand was the only one raised, and I got it for the bid price. No opposition! Who do you think assisted me?"[17]

The building, located at 171 Arcadia Avenue in Uniondale, was built mainly by the members of the branch under the direction of Otto Baumgart, then first counselor in the branch presidency.[18] By June 1951, enough of the building had been completed that meetings could be held there, and on June 24, 1951, the Oceanside Branch became the Uniondale Ward. However, Bishop Soper's tenure was short lived. In September he moved to Los Angeles (he returned after just a few months), and Otto Baumgart was called as the new ward's second bishop.[19]

Construction on the building continued, interrupted by the "Big Wind" of 1952, which blew down the steeple. It wasn't until 1954, with the steeple replaced, the building completed and all debts satisfied, that the Uniondale chapel was dedicated.

The ward's third bishop, William McKinley Guest, put a strong emphasis on home teaching, and as a result the ward's home teaching seldom went below 95%, and often reached 100%. This was true even when one ward member was in Japan. Another ward member, Keith Evans–an airline pilot—visited Brother Gilliland there. The emphasis on home teaching paid off, and by 1960, sacrament meeting attendance reached 238 (51% of the ward), in spite of a division that created the Suffolk Branch on February 3, 1957.

Long Island benefited directly from the World's Fair in 1964, and not just through convert baptisms. Knowing that the fast-growing area would soon need another building, the Church designed the Mormon Pavilion at the Fair so that it could be dismantled and used in constructing a building in Plainview, Long Island.

When the Plainview building was nearly complete, the New York Stake was again split, forming the Plainview Stake.[20] The new stake took in not only the Uniondale and Plainview Wards and the Suffolk Branch (now the Suffolk Ward), but also the Queens Ward, the Rego Park Branch (also now a ward) and a new branch, the Patchogue Branch.

Over the next two decades the Plainview Stake slowly grew and changed. The Patchogue Branch became the Terryville Ward in March 1970, and in 1978 was divided to form the Riverhead Branch, presided over by President Smalls, who was among the first African-American branch presidents in the Church. However, many Long Island units saw their numbers dwindle throughout the 1980s, and members struggled to cover long distances.

Starting in 1993, the stake examined what to do about decreases in membership, and even considered consolidating units. Leaders took a cue from Brooklyn's seemingly successful strategy of dividing wards into smaller branches. A Long Island committee that involved the entire stake council except the stake presidency reviewed geographic and census data and sought inspiration. Then it recommended dividing the Uniondale Ward into five different branches, along with other boundary changes that brought the stake up to a total of 17 units.

Initially, the Plainview stake presidency disagreed, and asked bishops and branch presidents in the stake to look at the issue. When this group unanimously agreed with the stake council's original recommendation, the proposal was presented to Elder Henry B. Eyring of the Quorum of the Twelve.

Focusing in on the smallest of the units in the proposal, Elder Eyring asked about its membership and was told it had just 30 active members, four Melchizedek Priesthood holders and one sealed couple. While the stake presidency braced for disagreement from the Apostle, he paused before responding, "It will be a stake." Within two weeks, Church leaders approved the recommendation. In 1999 six of the small branches, those that had been the Uniondale Ward, were combined with three branches from the Queens East District (which was then dissolved) to form the Lynbrook New York District—one step closer to becoming a stake.

## NEW JERSEY: BRANCHES AND A BUS CRASH

As in Long Island, a few members of the Church in New Jersey held meetings after the Eastern States Mission closed in 1869. At least one small group of Saints met in Perth Amboy as late as 1878, and a group of 10 members from New Jersey emigrated to Utah in 1896.

During most of the 1890s, however, no known branches were functioning in New Jersey. Starting around 1918, small groups of members met in several rented buildings in Hoboken (including the Odd Fellows Hall on Washington Street).

In 1922, the Eastern States Mission started a branch in Newark, consisting of about 15 active families led by presiding elder G. Stanley McAllister. The branch's Sunday meetings were held in rooms above Achtelstetter's Restaurant on Broad Street in Newark, while weekday meetings, such as Primary and Relief Society, were held in the homes of various members.[21]

As elsewhere, growth in the 1920s in New Jersey was rapid, with new members immigrating from the West and from Holland and Germany.[22] As attendance at Sunday meetings reached nearly 200, this growth forced the branch to move its Sunday meetings in January 1928 to the Junior Masonic Hall on the corner of Sixth and Orange Streets. Weekday Primary and Relief Society meetings were moved to the Robert Treat Hotel and the Women's Club.[23] By 1932, the branch had again outgrown its rented facilities and purchased a small church located at 40 Whittlesey Avenue in East Orange, which was remodeled using members' time, money and effort.

After the stake was organized in New York City in 1934, New Jersey members faced acute travel difficulties. The East Orange Ward's 245 members traveled from all over northern New Jersey to meet in the ward's new building in East Orange. In 1936, the stake and the Eastern States Mission addressed the problem by creating the North Jersey dependent branch, which met in Hackensack and in Union City, and the Metuchen Branch, which met in the Roger Smith Hotel in New Brunswick, and was part of the Eastern States Mission instead of the New York Stake.

Even with a smaller congregation, the East Orange Ward still faced the difficulty of a building that was too small for its congregation. In 1952, when members learned that construction of the Garden State Parkway would require the demolition of the Church's East Orange building, the ward purchased land at 140 White Oak Ridge Road in Short Hills.[24]

In September 1953, the ward's name changed to the Short Hills Ward, in preparation for the construction of the new building. Ground was broken for that building on September 26. By July 1955, the ward was holding meetings in the new chapel, which was dedicated September 16, 1956, by Elder Ezra Taft Benson of the Quorum of the Twelve Apostles.[25]

The North Jersey Branch was made an independent unit on January 13, 1952. At this time the branch was meeting in the Girl Scout Little House in Leonia, New Jersey. That building was so small for the branch, which had average attendance of 100, that classes were even held in the broom closet and the furnace room. By 1957, the branch had moved to the Ridgewood YMCA, but that space wasn't big enough either—so classes were held in broom closets and even the shower rooms.[26] The branch approved the purchase of property in Emerson for $30,000 that year, and became the North Jersey Ward the following year (1958).

At the same time, growth in both the North Jersey Branch and the Short Hills Ward led the stake to create the Montclair Ward.[27] The Montclair Ward likewise sought and found property for a building, on Mountain Avenue in North Caldwell. Upon that building's completion and dedication in 1962, the ward became the Caldwell Ward.

Meanwhile, the Metuchen Branch (also known as the New Brunswick Branch) started with just 17 members but soon increased to 30, and enjoyed perfect attendance at its meetings for several years. The branch was divided as a result of gasoline shortages during World War II, creating branches in Princeton, Plainfield and Monmouth in December 1942. These branches formed the New Jersey District of the Eastern States Mission, headed by scientist Henry Eyring. As the war ended, the branches were one by one merged together again.[28]

Then, despite the relatively small size of the collective branch, it was divided to form the Trenton Branch on November 1, 1953. The Metuchen Branch once again had just 30 members.

The next six years brought incredible growth.[29] Despite the division of the branch to create the Princeton Branch in 1959[30] and the Monmouth Branch in 1960, the Metuchen Branch became the New Brunswick Ward on February 28, 1960 (when the New Jersey Stake was created). New Brunswick reported 225 members at the time, while Monmouth recorded 194 and Trenton, now also a ward, reported 309.[31]

The creation of the New Jersey Stake was a milestone for the region, as it was the first time the New York City Stake was divided. In this split, the Short Hills, North Jersey and Montclair Wards, which were part of the New York Stake, were combined with the New Brunswick, Monmouth and Trenton branches from the New Jersey District of the Eastern States Mission to form the New Jersey Stake (total membership 2,046). New York Stake President George Mortimer continued as president of the New Jersey Stake, while his counselor, G. Stanley McAllister, was called as president of the New York Stake.

After the 1964 World's Fair, the New Jersey Stake saw its baptisms nearly double from 154 to 291 in a single year.[32] By 1967, the New Jersey Stake was ready to be split after five new wards and branches had been created. The Newark Branch was split off of the Short Hills Ward, and the Caldwell Ward produced two new units: the Dover Branch (later called the Ledgewood Ward) and, with the Emerson Ward, the Wyckoff Ward (later called the Fardale Ward).

Branches were also created from the Trenton Ward (the Dix-McGuire Branch) and the New Brunswick Ward (the Martinsville Branch, later called the North Branch Ward). Less than six months before the Plainview Stake was created on Long Island, the New Jersey Stake was split, creating the New Jersey Central Stake (now the East Brunswick New Jersey Stake).

Like the rest of the area, New Jersey benefited from the dedication of the Washington, D.C., temple in 1974, and members started making regular bus trips to the Temple. Unfortunately, these trips were not always with mishap. Perhaps the most dramatic incident occurred in 1979, when a bus carrying members from the Emerson Ward was involved in a head-on collision. While nearly everyone on the bus was injured in some way, no one was killed. Members counted—and recounted—their blessings, along with their broken noses, black eyes, bruises, stitches and aches and pains the next day in sacrament meeting.

Growth led to the creation of a new stake in 1981, the Morristown New Jersey Stake. Consisting of four wards and three branches, the new stake pulled membership from the New Jersey Stake (renamed first the Morristown New Jersey Stake and later the Caldwell New Jersey Stake) and the New Jersey Central Stake (renamed the East Brunswick New Jersey Stake).

A similar change occurred in 1996, when parts of the Caldwell and Morristown stakes combined to produce the Scotch Plains New Jersey Stake. In 1999, five branches from the Caldwell stake became the Paterson New Jersey District of the Morristown New Jersey Mission.

## QUEENS AND WESTCHESTER: NEW YORK PIONEERS

Following a surge of Church growth in Brooklyn and Manhattan during the roaring 20s, a nucleus of Saints formed in Queens and western Nassau County, including members who moved from other areas. The Ernest L. Wilkinson family moved from New Jersey to Queens, and the H. H. Haglund family moved to Flushing from Brooklyn. These families attended the Manhattan Branch.

Seeing this concentration of members in the Queens area, the district Relief Society president encouraged the women there to form a Relief Society in 1928, even though there was no organized branch in the area. The first presidency of the Queens Relief Society was Lousea Macdonald, president, with Alice Wilkinson and Elva Olpin as counselors.[33]

Soon many members in the group petitioned the district president, Fred G. Taylor, for a branch, but not everyone agreed. Eva Haglund, president of the district Young Ladies' Mutual Improvement Association and wife of H. H. Haglund, a counselor in the district presidency, objected, fearing that the division of the Manhattan Branch would weaken the MIA program just recently established.

President Taylor wrote to Eva Haglund about the idea, praising her service to the YLMIA in a letter on December 6, 1932. Eva was persuaded to continue her efforts, and the youth of the Manhattan Branch and the new Queens Branch found ways to continue their MIA work. Ernest L. Wilkinson became president of the Queens Branch when it was formed in 1932. The branch first met in the Good Citizenship League Hall in Flushing.

However, the Haglund family wasn't able to stay long. Their seven-year-old daughter, Jeanne, was blind and doctors recommended that she attend the New York Institute for the Education of the Blind in the northern Bronx. Her family moved nearby so that Jeanne could attend school as a day student. Like all active members in the northern Bronx and Westchester, the family continued to attend church in Manhattan.[34]

The Haglunds weren't the only family to move to the area. Stanley McAllister and his family moved to Mount Vernon in 1932, where they discovered five or six other Latter-day Saint families in Westchester County. They weren't attending church because, they said, it was too far to travel to Manhattan. McAllister brought the situation to the attention of President Taylor and a Eastern States Mission President Don B. Colton, who agreed that if support from the members were given, a branch could be started in Westchester.[35]

On November 26, 1933, some 60 adults and children responded to letters from President Taylor, and met in Mount Vernon's Masonic Temple to start the branch. G. Stanley McAllister, who more than 10 years earlier was the first leader of the New Jersey Branch, was proposed and sustained as the Westchester Branch's presiding elder. Unfortunately, few of the original members continued to attend after the branch was established. In one case, some of the children in the Haglund family didn't attend because they wanted to attend in Manhattan with their friends.[36]

Unlike Brooklyn, Queens maintained a stable membership through World War II and began to grow significantly by the early 1950s. Before the war broke out, the congregation purchased a house on Sanford Avenue in Flushing to be used for weekday meetings. Since the house wasn't big enough, sacrament services remained in the Good Citizenship League Hall and baptisms were held in the YMCA swimming pool or in Manhattan.[37]

In 1950, the ward purchased property for its own building on Bates Road in Little Neck, just inside the New York City limits. The Church sent Leonard Larsen to supervise the meetinghouse construction process. The task proved more complicated that anyone imagined. New York City regulations and building codes were so different from those encountered by the Church elsewhere that the project suffered many delays. Larsen's experience proved valuable in other building projects in the area and around the nation.[38]

In 1954, the first meetings were finally held in the Little Neck building. While the building was complete, however, it hadn't yet been completely paid for, delaying the dedication. Queens Ward members took on many projects to help pay for the building, including the sale of hundreds of yards of silk that had been donated to the cause. Finally, construction was paid for and in 1955, Elder Henry D. Moyle dedicated the building.[39]

The Westchester Branch started later than Queens but, like most of the wards and branches in the suburbs, its growth was faster. By 1939, the branch's attendance at sacrament meetings had increased from about 25 or less to 40.[40]

H. H. Haglund succeeded Stanley McAllister as branch president that year, and the branch saw a spurt in numbers and activity. Haglund called a less-active member to lead the Sunday School and saw that member resolve personal problems, baptize his wife and get sealed in the temple. Later growth came from an influx of members from Queens and from Manhattan.[41]

In 1942, a surprise gift from an anonymous donor started the branch's building fund.[42] Ten years later, in January 1952, the branch purchased property for a chapel on Wayside Lane in Scarsdale and the Westchester Branch began constructing its own building. A groundbreaking was held in August 1953, and meetings were held at the new building beginning in September 1954. President J. Reuben Clark, Jr., of the First Presidency dedicated the building on May 22, 1955.[43]

Just a year and a half later, on December 9, 1956, the Westchester Branch became the Westchester Ward. The Mount Kisco Branch was divided from the ward on January 14, 1962.[44]

As with other units, the World's Fair was a catalyst for growth in Queens and Westchester. The West Point Branch was organized in 1967, and the Poughkeepsie Branch, part of the Eastern States Mission, became a ward and was added to the New York Stake in 1970. A Spanish-speaking branch in Queens was created in 1971 out of the Manhattan Spanish-speaking branch and from the Rego Park Ward (a second Spanish-speaking branch was created in 1980 in Uniondale).

In 1975, the Bridgeport Connecticut Ward, comprising the area of the Hartford Stake closest to New York City, was divided, creating the Merritt First and Second Wards. The Mount Kisco Branch was made the Kitchawan Ward. With five wards now in existence in the area north of New York City, the Kitchawan Stake was created in 1978.

Just five years later, when the stake was renamed the Yorktown New York Stake, it consisted of wards in Westchester, Yorktown (former Kitchawan Ward), Newburgh, Poughkeepsie and New Canaan, Connecticut (former Merritt Wards), along with a Spanish-speaking branch in Westchester and branches in West Point and Middletown.

In the early 1980s the Westchester Ward experienced an influx of young women working as nannies in the area. By the late 1980s the number of nannies had increased to more than 150 in the Westchester Ward, while other wards and branches in the stake also saw a number of nannies move in. This influx led to the creation of a young single adult ward, now the Stamford Third Ward.

By 1992, the Yorktown stake included eight wards and four branches in both New York and Connecticut, and by 1997 the Middletown Branch had become a ward and new branches had been created in Newburgh (Spanish-speaking) and Liberty.

In 1992 the Yorktown Stake was divided, creating the Newburgh New York Stake from the Newburgh, Middletown and Poughkeepsie First and Second Wards and the Newburgh, West Point and Liberty Branches, with the addition of the Kingston Ward from the Albany stake. A branch in New Paltz was subsequently created in the Newburgh stake.

Later that same year, the Westchester new York Stake was created, with units from the New York New York Stake, the Bronx New York District and the Yorktown Stake The original Westchester Ward became two wards, and the new stake included units in Yonkers and four units in the Bronx.

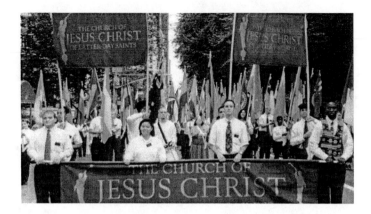

Members and missionaries march in the Columbus Day parade, October 12, 1998. Photo courtesy of Lisa Anderson.

Jim Lucas of the Manhattan First Ward marching in Scottish costume in the Columbus Day parade, October 9, 2000. Photo courtesy of Public Affairs, The Church of Jesus Christ of Latter-day Saints.

Dr. Morewedge, Dan Peterson, the Ambassador from Djibouti, Elder Neal A. Maxwell, Elder Merrill and Sister Marilyn Bateman at a reception for the Islamic Translation Series, February 2000. Photo courtesy of Public Affairs, The Church of Jesus Christ of Latter-day Saints.

Elder and Sister Maxwell greet Adela Farhadi and Ambassador Dr. Ravan A. G. Farhadi, Permanent Representative of Afghanistan to the United Nations, at the Islamic Celebration, March 17, 1999. Photo courtesy of Public Affairs, The Church of Jesus Christ of Latter-day Saints.

Richard Bushman, Manhattan First Ward, talks with Sheri Dew at the LDS Professionals Conference on October 19, 2000. Photo courtesy of Public Affairs, The Church of Jesus Christ of Latter-day Saints.

At a press conference on Ellis Island where the Statue of Liberty-Ellis Island Foundation announced plans to open the American Family Immigration History Center. The October 28, 1998, press conference announced public access to a computerized database containing 17 million U.S. immigration records. For the previous five years, Church members had worked with the Foundation and the National Park Service for more than two million volunteer hours digitizing immigration records from Ellis Island. Their work created a database reflecting 60% of all American immigration records between 1892 and 1924. Lee Iacocca, who is the chairman emeritus of the Statue of Liberty-Ellis Island Foundation, stands with a ship's manifest with Iacocca's father listed on line 9. Photo courtesy of Public Affairs, The Church of Jesus Christ of Latter-day Saints.

Keith Wright, Assemblyman from Harlem, with Elder Earl C. Tingey at the VIP reception for the Manhattan New York Temple, May 2004. Photo courtesy of Public Affairs, The Church of Jesus Christ of Latter-day Saints.

Mike Wallace and Elder and Sister Richards at the VIP reception for the Manhattan New York Temple, May 2004. Photo courtesy of Public Affairs, The Church of Jesus Christ of Latter-day Saints.

Jane Clayson greets Ambassador Slade, Samoa's Permanent Representative to the UN at a reception following the Radio City Music Hall Christmas Spectacular Event, November 30, 2000. Photo courtesy of Public Affairs, The Church of Jesus Christ of Latter-day Saints.

New York Governor George Pataki and actress Cicely Tyson (with friend) at a reception for the Mormon Tabernacle Choir after a performance at Lincoln Center, July 2003. Photo courtesy of Public Affairs, The Church of Jesus Christ of Latter-day Saints.

# APPENDIX

# 1997-2004
# NEW YORK STAKE TIMELINE

| | | |
|---|---|---|
| 1997 | NOVEMBER 8-9 | Elder Marlin K. Jensen divides the stake to form the New York New York Stake within the island of Manhattan |
| | DECEMBER 6 | Christmas concert and reception for prior stake presidency |
| 1998 | APRIL 26 | Regional fireside at Madison Square Garden with President Gordon B. Hinckley |
| | MAY 16 | First stake Primary book fair in the new stake |
| | JUNE 10 | Ship *Brooklyn* Commemoration at South Street Seaport; members reenact event wearing period costumes and sailing on the *Lettie G. Howard* |
| | JUNE 13 | Stake family history seminar with keynote speaker David Rencher; approximately 240 people, mostly non-LDS, attend; 32 presentations, including 10 in Spanish |
| | JUNE 27 | First stake LDS historical sites walking tour of Lower Manhattan |
| | JULY 25 | Stake Pioneer Day picnic at Central Park |
| | OCTOBER 12 | Stake marches in Columbus Day Parade for the first time; members carry flags of 130 nations up Fifth Avenue |
| | OCTOBER | Plans announced to build fifth and sixth floor meeting space at the stake center |
| | DECEMBER | Manhattan Ninth Branch moves from Sylvia's Restaurant to 129th Street |
| | | Living Nativity at the stake center |
| 1999 | JANUARY 18 | Martin Luther King, Jr. Vigil Concert |
| | MARCH 17 | Islamic Translation Series event at the Waldorf-Astoria Hotel with Elder Neal A. Maxwell |
| | NOVEMBER | Manhattan Sixth Branch becomes the Inwood First Ward |
| | | Chinese group begins meeting on its own at 401 Broadway |
| | DECEMBER 10 | Public Affairs U.N. diplomatic reception at Radio City Music Hall |
| 2000 | FEBRUARY 10 | Islamic Translation Series event at the United Nations with Elder Neal A. Maxwell and BYU President Merrill J. Bateman |
| | MARCH 4 | First stake arts festival with children's art fair |
| | MARCH 18 | Last stake temple trip to the Washington temple |
| | APRIL | Manhattan Fifth Branch becomes the Inwood Second Ward |

| | | |
|---|---|---|
| | MAY | Chinese group moves into larger space at 401 Broadway, 10th floor |
| | JUNE 11 | Inwood meetinghouse dedication with Bishop Richard C. Edgley of the Presiding Bishopric |
| | JULY 22 | Stake Pioneer Day and service day at Fort Tyron Park; dedication of ship *Brooklyn* plaque to be installed later |
| | OCTOBER 20 | First recital in stake series |
| | NOVEMBER 30 | U.N. diplomatic reception and Christmas Spectacular at Radio City Music Hall |
| | DECEMBER | Manhattan Second Ward splits, creating the Manhattan Fifth Ward, including the Chinese group |
| | DECEMBER 17 | Stake Handel's *Messiah* sing-along |
| 2001 | FEBRUARY | Manhattan Sixth (YSA) Ward created from the Manhattan Eighth (YSA) Ward |
| | MARCH 17 | First stake temple trip to the Boston temple |
| | APRIL 17 | Press conference at Ellis Island with Elders Russell M. Nelson, D. Todd Christofferson and W. Craig Zwick announcing the completion of the Church's digitizing project of Ellis Island passenger ship manifests |
| | MAY | Harlem meetinghouse property purchased at 128th Street and Lenox Avenue |
| | SEPTEMBER 11 | Terrorist attacks on World Trade Center; stake center turned into temporary emergency shelter |
| | SEPTEMBER 15 | Stake Young Men/Young Women opening social beach trip |
| | NOVEMBER 10 | Stake center fifth and sixth floors are dedicated and entire stake center is rededicated |
| 2002 | FEBRUARY | East 87th Street meetinghouse property purchased |
| | MARCH 24 | Special regional meeting with President Gordon B. Hinckley broadcast from stake center with overflow at the Inwood meetinghouse |
| | MARCH 31 | Canal Street (Chinese) Branch is created |
| | | Easter concert |
| | APRIL | Property located for the Canal Street Branch at 41 Elizabeth Street |
| | AUGUST 4 | Stake center fifth and sixth floors closed; eight units meeting at stake center alter meeting times and some units meet together until November 2003 as follows: three singles wards (Manhattan third, Manhattan sixth, Manhattan eighth) meet in combined "megaward" sacrament meeting; Manhattan Fourth and Fifth Wards meet together for sacrament meeting |
| | AUGUST 7 | Manhattan New York Temple publicly announced |
| 2003 | FEBRUARY | Church signs lease for property in Chinatown at 41 Elizabeth Street |
| | JULY 2 | Mormon Tabernacle Choir performs at Avery Fisher Hall |
| | NOVEMBER 16 | Manhattan Fifth and Sixth Wards are renamed the Union Square First and Third Wards, respectively; Manhattan Seventh (Deaf) Branch is renamed the Union Square Second Branch |

| | NOVEMBER 23 | Union Square meetinghouse is used for the first time |
|---|---|---|
| 2004 | JANUARY 18 | Union Square meetinghouse is dedicated |
| | JANUARY 26 | Stake center third floor renovation commences |
| | FEBRUARY 7 | Ship *Brooklyn* plaque dedication at 32 Old Slip in Lower Manhattan |
| | MARCH 13 | Last stake temple trip to the Boston temple |
| | MAY 1 | First Manhattan New York Temple tours for construction workers and neighbors |
| | MAY 3-7 | Manhattan New York Temple VIP tours |
| | MAY 8 | Manhattan New York Temple open house public tours begin |
| | JUNE 5 | Manhattan New York Temple open house public tours end |
| | JUNE 12 | Temple Jubilee and special youth fireside with President Gordon B. Hinckley at Radio City Music Hall |
| | JUNE 13 | Manhattan New York Temple dedication by President Gordon B. Hinckley |
| | JUNE 26 | Canal Street Branch meeting space dedicated at 41 Elizabeth Street |
| | OCTOBER 9 | Angel Moroni statue is placed on Manhattan New York Temple steeple |

# 1934-2004 NEW YORK STAKE
# PRIESTHOOD AND AUXILIARY LEADERS

*Following is a partial list of stake leaders in the Manhattan and New York City region since the New York New York Stake was created in 1934. Names were taken from stake reports and directories. Generally, dates given are when Church members were officially sustained and/or officially released (not dates on which members were called, ordained, or set apart). Dates in brackets [ ] are approximate.*

## STAKE PRESIDENTS

**1931-1934** President Fred G. Taylor, 1931-1934 (District President)

**1934-1936** President Fred G. Taylor, Howard S. Bennion, First Counselor, 1934 - 1936, Hakon H. Haglund, Second Counselor, 1934 - 1936

**1936-1942** President Harvey Fletcher, William L. Woolf, First Counselor, 1936 - 1942, Ivor Sharp, Second Counselor, 1936 - 1938, Guy B. Rose, Second Counselor, 1938 - 1942

**1942-1948** President Howard S. Bennion, Guy B. Rose, First Counselor, 1942 - 1948, Carl J. Christensen, Second Counselor, 1942 - 1946, William F. Edwards, Second Counselor, 1946 - 1948

**1948-1950** President William F. Edwards, George Harding Mortimer, First Counselor, 1948 - 1950, David D. Paine, Second Counselor, 1948 - 1950

**1950-1960** President George Harding Mortimer, David D. Paine, First Counselor, 1950 - 1960, G. Stanley McAllister, Second Counselor, 1950 - 1960

**1960-1967** President G. Stanley McAllister, George E. Watkins, First Counselor, 1960 - 1967, William M. Guest, Second Counselor, 1960 - 1961, Gordon E. Crandall, Second Counselor, 1961 - 1967

**1967-1975** President George E. Watkins, Victor B. Jex, First Counselor, 1967 - 1975, H. Darcy Clawson, Second Counselor, 1967 - 1975

**1975-1978** President Victor B. Jex, S. Sterling Lichfield, Jr., First Counselor, ____ - ____, Terrell (Ted) A. Lasseter, Second Counselor, ____ - ____

**1978-1985** President Frank W. Miller, Albert S. Woodhouse, First Counselor, 1978 - ____, Luis A. Rojas, Second Counselor, 1978 - ____, Michael K. Young, First Counselor, 1983 - ____ 198[5], Daniel A. Salcedo, Second Counselor, 1983 - ____ 198[5]

**1985-1989** President Michael K. Young, Luis A. Rojas, First Counselor, 198[5] - 1987, Eliot Ashby Brinton, Second Counselor, 198[5] - 1987, Eliot Ashby Brinton, First Counselor, 1987 - 1989, Justo G. Huapaya, Second Counselor, 1987 - 1989

APPENDIX 247

1989-1991　President Eliot Ashby Brinton, Matthew Sander Hosford, First Counselor, 1989 - 1991, John Roger Stone, First Counselor, 1991 - 1991, Rafael Ortiz, Second Counselor, 1989 - 1991

1991-1997　President John Roger Stone, Ronald N. Inouye, First Counselor, 1991 - 1994, Rafael Ortiz, Second Counselor, 1991 - 1992, LaMar Orbit Hill, Second Counselor, 1992 - 1993, Luis Alfredo Gallegos, Second Counselor, ___ - 1994, Luis Alfredo Gallegos, First Counselor, 1994 - ___, Clinton Scott Baxter, Second Counselor, 1994 - 1995, Clinton Scott Baxter, First Counselor, 1995 - 1997, Carlos G. Quiroa, Second Counselor, 1995 – 1997

1997-PRESENT　President Brent Jay Belnap, Clinton Scott Baxter, First Counselor, 1997 - 2000, David Santamaria, Second Counselor, 1997 - 2000, David Santamaria, First Counselor, 2000 - 2001, Yoshiya (Josh) Yamada, Second Counselor, 2000 - 2001, Yoshiya (Josh) Yamada, First Counselor, 2001 - PRESENT, James Carlyle Green, Second Counselor, 2001 - 2003, Stephen Martell Hodson, Second Counselor, 2003 - PRESENT

## STAKE RELIEF SOCIETY PRESIDENTS

| | | | |
|---|---|---|---|
| 1934 | Lorena C. Fletcher | 1974 | Alma Bonner |
| 1942 | Eva F. Haaglund | 1978 | Thora W. Allan |
| 1945 | Grace C. Woolley | 1980 | Diane Anderson |
| 1947 | Louisa R. Macdonald | 1985 | Cyndey Quinn |
| 1949 | Vera Hales | 1987 | Lynda Gunther |
| 1956 | Margaret Stephenson | 1992 | Joan Jackson |
| 1957 | Anna Laura Cannon | 1994 | Sally Harker |
| 1958 | Bessie W. Thomas | 1996 | Linda Inouye |
| 1959 | Lyle N. Paine | 1997 | Marilyn Higbee Walker |
| 1967 | Ada H. Miller | 2000 | Susan Robison |
| 1971 | Lilly Jespersen | | |

## STAKE SUNDAY SCHOOL SUPERINTENDENTS/PRESIDENTS

| | | | |
|---|---|---|---|
| 1934 | Guy B. Rose | 1954 | Arch Madsen |
| 1936 | O. Wendell Hyde | 1954 | Robert C. Fletcher |
| 1939 | O. Preston Robinson | 1957 | Darrell H. Spackman |
| 1941 | H. Wayne Driggs | 1958 | Joseph Willard Tingey |
| 1942 | George H. Mortimer | 1959 | Howard B. Anderson, Jr. |
| 1944 | Stephen H. Fletcher | 1960 | H. Gregertson Rose |
| 1946 | Leishman R. Wrathall | 1961 | Melvin C. Miller |
| 1947 | Milton R. Mason | 1965 | Homer M. LeBaron |
| 1948 | Carl Erwin Nelson | 1972 | Jed R. Robinson |
| 1951 | W. Kenneth Firmage | 1974 | J. Martin Pond, Jr. |
| 1953 | Walter M. Soper | 1978 | William Quale |

## STAKE SUNDAY SCHOOL SUPERINTENDENTS/PRESIDENTS

| | | | |
|---|---|---|---|
| 1980 | Neil Thompson | 1993 | Greg Klomp |
| 1983 | Greg Klomp | 1994 | Ned Butikofer |
| 1984 | Ken Shelly | 1995 | Hans Klarer |
| 1987 | Todd Peterson | 1998 | Matt Downs |
| 1990 | David Edwards | 2000 | Thomas Vogelmann |
| 1992 | Rob Wright | 2002 | Noboru Takahashi |
| 1992 | C. Scott Baxter | | |

## STAKE YOUNG WOMEN PRESIDENTS

| | | | |
|---|---|---|---|
| 1934 | Eva F. Haaglund | 1968 | Martha Lassetter |
| 1939 | Louise Luke | 1969 | Maren Mouritsen |
| 1941 | Charlotte H. Knight | 1972 | Charlene Holmstrom |
| 1942 | Fay C. Bolin | 1976 | Sue Hickenlooper |
| 1946 | Olive Laurenson | 1978 | Jean Woodhouse |
| 1948 | Louise Greenwood | 1980 | Anne Knight |
| 1951 | Shirlee Robison | 1982 | Janice M. Crabb |
| 1953 | Rita Soper | 1984 | Ellen McCall |
| 1954 | Claire Dyreng Richards | 1986 | Joan Nicholson |
| 1956 | Veda J. Mortimer | 1989 | Doris Cottam |
| 1960 | Jean Dorny | 1991 | Royce Twitchell |
| 1961 | Rosa J. Huber | 1992 | Judy Davis |
| 1963 | Eleanor Knowles | 1997 | Jennifer Buckner |
| 1965 | Winnifred Bowers | 1999 | Marilee Moe |

## STAKE YOUNG MEN MIA SUPERINTENDENTS/PRESIDENTS

| | | | |
|---|---|---|---|
| 1934 | David D. Paine | 1957 | Fred K. Holbrook |
| 1938 | William F. Edwards | 1958 | David R. Fry |
| 1941 | G. Stanley McAllister | 1960 | John C. Schreiner |
| 1942 | G. Earl Stoddard | 1962 | Lynn L. Davis |
| 1947 | Webster W. Decker | 1963 | Don Lee Tobler |
| 1948 | Marlin L. Dittmore | 1966 | J. Martin Pond, Jr. |
| 1950 | Gordon L. Wright | 1967 | Robert R. Webber |
| 1952 | Richard Burt | 1969 | Monte P. Hickenlooper |
| 1953 | Jack R. Laney | 1970 | John Evans |
| 1955 | Kenneth R. Madsen | 1972 | Douglas Jackson |

## STAKE YOUNG MEN MIA SUPERINTENDENTS/PRESIDENTS

| | | | |
|---|---|---|---|
| 1973 | Kenneth Thiess | 1991 | Tony Fennimore |
| 1974 | Henry E. Heilesen | 1992 | Kevin Kelly |
| 1978 | George Arrington | 1995 | Malcolm Draper |
| 1980 | Michael Jeffries | 1996 | Doug Ellis |
| 1983 | Scott Rasmussen | 1997 | David Buckner |
| 1985 | Gilberto Perea | 1998 | Thomas Epting |
| 1986 | Eric Hyer | 2003 | Justin Rucker |
| 1988 | Mark Graham | 2004 | Justin Hohl |
| 1990 | Steven Toronto | | |

## STAKE PRIMARY PRESIDENTS

| | | | |
|---|---|---|---|
| 1935 | Lydia A. Stephens | 1973 | Margaret Bown |
| 1941 | Leone A. Rose | 1978 | Clara Neu |
| 1943 | Louise B. Greenwood | 1980 | Florencia Rodriguez |
| 1947 | Olive Harris | 1983 | Linda Pinkerton |
| 1949 | Ellis Cullimore | 1986 | Mary Bell |
| 1950 | Pauline Thomander | 1988 | Martha Barrett |
| 1954 | Adelaide N. McAllister | 1990 | Candida Bonet |
| 1959 | Gertrude R. Nelson | 1992 | Dorothy Larson |
| 1961 | Jean D. Griffith | 1994 | Betsi Ricks |
| 1964 | Claire H. Freedman | 1995 | Diana Murphy |
| 1965 | Barbara Sheets | 2001 | Joanne Rowland |
| 1967 | Jeanne G. Loso | 2004 | Michelle Larsen |

## STAKE PATRIARCHS

| | | | |
|---|---|---|---|
| 1934-1938 | James S. Knecht | [1977] | George E. Watkins |
| 1947- | LeRoy A. Wirthlin | [1977] | James Bonner |
| 1950-1956 | Howard S. Bennion | [1980] | George Harding Mortimer |
| 1956-1959 | Cyril D. Pearson | [1984] | Manuel D. Nieto |
| 1959-1960 | DeWitt Paul | [1984] | F. Anthony Santangelo |
| 1961-1963 | Earl B. Snell | [1987] | Jaime Mir (Spanish) |
| 1963-1967 | Owen S. Cullimore | [1988-1989] | Gilberto Perea (Spanish) |
| 1967-1972 | Arthur B. Erekson | 1989-PRESENT | Richard Lyman Bushman (English) |
| 1971- | Paul W. Jespersen | -1994 | George E. Watkins (English) |
| [1977] | John E. Griffith | 1994-1997 | Ronald N. Inouye (English) |

## MISSION PRESIDENTS, NEW YORK NEW YORK MISSION

| | | | |
|---|---|---|---|
| 1933-1937 | Don B. Colton | 1968-1971 | Harold N. Wilkinson |
| 1937-1940 | Israel F. Evans | 1971-1974 | David L. McKay |
| 1940-1944 | Gustave A. Iverson | 1974-1977 | Thomas B. Neff |
| 1944-1948 | Roy W. Doxey | 1977-1980 | Roland R. Wright |
| 1948-1952 | George Q. Morris | 1980-1983 | Albert Choules, Jr. |
| 1952-1955 | Delbert G. Taylor | 1983-1986 | W. Boyd Christensen |
| 1955-1959 | Theodore C. Jacobsen | 1986-1989 | Willard B. Barton |
| 1959-1962 | Gerald G. Smith | 1989-1991 | Cree-L Kofford |
| 1962-1965 | Wilburn C. West | 1991-1994 | Sheldon F. Child *(last year as president of south mission)* |
| 1965-1968 | Walter J. Eldredge | | |

## MISSION PRESIDENTS, NEW YORK NEW YORK NORTH MISSION

| | | | |
|---|---|---|---|
| 1993-96 | Parley L. Howell | 2002-03 | Scott S. Parker |
| 1996-1999 | Ronald A. Rasband | 2003 | Robert E. Sorenson |
| 1999-2002 | Noel G. Stoker | 2003-PRESENT | Nelson M. Boren |

## MISSION PRESIDENTS, NEW YORK NEW YORK SOUTH MISSION

| | | | |
|---|---|---|---|
| 1994-1997 | Walter John Bailey | 2000-2003 | G. Lawrence Spackman |
| 1997-2000 | Dean W. Croft | 2003- | Jeffrey R. Morrow |

1837-2004 MANHATTAN
# MEETING LOCATIONS

| | |
|---|---|
| 1837 | Goerck Street (in upper room)—first meeting site<br>Chair warehouse provided by David Rogers—second meeting site |
| 1838 | Wandall Mace home, 13 Bedford Street |
| 1841-1842 | 31 Canal Street (old style numbering) |
| 1842-1843 | 29 Canal Street (old style numbering) |
| 1843-1844 | 263 Grand Street (between Forsythe and Eldredge) |
| 1844 | Marion Temperence Hall, 183 Canal Street (old style numbering—now at Holland Tunnel exit) |
| 1845 | Houston & First Street (East River Branch established at this intersection) |
| 1900 | 70 West 125th Street |
| 1901 | 33 West 126th Street |
| 1901-1903 | 172 West 81st Street |
| 1905 | 33 West 126th Street |
| 1906 | Hawthorne Hall, 153 West 125th Street |
| EARLY 1920S | Steinway Hall, 109 West 57th Street; Carnegie Hall, 57th Street at 7th Avenue; Rented hall, Broadway and 103rd Street; Leslie Hall, 83rd Street West of Broadway |
| 1925 | "Beer hall," Broadway and 80th Street |
| 1928-1943 | 316 West 57th Street<br>Hotel, 2166 Broadway between 76th and 77th Streets |
| 1943-1945 | Steinway Hall, 109 West 57th Street |
| 1945-1975 | 142 West 81st Street |
| 1975-PRESENT | 2 Lincoln Square, 125 Columbus Avenue |
| 1996-2000 | Herbert L. Birch Manhattan Early Childhood Center, 554 Fort Washington Avenue |
| 1997-1999 | Sylvia's Restaurant, 328 Lenox Avenue |
| 1999-PRESENT | West 129th Street, near Lenox Avenue |
| 1999-2000 | 401 Broadway, 12th Floor |
| 2000-2004 | 401 Broadway, 10th Floor |
| 2000-PRESENT | Inwood Building, 1815 Riverside Drive |
| 2003-PRESENT | Union Square Building, 144 West 15th Street |
| 2004-PRESENT | Canal Street Building, 41 Elizabeth Street |

*Pending Locations Under Construction: Harlem Building, Lenox Avenue and 128th Street; East Side Building, 217 East 87th Street, between 2nd and 3rd Avenues*

Y OF KENT LARSEN

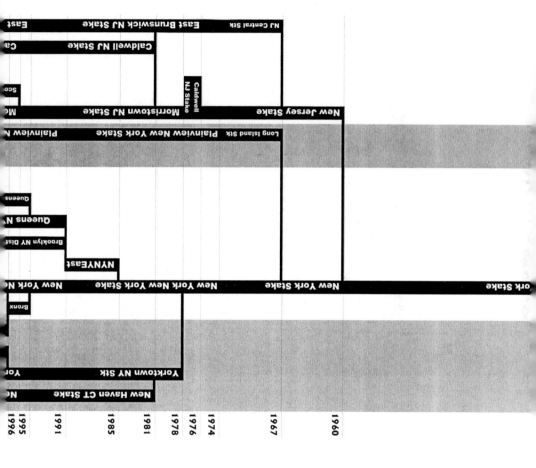

# The Early Church in New York City

## A Walking Tour

1. #7 College Green - Residence of Professor Charles Anthon (Columbia College).

2. #7 Spruce Street - The Prophet and The New York Messenger were published here (1844-1845).

3. Corner of Ann and Nassau - The Mormon was published here (1855-1857).

4. 29 Ann Street - A Voice of Warning was published here in 1837.

5. 46 1/2 John Street - residence of Elijah Fordham.

6. 20 Wall Street - Machinist Shop of Wandle Mace.

7. 88 Pearl Street - Joseph Smith and Newel K. Whitney boarded here in 1832.

8. Old Slip - The Ship Brooklyn set sail carrying about 238 Mormon pioneers on February 4, 1846.

Time: 1-2 Hours          Distance: 1.0-1.1 miles

Getting There:
* Subway:
  1,2,3 to Chambers St.
  2,3 to Park Place
  4,5,6 to Brooklyn Bridge
  A,C to Chambers St.
  J,M,Z to Chambers St.
  N, R to City Hall

* Car:
  FDR Drive South to Wagner Pl (Brooklyn Bridge) r. on St. James Pl., l. on Worth St., l. on Broadway
  (not recommended during business hours due to traffic and lack of parking)

# Columbia College

## Martin Harris Meets Charles Anthon

One of the best-known stories about the coming forth of the Book of Mormon happened in New York City when Martin Harris (1783-1875), Joseph Smith's scribe and benefactor, visited Charles Anthon (1797-1867), a professor at Columbia College.

Harris obtained a transcription and translation of characters from the golden plates and, in February 1828, took the two documents to at least three "learned men" in Utica, Albany, and New York City. They were examined by well-known scholars Samuel Latham Mitchill (1764-1831) and Charles Anthon. Harris hoped that the scholars' comments would support Joseph Smith's translation.

Harris and Anthon's accounts of their meeting differ substantially, with Harris claiming that Anthon gave him a certificate verifying the authenticity of the characters, only to tear it up when he heard their origin.

Anthon claimed in written accounts from 1834 and 1841 that he told Harris he was the victim of a fraud, but contradicted himself in the accounts about whether or not he had given Harris a written opinion.

Given the state of knowledge of the Egyptian language in 1828, it is unlikely that Anthon's views would be more than opinion.

In December 1844, the New York LDS newspaper *The Prophet* printed what it said was a copy of the characters Harris showed Anthon from a document now owned by the Community of Christ (RLDS Church).

### Columbia University

Columbia founded in 1756 as King's College, affiliated with Trinity Parrish.

Alumni include:
- Alexander Hamilton
- John Jay
- J. Reuben Clark

### Extent of New York City, 1828

- Street grid planned to upper Manhattan in 1811.
- City Hall completed 1812.
- City extends to 16th Street, Union Square. Fifth Avenue extends to 13th Street.
- First gas pipes laid in 1825.
- Erie Canal was completed in 1825, reducing travel time from Buffalo from three weeks to eight days. (Palmyra, New York is located on the Erie Canal.).

### In New York and U.S. History

1810 – In U.S. Census, New York City passes Philadelphia as most populous U.S. city.

3 July 1824 – Castle Clinton opens as Castle Garden, an entertainment house.

4 July 1827 – Slavery abolished in New York. First black newspaper in U.S., *Freedom's Journal*, established that year in New York City.

4 July 1828 – First passenger railroad, the Baltimore & Ohio, begins operation.

*This document represents the Book of Mormon characters on the gold plates, but is probably not the transcript taken by Martin Harris to Charles Anthon in 1828. The heirs of David Whitmer sold this document to the Reorganized Church of Jesus Christ of Latter Day Saints (now the Community of Christ).*

*Martin Harris at about age 87*

*Charles Anthon*

## In LDS Church History

June 1828 – Martin Harris borrows and loses 116 manuscript pages of Book of Mormon.

15 May 1829 – Joseph Smith and Oliver Cowdery receive Aaronic Priesthood.

May or June 1829 – Joseph Smith and Oliver Cowdery receive Melchizedek Priesthood.

June 1829 – The three witnesses see the golden plates.

## Further Reading

Roberts, B. H. *History of the Church* (Salt Lake City: Deseret Book, 1978).

Roberts, B. H. *Comprehensive History of the Church* (Salt Lake City: Deseret Book, 1978).

*Encyclopedia of Mormonism* (New York: Macmillan, 1992).

Kimball, Stanley B. "I Cannot Read a Sealed Book." *IE* 60 (Feb. 1957):80-82, 104, 106.

Kimball, Stanley B. "The Anthon Transcript: People, Primary Sources, and Problems." *BYU Studies* 10 (Spring 1970):325-52.

"Martin Harris' Visit to Charles Anthon: Collected Documents on Short-hand Egyptian." F.A.R.M.S. Provo, Utah, 1985.

# Printing House Square

## New York LDS Newspapers and Pamphlets

Unlike today, 150 years ago New Yorkers published a weekly LDS newspaper. *The Prophet*, first of three LDS newspapers, was published every week from a printing press located at 68 Commercial Street and issued at 7 Spruce Street, right here in the city. *The Prophet* was succeeded by *The New York Messenger* and later, *The Mormon*.

The first issue of *The Prophet* was published May 24, 1844, by Parley P. Pratt and Orson Pratt, after which it was run by Samuel Brannan, presiding elder of the branch in Manhattan. The newspaper contained essays from Church leaders and members as well as general and Church-specific news, and official Church announcements. The audience was mostly LDS, and the paper was supported entirely by the subscription fees of its readers, which were one dollar a year.

By the middle of 1845, *The Prophet* had published 52 issues, but with the 53rd issue, published July 5th, the newspaper's name changed to *The New York Messenger*, and the cost of an annual subscription was raised to two dollars. Publication ended early in 1846 when Brannan took the press to California with the group of Mormons he led on the ship *Brooklyn*. There the press was used for *The California Star*, a general newspaper.

It wasn't until 1855 that a replacement newspaper was started. Elder John Taylor, president of the Eastern States Mission, started *The Mormon* in February 1855. Located near the buildings that housed the New York Herald and New York Tribune, *The Mormon* sought to unapologetically defend the Church and its doctrines.

However, in September 1857, Elder Taylor and the missionaries in the Eastern States Mission were recalled to Utah because of the Utah War, ending the publicaton of LDS newspapers in New York City.

### Extent of New York City, 1857

- City extends to 59th Street.
- Construction on Central Park begins in 1857.
- New York has 10 to 15 daily newspapers throughout the 1840s and 1850s, including at least 6 major newspapers: the *Sun, Post, Tribune, Herald, Observer* and the *Courier & Enquirer*. *The New York Times* was started 18 August 1851.

### In New York and U.S. History

1855 – Castle Clinton becomes New York City immigration station.

Aug. 1857 – Financial panic of 1857 and runs on the banks. Subsequent depression improves just before the Civil War.

12 Apr. 1861 – Confederate forces fire on Ft. Sumpter, in South Carolina. Significant portion of U.S. troops are still stationed in Utah.

20 Aug. 1859 – First ever question & answer interview published: Horace Greely's interview of Brigham Young in *New York Tribune*.

*Masthead of* The Mormon

"*To keep the immigrants, who were coming into the country through the Port of New York, informed as to routes of travel and other matters pertaining to their welfare; to instruct the Saints and investigators; and to correct the many false and slanderous reports which were continually put in circulation and to advocate the interests of Utah and the Mormons generally,*"
Purpose of *The Mormon*,
as announced in its first edition.

*John Taylor*

## In LDS Church History

August 1852 – Elder Orson Pratt publicly announces doctrine of plural marriage.

9 June 1856 – First handcart company leaves Iowa City, Iowa, for Utah.

13 May 1857 – Elder Parley P. Pratt assassinated in Arkansas.

28 May 1857 – Acting on reports from non-Mormons, U.S. Pres. James Buchannan orders U.S. Army to Utah.

15 Sept. 1857 – Brigham Young puts Utah under martial law.

24 Feb. 1858 – Col. Thomas L. Kane brokers peaceful end to Utah War.

## Further Reading

Tiffany, Scott. LDS Newspapers of Nineteenth Century New York City. *The New York LDS Historian.* Winter 1999, Vol. 1 No. 2.

Pratt, Parley P., *The Autobiography of Parley P. Pratt* (Salt Lake City: Deseret Book).

Roberts, B. H. *History of the Church* (Salt Lake City: Deseret Book, 1978).

Roberts, B. H. *Comprehensive History of the Church* (Salt Lake City: Deseret Book, 1978).

*Encyclopedia of Mormonism* (New York: Macmillan, 1992).

# 46 ½ John Street

## Residence of Elijah Fordham

When Parley P. Pratt arrived in New York City in 1837, the only Mormon in the city was Elijah Fordham, a New York City native who had joined the Church in Michigan with his wife. In March 1834, his wife died, and Fordham relocated to Kirtland, Ohio and soon participated in Zion's Camp. In 1836 he was ordained an elder, and then a seventy later that same year.

It isn't clear why Elijah Fordham was in New York City in 1837 when Elder Pratt arrived, but he was staying with his sister-in-law and had just assisted the Apostles on their way to England.

Elijah Fordham was instrumental in helping Elder Pratt get missionary work started in New York City, preaching in meetings and assisting in the anointing of a sick child in the home of Wandle Mace, which led to the baptism of those in the house. Fordham later married Ann Shaffer, one of those present.

Elijah then moved to Missouri, where he was among the Saints expelled in the late 1830s. Arriving in Nauvoo, he settled across the Mississippi river in Iowa, and was on his death bed when he was miraculously healed by Joseph Smith.

He was then called to return to New York to support the candidacy of Joseph Smith for president of the United States. Following the Martyrdom, he returned with over $1,200 for the Nauvoo Temple, and also spent eight months carving the oxen for the baptismal font.

Elijah Fordham emmigrated to Utah, and died in Wellsville, Cache County in 1879.

*Of all the places in which the English language is spoken, I found the City of New York to be the most difficult as to access to the minds or attention of the people. From July to January we preached, advertised, printed, published,*

### Extent of New York City, 1837

- City extends to mid 20s. Fifth Avenue to 42nd Street.
- Construction on the Croton water system began in 1837.
- City boasts 17 daily newspapers.
- City's notorious prison, The Tombs, completed in 1838.

### In New York and U.S. History

16-17 Dec. 1835 – New York City's "Great Fire" decimates city below Wall Street, destroying 674 buildings and killing 2.

May 1837 – Financial panic of 1837 includes riots and runs on the banks. Subsequent depression lasts until early 1840s.

7 May 1838 – First transatlantic steamship, *The Great Western*, sails for Britain. Regular steamship service is in place by 1840.

1841 – John Street Methodist Church rebuilt.

testified, visited, talked, prayed, and wept in vain. To all appearance there was no interest or impression on the minds of the people in regard to the fullness of the gospel.
There was one member of the Church of the Saints living there, whose name was Elijah Fordham; he was an Elder, and assisted me. We had baptized about six members, and organized a little branch, who were accustomed to meet in a small upper room in Goerck street; sometimes two or three others met with us. ...
We had retired to our private room up stairs with the few members we had, to hold a last prayer meeting, as I was about taking leave for New Orleans. We had prayed all round in turn, when, on a sudden, the room was filled with the Holy Spirit, and so was each one present. We began to speak in tongues and prophesy. Many marvelous things were manifested which I cannot write; but the principal burthen of the prophesyings was concerning New York City, and our mission there.

*Parley P. Pratt*

The Lord said that He had heard our prayers, beheld our labors, diligence, and long suffering towards that city; and that He had seen our tears. Our prayers were heard, and our labors and sacrifices were accepted. We should tarry in the city, and go not thence as yet; for the Lord had many people in that city, and He had now come by the power of His Holy Spirit to gather them into His fold. ...
So we gave up going to New Orleans, and concluded to stay.

The Autobiography of Parley P. Pratt, Ch. 20

---

## In LDS Church History

27 March 1836 – Kirtland Temple dedicated.

May 1837 – Collapse of the Kirtland Safety Society brought on by Panic of 1837.

13 June 1837 – Mission of the Apostles to Britian, opening the British Mission.

October 1837 – Parley P. Pratt's *A Voice of Warning*, the first book for missionary use, was published in New York City.

6 July 1838 – LDS exodus from Kirtland, Ohio, begins.

## Further Reading

Pratt, Parley P., *The Autobiography of Parley P. Pratt* (Salt Lake City: Deseret Book).

Mace, Wandle. *Autobiography of Wandle Mace*. BYU Special Collections.

Communications. *The Evening and Morning Star* Vol. 2, No. 23, August 1834, Kirtland, Ohio.

Roberts, B. H. *History of the Church* (Salt Lake City: Deseret Book, 1978).

# 20 Wall Street

## Machinist Shop of Wandle Mace

One of the first converts to the LDS Church in New York City, Wandle Mace was at that time a successful machinist and coach maker. By 1830 he was listed as having a portable machinist shop at 20 Wall Street, on the northwest corner of Nassau and Wall Streets, just east of a Presbyterian church.

Born in 1809, Mace apprenticed as a wheelwright at age 13 and worked making wheels and coaches. He later had coachmaker's shops at 161 W. Broadway (1833-34) and at 249 Elizabeth St. (1838).

He patented two machines for post mortising and rail sharpening, and sold the patents. He also built a machine for sweeping the streets based on the design of a Mr. Kidder. "This was the first street sweeping machine ever made and used in NYC," Mace later wrote.

When Parley P. Pratt came to New York City, Mace was operating his shop at 20 Wall Street. He had purchased the patent on a portable mill called a conical grinder. In his shop he made and sold the grinders.

Mace had been excommunicated from the Presbyterian Church because he didn't believe some of its doctrines and was meeting privately with truth-seeking friends to discuss the scriptures. He also went from house to house preaching the gospel each Sunday for two years before deciding he didn't have the authority to preach.

At a private meeting Elijah Fordham introduced him to Parley P. Pratt and learned of Joseph Smith and the Book of Mormon. Parley P. Pratt later visited Mace's house at 13 Bedford Street, and there healed his son and a Mrs. Dexter and her daughter, leading to their baptisms.

### Extent of New York City, 1840s

- Construction of Lexington and Madison Avenues begins in 1840s.
- First water from Croton water system arrives at new Croton Aqueduct (Fifth Avenue at 42nd Street, site of current New York Public Library main branch) and at Croton Fountain in City Hall Park.
- Madison Square (24th Street) opens 10 May 1847.

### In New York and U.S. History

10 April 1841 – First issue of Horace Greeley's *New York Tribune*.

19 July 1845 – New York City's second "Great Fire" kills 30 and destroys 300 buildings in area extending from Wall Street to Coentie's Slip, east of Broad St.

1845 – New York Knickerbocker's Club accepts Abner Doubleday and Alexander Cartwright's rules for baseball.

"A child of Mr. Wandle Mace, of No. 13 Bedford street, was healed of brain fever in the last stage, when he doctors had given it over, and the kindred and neighbors had gathered in to see it die. I laid my hands on it, in the presence of the all, and it was healed, and in a few hours took nourishment, and commenced to play and run about the floor.

In the same house, in an upper chamber, lay a woman, by the name of Dexter, sick, who had not left her room, nor scarcely her bed, for some six months; she was at the point of death, and her babe also, who had taken the disease from her. Her mother, who had the care of her, was present when the child was healed, and she ran up stairs and told the woman that there were men below who healed the sick, as in days of old, by the laying on of hands in the name of Jesus. The woman exclaimed, "Thank God, then I can be healed." She sent for us, and was from that hour restored to health, and the child also.

Margaret Mace

Wandle Mace

She walked about two miles to the East River and was baptized, and then walked home again–it being a very wet day with snow and rain, and the sidewalks about shoe deep in snow and mud. After these three miracles of healing had been witnessed in that house in Bedford street, six persons who witnessed them were baptized, viz: Wandle Mace and wife, Theodore Curtis and wife, and the sick woman and her mother, before named."

Parley Pratt Autobiography (1985), pp. 146-148

## In LDS Church History

November 1839 – Parley P. Pratt arrives back in New York City, staying six months before leaving for England.

20 July 1840 – Ship *Britannia* arrives in New York City with 41 Mormon immigrants, first of more than 85,000 to arrive through New York City by 1890.

April 1841 – The Quorum of the Twelve meet in England, the only time the quorum has met outside the U.S.

27 June 1844 – Joseph and Hyrum Smith martyred in Carthage, Illinois.

## Further Reading

Pratt, Parley P., *The Autobiography of Parley P. Pratt* (Salt Lake City: Deseret Book).

Mace, Wandle. *Autobiography of Wandle Mace*. BYU Special Collections.

Roberts, B. H. *History of the Church* (Salt Lake City: Deseret Book, 1978).

# Pearl Street House

## Lodging for Joseph Smith

Joseph Smith and Bishop Newel K. Whitney came to New York City in October 1832 to purchase goods for Whitney's store in Kirtland. While there, they lodged temporarily at Pearl Street House.

The location was very good for Bishop Whitney's purchasing. By 1832, New York City's dry goods merchants had concentrated on Pearl Street, and public markets were nearby on Old Slip and Coenties Slip.

The Prophet and Bishop Whitney arrived back in Nauvoo from their trip on Novermber 6, 1832.

*Emma Hale Smith*

*Oct. 13, 1832*
*Pearl Street House*

*My Dear Wife,*

*This day I have been walking through the most splendid part of the city of New York. The buildings are truly great and wonderful, to the astonishing of every beholder. And the language of my heart is like this: Can the great God of all the earth, maker of all things magnificent and splendid, be displeased with man for all these great inventions sought out by them? My answer is no, it cannot be, seeing these works are calculated to make men comfortable, wise and happy. Therefore, not for the works can the Lord be displeased.*

*I hope you will excuse me for writing this letter so soon after writing, for I feel as if I wanted to say something to you to comfort you in your peculiar trial and present afflic-*

### Extent of New York City, 1832

- City extends to above Union Square. Fifth Avenue extends to 23rd Street.
- Union Square (16th Street and Fourth Avenue) opened in 1831.
- Construction on the city's first railroad, the New York & Hudson, began in 1831.

### In New York and U.S. History

26 June 1832 – Cholera epidemic hits New York City. 3,513 die by epidemic's end in August.

26 Nov. 1832 – New York & Harlem railroad opens from Prince Street to the Harlem River.

16-17 Dec. 1835 – New York City's "Great Fire" decimates city below Wall Street, destroying 674 buildings and killing 2.

tion. I hope God will give you strength that you may not faint. I pray God to soften the hearts of those around you to be kind to you and take the burden off your shoulders as much as possible and not afflict you. I feel for you, for I know your state and that others do not. But you must comfort yourself, knowing that God is your friend in heaven, and that you have one true and living friend on earth.

Your husband,
Joseph Smith Jr.

P.S. While Brother Whitney is selecting goods I have nothing to do but to sit in my room and pray for him that he may have strength to endure his labors, for truly it is a tedious job to stand on the feet all day to select goods. It wants good judgement and a long acquaintance with goods to get good ones and man must be his own judge, for no one will judge for him and it is much perplexity of mind. I prefer reading and praying and holding communion with the holy spirit and writing to you then walking the streets and beholding the distraction of man. . . . Brother Whitney is received with great kindness by all his old acquaintances. He is faithful in prayer and fervent in spirit and we take great comfort together. There is about one hundred boarders and sometimes more in this house every day from one to two from all parts of the world. I think you would have laughed right hearty if you could have been where you could see the waiters today, noon, as they waited on the table, both black and white and mulato running, bowing and maneuvering. But I must conclude. I remain your affectionate Husband until Death.

Joseph Smith Jr.

*Joseph Smith Jr.*

## In LDS Church History

30 Dec. 1830 – The Saints are commanded to gather in Kirtland, Ohio (D&C 37).

7 June 1831 – The Saints are commanded to gather in Missouri, "the land of your inheritance."

June 1832 – First LDS missionaries preach in a foreign country, Canada

1 June 1832 – First LDS periodical, *The Evening and Morning Star*, issued at Independence, Missouri.

## Further Reading

Joseph Smith to Emma Smith, 13 October 1832; in Dean Jessee, ed., *The Personal Writings of Joseph Smith* (Salt Lake City, Utah: Deseret Book 1984) pp. 252-254.

Newell, Linda King and Valeen Tippetts Avery, *Mormon Enigma: Emma Hale Smith* (Garden City, NY: Doubleday & Co., 1984) p.45-6.

# Old Slip

## Starting Point for the *Brooklyn*

"Brethren Awake! Be determined to get out of this evil nation by next spring," came the cry from Orson Pratt on November 8, 1845, at American Hall in New York City. Pooling their resources, Church members rented the ship *Brooklyn* and made the journey by sea from New York City to Upper California (present-day California, Nevada, Utah, and Arizona).

Each family paid fare of $75 for adults and half that for children. They packed agricultural and mechanical tools to equip at least 800 workers with everything from ploughs, hoes, and shovels to glass, paper, a printing press, school books and twine. They included about seventy men, sixty women and one hundred children, plus a dozen non-Church members, including the crew and a few business people. They sailed on Wednesday, February 4, 1846, the same day the first Saints left Nauvoo on the journey west.

After five months and twenty-seven days, traveling over 24,000 miles, the New York Mormons sailed into the harbor of Yerba Buena, California, now known as San Francisco, on July 31st. There they established industries and built houses. They became local craftsmen, tailors, bakers, surveyors, masons, carpenters, cobblers and attorneys. They opened the first local bank, post office, library and the first public school in California.

Not all of the passengers remained faithful after arriving in California, however. Sam Brannan, in particular, became rich after opening a store at Sutter's Fort following the discovery of gold. However, he eventually lost not only his faith, but his wife and his fortune. About one-third of the Brooklyn Saints remained faithful and eventually moved to Salt Lake City.

### Extent of New York City, 1846

- The Croton Water System was completed in 1842, bringing water to the Croton Aqueduct (42nd Street and Fifth Avenue, current site of New York Public Library main branch) and the Croton Fountain in City Hall Park.
- City extends to just north of 30th Street by 1846.
- Madison Square (23rd Street and Madison Avenue) opened in 1847.
- More than 100 horsedrawn omnibuses transported passengers around the city.

### In New York and U.S. History

4 Mar. 1845 – James K. Polk inaugurated as U.S. President.

4 July 1845 – The ten-year-old Republic of Texas accepts annexation into U. S., leading to Mexican War.

19 July 1845 – New York City's second "Great Fire" kills 30 and destroys 300 buildings in area extending from Wall Street to Coentie's Slip, east of Broad St.

13 May 1846 – U.S. declares war on Mexico.

14 June 1846 – American settlers in California start Bear Flag Revolt against Mexico.

Of the 230 who sailed, all but 12 were Latter-day Saints. There were 70 men, 60 women, and 100 children. Adults paid $75 and children $37.50. They brought books, a printing press, guns, 800 pounds of paying freight bound for the Sandwich Islands, and enough agricultural and mechanical tools to equip 800 laborers. All of the people and cargo were crammed onto the ship Brooklyn, which Brannan had leased at the inexpensive rate of $1,200 per month plus expenses. An average-size ship for its day, the Brooklyn was 125 feet long and 28 feet across the beam and weighed about 445 tons.

Historical Atlas of Mormonism, p. 78.

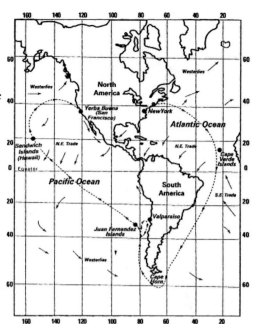

*Voyage of the* Brooklyn

---

## In LDS Church History

27 June 1844 – Joseph and Hyrum Smith martyred in Nauvoo, Illinois.

9 Sep. 1845 – Church leaders state their intention to leave Nauvoo.

4 Feb. 1846 – First Mormon wagons cross the Mississippi river, starting the Mormon trek west.

13 July 1846 – Mormon Battalion enlisted.

17 Sept. 1846 – Remaining poverty-stricken Mormons driven from Nauvoo in violation of "treaty of surrender."

## Further Reading

Hansen, Lorin K., "Voyage of the Brooklyn," *Dialogue: A Journal of Mormon Thought*. 21:3 Aug 1988.

Roberts, B. H., *Comprehensive History of the Church*, Vol. 3, Ch. 71, p. 39.

"Bay Area's First Farmer," Program for *150 Years in California* celebration, June 26-Oct. 1, 1996.

Tiffany, Scott. "The Voyage of The Ship Brooklyn," *The New York LDS Historian*, Vol.1, No. 1, Spring 1998.

# Some Other Early LDS Sites on Manhattan

1. Residence of Wandle Mace, 13 Bedford Street
2. Residence of S. Mitchell, 47 White Street
3. Location where First LDS meetings held, Goerck Street
4. Lodgings of Parley P. Pratt, 58 Mott Street
5. Printing Office of *The Prophet*, 68 Commerical Street
6. Wandle Mace's Coach Maker's Shop, 249 Elizabeth Street
7. Residence of cousin of Parley P. Pratt, 89 Gold Street
8. Castle Garden, U.S. Immigration Station 1855-1890, Battery Park
9. Tammany Hall (where Parley P. Pratt spoke to the Free Thinkers), Nassau and Frankfort
10. Wandle Mace's Grocery Store, 44 Bayard
11. Wandel Mace's Coach Maker s Shop, 161 West Broadway
12. Joshua Parker Cabinet Shop, 266 Hudson, and Residence, 29 Charlton
13. Marion Temperance Hall, site of LDS meetings in 1844, 183 Canal Street (old style numbers).
14. 263 Grand Street. (between Eldredge and Forsythe), LDS services held 1843-44
15. 31 Canal Street, LDS services held 1841-42
16. 29 Canal Street LDS services held 1842-43
17. Houston and 1st St., East River branch established 1845.

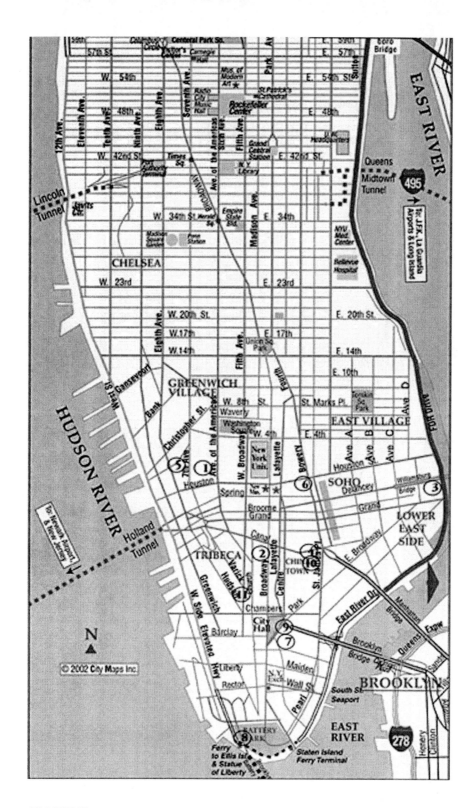

APPENDIX

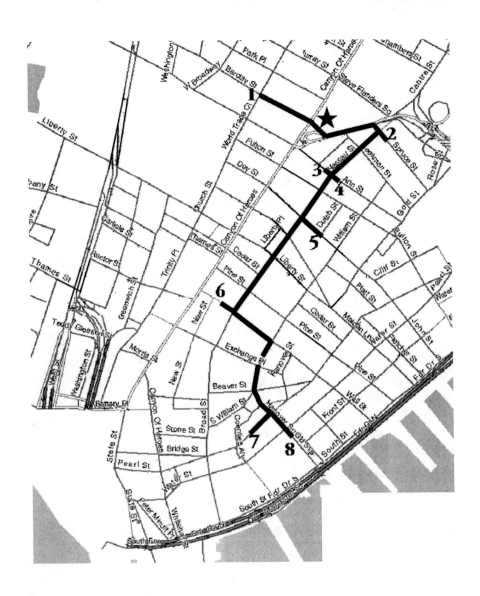

Published by:
New York Stake History Group
Based on the group's research.

© 1999, 2000, 2001, 2002, 2004
New York Stake History Group

Version 4.2, 25Oct2004

# NOTES

## PART 1: THE CITY SAINTS STORY

**MORMONITES IN MANHATTAN**

1. Morning Courier and Enquirer, August 31 and September 1, 1831.

2. Leonard J. Arrington, "James Gordon Bennett's 1831 Report on the 'Mormonites'" *BYU Studies,* (Spring 1970): 354-7.

3. ibid., 363.

4. Jessee, ed., Personal Writings of Joseph Smith, Salt Lake City: Deseret Book, 1984, p. 278. A few months after his visit to New York City, Joseph Smith received the revelation that "every man shall hear the fullness of the gospel in his own tongue, and in his own language" (Doctrine & Covenants 90:11).

5. Orson F. Whitney, Conference Report, October 1920, p. 32.

6. Parley P. Pratt The Autobiography of Parley Parker Pratt, Salt Lake City: Deseret Book, 1985, p. 144

7. ibid., 145.

8. ibid.

9. ibid.

10. ibid., pp. 145-46.

11. ibid.

12. ibid, pp.146-47.

13. Wandle Mace, Autobiography, typescript, BYU-S, p. 14-17.

14. Pratt, Autobiography, p. 146-47 and Mace, Autobiography, p. 20-21.

15. Mace, Autobiography, p. 22.

16. This book sold for 12 cents and was published at 162 Nassau Street in February of 1838. For more information, see Francis W. Kirkham, *A New Witness for Christ in America,* Salt Lake City: Utah Printing Co., 1967 Vol. 2 p. 159.

17. Kirkham, 162-63.

18. Millennial Star vol. 26 (1864), p. 824.

19. Matthias F. Cowley, Wilford Woodruff—His Life and Labors, Salt Lake City: Bookcraft, 1986, p. 90.

20. Pratt, Autobiography, p. 259.

21. Published in New York City in 1840.

22. Pratt, Autobiography, p. 261.

23. Andrew Jenson, Encyclopedic History of the Church, Salt Lake City: Deseret News, 1941, p. 579.

24. Times and Seasons, Vol. 3, 1842, pp. 844-45.

25. Encyclopedia of Mormonism, Daniel H. Ludlow (ed.), New York: Macmillan, 1992 Vol. 3, "Proclamations of the First Presidency and the Quorum of the Twelve Apostles,"

26. Jenson, p. 579; see also Lyondon W. Cook, The Revelations of the Prophet Joseph Smith, Salt Lake City: Deseret Book, 1985, p. 45

27. Pratt, Autobiography, p. 402.

28. ibid. Elder John Taylor of the Quorum of the Twelve Apostles was then based in New York City and presiding over the Church in the northeastern US. Among other activities, for two and a half years beginning in 1855, Elder Taylor published The Mormon, the successor to Parley's newspaper, The Prophet.

29. Jenson, Conference Report, April 1917, p. 101.

## NEW YORK CITY'S OCEAN PIONEERS

1. New York Messenger 15 Nov. 1845.

2. Times and Seasons, 1 Dec. 1845; History of the Church 7: 520-22; CHC, V.3, Ch.71, p.26

3. Samuel Brannan, Scoundrel's Tale: The Samuel Brannan Papers, William Bagley (ed.), Spokane, WA: The Arthur H. Clark Company, 1999, p. 101

4. Scoundrel's Tale, p. 23

5. History of the Church, 2:205-6.

6. Kemble Reader, 1963, p. 22

7. Scoundrel's Tale, p. 123

## A RISING OR SETTING SUN?

1. The number of active missions declined from a high of 15 in 1855 to a low of seven in 1870.

2. Roberts, B. H., Life of John Taylor, Salt Lake City: Bookcraft, 1963, p.243.

3. Andrew Jenson, Encyclopedic History of the Church, p.213.

4. Deseret News 1997-98 Church Almanac, p. 410. There is also anecdotal evidence that some converts were made during the time that the mission was supposedly closed. For example, the Schlesselman family was baptized about 1858, when some sources say the mission was closed. John Schlesselman, a German immigrant, met and married his wife Mina in New York City in the late 1850s and they immigrated to Utah in 1861. See Hartley, William G.; Kindred Saints: Mormon immigrant heritage of Alvin & Kathryne Christenson, Salt Lake City, Eden Hill, 1982, p.122-135.

5. Deseret News 1997-98 Church Almanac p. 410. The only other U.S. missions at the time, in Hawaii and in the Indian Territories, were also closed just prior to the Civil War.

6. Andrew Jenson, Encyclopedic History of the Church, p.213.

7. Deseret News 1997-98 Church Almanac, p.241, p. 410.

8. Jenson, Andrew, LDS Biographical Encyclopedia, Vol. 2, 1951, p. 604. Henry G. Bywater reportedly presided over the annual district conference from as early as 1873 through 1883.

9. Deseret News 1997-98 Church Almanac, p.162-167.

10. Letters of Brigham Young to his Sons, Dean Jessee (ed), Salt Lake City: Deseret Book, 1974, p.347-8.

11. For example, Orson F. Whitney records meeting the immigration agent, James H. Hart, and friends from Salt Lake City in New York before boarding a ship for England in 1881.

12. Letters of Brigham Young to his Sons, p. 345.

13. Gibbs, Linda Jones, Masterworks (catalog of the Masterworks exhibit at the LDS Church Museum of History and Art), p. 44.

14. Heber J. Grant, Gospel Standards, p.267-268.

15. Letters of Brigham Young to his Sons, p. 275.

16. Letters of Brigham Young to his Sons, p. 21.

17. Letters of Brigham Young to his Sons, pp. 91, 95.

18. Heber J. Grant, Gospel Standards, pp.317-323, 339.

## SAINTS IN THE CITY

1. Although members had met sporadically in Brooklyn, in 1900 the Church began meeting in Manhattan for the first time in more than 25 years. The services were held at 170 West 125th Street.

2. In addition, the Herald Tribune featured two articles on the new stake and the Church in general. One of the Herald Tribune articles described New York City Mormons as presenting "a complete, though small, cross-section of metropolitan life," noting that Columbia, NYU, music, drama, and art students "probably represent a third of the membership" in New York City, still today perhaps an apt description of Latter-day Saints in much of the City. See John Walker Harrington, "Mormonism Retraces Its Steps to Evangelize New York State," New York Herald Tribune, 16 December 1934, 2nd Section, pp. 3, 10.

## A STAKE IN BABYLON

1. The New York Stake apparently performed well enough to show that the idea of setting up stakes so far from Church headquarters was sound because just over six months later, they formed a stake even farther away – in Hawaii. Stakes in Chicago (1936) and Washington, DC (1940) soon followed.

## VISITING THE MORMON PAVILION (SIDEBAR)

1. In a letter dated October 16, 1975, David Evans said President David O. McKay called the Mormon Pavilion "one of the most unique and effective missionary efforts in [LDS Church] history."

2. Bernard B. Brockbank, "The Church at the New York World's Fair", Improvement Era, April 1964, p. 281.

3. The New York Times, May 19, 1964, 34:2.

4. The Easterner, November 1965 (Eastern States Mission Newsletter).

5. A well-known copy of the World's Fair "Christus" now stands in the Salt Lake Temple Visitor's Center. The actual 1964 World's Fair sculpture is in the visitors' center at the Los Angeles Temple.

### WELCOME TO THE WORLD

1. Except as otherwise noted, information in this article comes from the personal knowledge of the author and from a series of approximately 20 interviews conducted in 1999 and 2000 with Church members and leaders throughout New York City. Additional information is available in the author's article "Mormons in New York City" in Tony Carnes and Anna Karpathakis (ed), New York Glory: Religions in the City, New York: New York University Press, 2001, pp. 196-211.

2. Quoted in Brent L. Top. "Legacy of the Mormon Pavilion." Ensign 19 (October 1989) p. 28.

3. President Lee and Brother Mortimer were accompanied by Church architect Emil Fetzer who later recounted the episode similarly. See Shaun D. Stahle, "'Not that we're back, it's that we're still here,'" Church News, 12 June 2004, pp. 4-5.

4. Tim B. Heaton. "Vital Statistics." In Encyclopedia of Mormonism, 1520-1521, general editor Daniel H. Ludlow. New York: Macmillan, 1992.

## PART 2

### BUILDING FAITH: MANHATTAN REACHES NEW HEIGHTS

1. At the time, President Santamaría's wife, Patricia, was not a member of the Church. When President Santamaría was set apart at Elder Jensen's direction by President Belnap, he was told his wife would become a member of the Church. Within the year she was baptized

2. At the time there were tow Spanish-language units: the Manhattan Fourth Ward and the Manhattan Fifth Branch, which later became the Inwood Second Ward.

3. Translation was provided for American Sign Language, Cambodian, Cantonese, Haitian French Creole, Korean, Laotian, Mandarin, Portuguese, Russian, Spanish and Vietnamese.

4. At the time of the announcement, only the fifth floor was slated for renovation, although the entire air space for the fifth and sixth floors had been acquired. Shortly before construction was completed on the fifth floor, the sixth floor construction began. At President Belnap's insistence, a cement floor was poured for the sixth floor during the renovation of the fifth floor, later essential for the construction of the temple.

5. For more information about the Chinese group's formation, please see the unit history in Part 4 of this book.

6. The two stores were Orloff's Delicatessen, a generic low-priced New York City diner, and Burke & Burke, an upscale food establishment.

## SELFELSS SERVICE: ST. ZITA'S CONVENT AND THE LDS CHURCH AT UNION SQUARE

1. Pamphlet "St Zita's Home", (undated) produced by "The Sisters of Reparation of the Congregation of Mary", p1.

2. Pamphlet, "St Zita's Home", p2.

3. New Advent website, entry on St Zita: , The Catholic Encyclopedia, Volume XV Copyright © 1912 by Robert Appleton Company, Online Edition Copyright © 2003 by K. Knight

4. Pamphlet, "St Zita's Home", pp 1 - 2.

5. New Advent website, entry on St Zita:

6. Booklet, "Help Us To Help Them", (undated) p 2 – 5.

7. NY Post, December 26, 2001 --Lois Weiss, "Nun of the Above to Developer's Plans"

## A TEMPLE IN THE CITY

1. The New York Times, November 10, 1869. Special thanks to Kent Larsen for uncovering this interesting article.

2. Stake President Brent J. Belnap's recollections taken in an interview with Scott D. Tiffany on November 13, 2002.

3. A stake high priests' quorum meeting and "luau" were held on the fifth floor of the stake center on the last Saturday before the fifth and sixth floors were officially closed down. A new outdoor "patio" that exited off the fifth floor above the current stake offices was used for the first—and only—time.

## PART 3

### SINGLE IN THE CITY

1. As construction on the Manhattan New York Temple began in late summer 2002, the chapel and meeting space on the second, fifth and sixth floors were closed. Consequently, the eight units meeting in the stake center were combined in various ways so that Sunday services could take place for all of them using only the chapel and meeting space on the third and fourth floors. For many months all three singles wards met together for church meetings in what was commonly nicknamed the "megaward." More than 500 people frequently attended sacrament meeting.

### VARIATIONS IN THE CITY

1. Source: Dean Jessee, ed. Personal Writings of Joseph Smith, rev. ed. (Salt Lake City: Deseret Book, 2002), 278-79

### ARTISTS IN THE CITY

1 The principal repository of LDS art is the Church Museum of History and Art in Salt Lake City. For a complete survey of early LDS artists, see "The Foundation of Latter-day Saint Art, 1835-1890" by Richard G. Oman in Images of Faith: Art of the Latter-day Saints, 4-39.

2. Robert O. Davis, "The Impact of French Training on Latter-day Saint Art, 1890-1925" Images of Faith: Art of the Latter-day Saints. 41. The Academie Julian was created for international students, mostly British and American. Its open enrollment

policies admitted many students who would otherwise have been forbidden access to the formal French academies.

3. Robert O. Davis, 41-44.

4. Thomas E. Toone, Mahonri Young: His Life and Art, Salt Lake City: Signature Books, 1997, 46.

5. Thomas E. Toone, 30.

6. Thomas E. Toone, 103-107.

7. Robert O. Davis, 50-53.

8. Robert O. Davis, 41.

9. Robert O. Davis, "Developing a Regional Latter-day Saint Art, 1925-1965" Images of Faith: Art of the Latter-day Saints, 71-111.

10. The Art Students League of New York, 2001-2002 catalog, 127th Regular Session, 89-94.

11. Images by these painters and many others are available online at the Museum of Church History and Art (http://www.lds.org/museum), in the volume by Richard G. Oman in Images of Faith: Art of the Latter-day Saints, and at the Springville Museum of Art which focuses on Utah painters. The SMA website includes hundreds of images. See http://www.sma.nebo.edu/

12. Mahonri Young, "Notes at the Beginning," Mahonri M. Young: Retrospective Exhibition, 56.

13. Spencer W. Kimball, "Education for Eternity," address to faculty and staff, Brigham Young University, Provo, Utah, September 12, 1967.

**PART 4**

SEVENTY YEARS LATER

1. Woolf, William L., The Church in New York City in Improvement Era, Dec 1938 pp728-730, 754-756

2. At the close of 1893, the Eastern States Mission reported a total of 55 members in the entire area, including all of New York, New Jersey and Pennsylvania. Smith, Louise S. "The History of the Church of Jesus Christ of Latter-day Saints in New Jersey." 9 May 1984.

3. Brooklyn Chapel: Twenty-first Anniversary 1919-1940. p76.

4. Brooklyn District History Committee, Zion in the Brooklyn District: One Heart, Many Voices, 1997. p 13

5. Ibid

6. Brooklyn Chapel: Twenty-first Anniversary 1919-1940. pp76.

7. This situation also existed in Manhattan, where Bishop William L. Woolf reported that in the 1930s and early 1940s half the active families in the ward – 25 to 30 families – were German.

8. Jackson, Kenneth T., ed., The Encyclopedia of New York City

9. Brooklyn District History Committee, Zion in the Brooklyn District: One Heart, Many Voices, 1997. pp14

10. Brooklyn Chapel: Twenty-first Anniversary 1919-1940. pp84-93.

11. Brooklyn District History Committee. Zion in the Brooklyn District: One Heart, Many Voices, 1997. p15.

12. Ibid.

13. Brooklyn District History Committee. Zion in the Brooklyn District: One Heart, Many Voices, 1997. p. 5-6, 21.

14. Brooklyn District History Committee. Zion in the Brooklyn District: One Heart, Many Voices, 1997. p. 5-6. The building, constructed in 1912, was the former home of the Wells Memorial Presbyterian Church, named in honor of Dr. John D. Wells, pastor of the South Third Street Presbyterian Church in Brooklyn.

15. History of the Church V4 pg88, entry for Tuesday, 25 February 1840. Brigham Young was en route to England along with most of the Quorum of the Twelve.

16. The Oceanside branch was made a dependent branch of the Queens Ward on January 20, 1935.

17. Beginnings and New Beginnings: A short history of The Church of Jesus Christ of Latter-day Saints on Long Island, not dated (apparently 1981), pp 3.

18. Ibid.

19. Ibid

20. Ibid.

21. Smith, Louise S. "A History of the Church of Jesus Christ of Latter-day Saints in New Jersey." May 9, 1984. pp14.

22. Ibid.

23. Interview of Gilbert Moen by Louise Smith, cited in Smith, Louise S. "A History of the Church of Jesus Christ of Latter-day Saints in New Jersey." May 9, 1984. p15.

24. Louise S. Smith, A History of the Church of Jesus Christ of Latter-day Saints in New Jersey. Unpublished school paper, 1984. p 17-18.

25. A Brief History of Short Hills Ward (author not indicated), submitted for the Manhattan New York Temple Cornerstone, 2004.

26. Mathusek, Luella. History of the Emerson Ward of the Caldwell New Jersey Stake, submitted for the Manhattan New York Temple Cornerstone, 2004.

27. Louise S. Smith, A History of the Church of Jesus Christ of Latter-day Saints in New Jersey. Unpublished school paper, 1984. p 18; LDS Church archives indicate that Montclair was created as a Ward, not a branch as Smith indicates.

28. East Brunswick New Jersey Stake History, (author not stated), submitted for the Manhattan New York Temple Cornerstone, 2004.

29. Ibid.

30. Ibid.

31. General Minutes, New Jersey Stake (now Morristown New Jersey Stake) February 28, 1960, LDS Church Archives, Microfilm LR 6026 11.

32. Nelson Wadsworth. Influence of Mormon Pavilion Felt Around Globe. Church News, December 26, 1964.

33. Ironically, the husbands of both counselors later became presidents of Utah's major universities, Brigham Young University and the University of Utah.

34. Haglund, Richard F., untitled family history pp. 3-4.

35. Ibid.

36. Ibid.

37. Cann, Damon. A Brief History of the Plainview, New York Stake. 2004, p. 2, submitted for the cornerstone of the Manhattan New York Temple.

38. Ibid.

39. Ibid.

40. Haglund, Richard F. untitled family history, p 5.

41. Haglund, Richard F. untitled family history, p 6.

42. Ibid.

43. Jean D. Griffith. Westchester Ward History, not dated.

44. Ibid.

## UNIT HISTORICAL OVERVIEWS

1. Kurt Wickham, interview with Sara Anderson, February 22, 2004.

2. Kurt Wickham, email, February 23, 2004.

3. Kurt Wickham, email, February 23, 2004.

4. Kurt Wickham, email, February 23, 2004.

5. Mission President Nelson Boren, as recalled by David Skouson, interview with Sara Anderson, 3 February 2004.

6. Note: The first Manhattan Sixth Branch was a Korean branch that included Korean-speaking members of the Church, primarily from Manhattan and Queens, as well as some from Westchester and New Jersey.

## NEW YORK NEW YORK STAKE AUXILIARIES

1. Marilyn Higbee Walker, interview by Anne Knight, 4 March 2004.

2. Susan Robison, interview by Sariah Toronto, 29 January 2004.

3. Marilyn Higbee Walker, interview by Anne Knight, 4 March 2004, and Susan Robison, interview by Sariah Toronto, 29 January 2004.

4. Marilyn Higbee Walker, interview by Anne Knight, 4 March 2004.

5. Marilyn Higbee Walker, interview by Anne Knight, 4 March 2004.

6. Susan Robison, interview by Sariah Toronto, 29 January 2004.

7. Susan Robison, interview by Sariah Toronto, 29 January 2004.

8. Susan Robison, interview by Sariah Toronto, 29 January 2004.

9. Susan Robison, interview by Sariah Toronto, 29 January 2004.

10. Marilyn Higbee Walker, interview by Anne Knight, 4 March 2004, and Susan Robison, interview by Sariah Toronto, 29 January 2004.

11. Marilyn Higbee Walker, interview by Anne Knight, 4 March 2004.

12. Marilyn Higbee Walker, interview by Anne Knight, 4 March 2004.
13. Susan Robison, interview by Sariah Toronto, 29 January 2004.
14. David and Jennifer Buckner, interviews by Sariah Toronto, 29 February 2004.
15. Jennifer Buckner, interview by Sariah Toronto, 29 February 2004.
16. Marilee Moe, interview by Anne Knight, 9 October 2003/
17. David and Jennifer Buckner, interviews by Sariah Toronto, 29 February 2004, and Marilee Moe, interview by Anne Knight, 9 October 2003.
18. David and Jennifer Buckner, interviews by Sariah Toronto, 29 February 2004.
19. Marilee Moe, interview by Anne Knight, 9 October 2003.
20. Thomas L. Epting, interview by Anne Knight, 12 March 2004.
21. Marilee Moe, interview by Anne Knight, 9 October 2003.
22. Meredith Higbee, telephone interview by Anne Knight, March 2004.
23. Debbie Bingham, reflections on 9/11, March 2004 e-mail in editor's possession
24. Marilee Moe, interview by Anne Knight, 9 October 2003.
25. Justin C. Rucker, interview by Anne Knight, 26 February 2004.
26. Marilee Moe, interview by Anne Knight, 9 October 2003.
27. Jennifer Buckner, interview by Sariah Toronto, 29 February 2004.
28. Jennifer Buckner, interview by Sariah Toronto, 29 February 2004.
29. Marilee Moe, interview by Anne Knight, 9 October 2003.
30. Marilee Moe, interview by Anne Knight, 9 October 2003.
31. Marilee Moe, interview by Anne Knight, 9 October 2003.
32. Jennifer Buckner, interview by Sariah Toronto, 29 February 2004, and Marilee Moe, interview by Anne Knight, 9 October 2003.
33. Jennifer Buckner, interview by Sariah Toronto, 29 February 2004.
34. Marilee Moe, interview by Anne Knight, 9 October 2003.
35. Chrysula Winegar, a former Young Women leader in the Inwood First Ward, May 2004 e-mail in editor's possession.
36. Thomas L. Epting, interview by Anne Knight, March 12, 2004.
37. Justin C. Rucker interview.
38. Justin C. Rucker interview.
39. Ibid, and Boy Scouts of America fact sheet.
40. Justin Rucker interview
41. Deseret News 2003 Church Almanac, p. 112.
42. Wayne Collier, Notes on Scouting.
43. Thomas A. Vogelmann, telephone interview by Anne Knight, March 2004.
44. Noboru Takahasi, interview by Sariah Toronto, 1 February 2004.

45. When the New York New York Stake was formed in 1997, Diana Murphy had been serving as Primary president since April 1995. She continued serving until April 2001, when Joanne Rowland, who had worked with Sister Murphy for approximately one year as stake Primary secretary, was called to preside.

46. Cards and letters were also sent by Young Men and Young Women organizations, by Relief Societies and by individual Church members.

# CONTRIBUTORS

The New York New York Stake History Group is a volunteer committee dedicated to researching and writing about LDS history in the New York City area. The committee produces *The New York LDS Historian,* a newsletter on aspects of Church life in the city. Current research projects include LDS history in Brooklyn, Hispanic Latter-day Saints in New York City, and New York Mormons in business and school. Committee volunteers comprise a cross-section of the stake: students, teachers, arts people, married and single, old-time members and recent converts, businessmen and lawyers, and a variety of ethnicities.

**NEW YORK NEW YORK STAKE LDS HISTORY COMMITTEE**

| Sara Anderson | Allison Clark | Joanna Legerski |
| Sarah Archer-Beck | Raquel Cook | Jim Lucas |
| Matthew Archer-Beck | América Cruz | Glen Nelson |
| Darrell Babidge | Todd Flyr | Taylor Petrey |
| Brent J. Belnap | Al Gámez | Jennifer Reeder |
| Amber Blakesley | Maria Hunter | Joanne Rowland |
| Claudia L. Bushman | Delia Johnson | Scott Tiffany |
| Richard L. Bushman | Anne Knight | Sariah Toronto |
| | Kent Larsen | |

**ADDITIONAL CONTRIBUTORS**

| Tara Bench | Laura Christofferson | Julie McAdams |
| Cindy Butikofer | Chad Donvito | Susan Robison |
| Ned Butikofer | Laurel Dougall | Sumer Thurston Evans |
| Linda Cameron | Kamla Fennimore | Chrysula Winegar |
| Kent David Christensen | Jordan Gunther | Kristopher Woolley |
| | Dan Hiatt | |

## CONTRIBUTORS TO CITY SAINTS

**SARA ANDERSON** Sara Anderson moved to New York in 1999 to pursue adventure with her husband Adam, a law student at Columbia. Originally members of the Manhattan First Ward, they now live in the Inwood First Ward with their three children, Adam, Abigail and Mark. Sara likes to read, swim, and ride her bike down the west side greenway.

**DARRELL BABIDGE** Darrell Babidge is a member of the Manhattan First Ward. He and his wife Jenny met each other in New York in 1999. They have two boys, John Chandler and Joseph. Darrell and Jenny are both professional opera singers.

**BRENT J. BELNAP** Brent J. Belnap was called as New York New York Stake president in November 1997, after having served as bishop of the Manhattan Third (Singles) Ward for almost five years. He moved to Manhattan in 1986 to study law at Columbia University. President Belnap currently works as senior vice president and associate general counsel with Citigroup. He married Lorinda (who grew up three houses away from President Belnap in Ogden, Utah) in 1991. They have five children.

**TARA BENCH** Tara Bench came to New York City in 1999 to work in the Martha Stewart kitchen. Today, she still works for the same company, now as an editor. She attends the Manhattan Eighth (Singles) Ward.

**AMBER BLAKESLEY** Amber Blakesley came to New York as an intern in the summer of 2001. She fell in love with the city and promptly moved back in the summer of 2002 after graduating from BYU, where she studied graphic design. She is currently an Art Director for Martha Stewart Living. Amber attends the Manhattan Eighth (Singles) Ward.

**CLAUDIA L. BUSHMAN** Claudia L. Bushman has been a member of the Manhattan First Ward in the first Eastern stake for more than 15 years. She teaches American Studies at Columbia University and chairs the Ship Brooklyn plaque committee and the Harlem Bridge Builders. She cooks for the history committee.

**RICHARD L. BUSHMAN** Richard Bushman, chair of the New York New York Stake history committee, retired from Columbia University in 2001 to work on a biography of Joseph Smith, which, by coincidence, he submitted to the publisher in the same week that the stake history was completed. He is stake patriarch and has lived in the Manhattan First Ward with his wife Claudia for 15 years.

**CINDY BUTIKOFER** Cindy Butikofer, who never wanted a yard, happily came to New York City with husband Ned in 1984. She is a learning specialist at Trinity School and mother of two born and bred New Yorkers–Ansel, who is currently in college, and Norma, a high school senior.

**NED BUTIKOFER** Ned Butikofer, president of the Canal Street (Chinese-language) Branch, arrived in New York City with an MFA in acting in 1984. He mostly recently appeared in two Double Helix Productions: *Trojan Women* and Chekhov's *Three Sisters*. Ned and his wife Cindy have raised two children in the city.

**LINDA CAMERON** After graduating from the University of California with a degree in musical theater, Linda Cameron came to New York City in 1990. She is currently the financial manager for a translation company. She and husband Craig Myers met in a singles ward in the stake and now attend the Inwood First Ward.

**KENT DAVID CHRISTENSEN** Kent David Christensen is a member of the Manhattan Second Ward. He was born in Los Angeles and attended BYU and Art Center College of Design before moving to New York in 1988, where he lives with his wife, Janet, and two daughters, Anne and Jane. He has created illustrations for many national publications, including *TIME, Sports Illustrated, BusinessWeek* and *The Wall Street Journal.*

**LAURA CHRISTOFFERSON** Laura Christofferson moved to New York City after graduating from college in May 2000 because it sounded more adventurous than moving home. She has worked for the Association of Art Museum Directors since then and recently began a Masters program in American Studies at Columbia. She is chair of the New York New York Stake Public Affairs committee and has been a member of three wards in the stake.

**ALLISON CLARK** A historian at heart and by profession, Allison Clark takes occasional breaks from writing her doctoral dissertation in medieval history to delve into LDS history. She has spent most of her six years in the city as a member of the Manhattan Third Ward, but she also likes to visit her neighborhood Inwood First Ward. She earns her keep at an educational non-profit and by giving tours at the Cloisters museum. For fun, she loves to ride her bike and talk politics.

**RAQUEL COOK** Raquel Cook left New York in 2002 and is now working on her Doctorate in Education at Utah State University. She also teaches college and high school courses, writes when she can and, most importantly, is Isabel's mom. She misses New York insanely.

**CHAD DONVITO** Chad Donvito moved from the left coast to the right coast just over three years ago. He currently does brand management for Kraft Foods. Chad and his wife Laura live in the Manhattan Second Ward, but attend the Manhattan Seventh (Deaf) Branch, where Chad serves as executive secretary and Laura is Relief Society president.

**LAUREL DOUGALL** Laurel Dougall grew up just outside of New York City. Upon graduating from BYU in December 1998, she and her husband hopped on a bus and rode back to the Big Apple. She now has two children, is a member of the Union Square First Ward and in her "spare time" teaches Kindermusik and sings and records with the group Ephraim's Harp.

**ÁLVARO GÁMEZ** In 1980 Álvaro Gámez came to the city from Colombia to complete a degree in business administration. He also served as project president to renovate an empty building purchased from the city on 107th Street. Coordinating the work of lawyers, architects and nine families contributing a wide range of skills, Al brought the project to successful completion. He currently works in the finance department of Columbia University and serves in the Manhattan Fourth (Spanish-language) Ward bishopric, while his wife Genny and daughters Katharine and Laura attend the Manhattan First Ward.

**DAN HIATT** Further education brought Dan Hiatt and family to the city in 1994, specifically a PhD in Political Science at Columbia University. Over time plans changed and Dan now does accounting for New York Life Insurance, plus he serves as president of the Harlem First Branch. He enjoys the outdoors—camping, hiking, rock climbing—and he and his wife Beth are parents of Jordan, Alexis, Caitlyn, Daniel and Nicholas, with a new baby expected in March 2005.

**DELIA JOHNSON** Delia and Woodrow moved to New York City in September 1997, and then to Eugene, Oregon, in August 2002. While living on 113th Street in Manhattan, Woodrow was a PhD student in finance at Columbia University's business school. Delia stayed at home with their two children, Sarah Naomi who was almost three years old when they moved there, and Ivan, who was three weeks old. In Oregon Woodrow is a professor of finance at the University of Oregon. Delia will soon begin working on a Masters of Accounting Degree. Sarah Naomi and Ivan are learning a lot at their Japanese immersion school.

**ANNE KNIGHT** A change from teaching high school French and German in Utah to working in administration at the United Nations (where every sound or thing ever learned came in handy) occurred for Anne Knight in 1979. She attends the Inwood First Ward and is now in pink cloud mode as a retiree.

**KENT LARSEN** Kent and his wife Michelle have lived in New York since 1988 and are the parents of Michael, Elizabeth, and Ruby–all Yankees fans and members of the Inwood First Ward. Kent owns and operates three businesses: Luso Brazilian Books (importing Portuguese language publications); Mormon Pavilion (selling LDS books); and Mormon Arts and Letters (a publishing venture). As an original member of the stake's history committee, he has contributed significant research as well as articles and has been part of the production team for all publications.

**JOANNA LEGERSKI** Joanna Legerski originally came to New York City in 1996 to work as a live-in nanny, and was a member of the Manhattan Third Ward for many years. After a brief foray into the corporate world, she made a career shift to examine the affects of 9/11 on youth for the State Office of Mental Health at Columbia University Division of Child & Adolescent Psychiatry. Currently Joanna is a clinical psychology PhD student at the University of Montana, looking forward to her first encounter with a grizzly bear.

**JAMES LUCAS** James Lucas is an attorney/businessman and member of the Manhattan First Ward. He is also the author of the chapter on "Mormons in New York City" in "New York Glory: Religions in the City," Tony Carnes and Anna Karpathakis (ed.), New York: New York University Press, 2001.

**JULIE MCADAMS** Ben and Julie moved to New York in August 2000 to study law at Columbia University Law School. They are currently practicing law in New York. Julie works at Baker & McKenzie and Ben at Davis Polk & Wardwell. They are members of the Manhattan Second Ward, but attend the Union Square Third Ward, where Ben is serving in the bishopric.

**GLEN NELSON** Glen Nelson arrived in New York City nearly 20 years ago as a graduate student of New York University. He is an author and father of two children. A frequent collaborator of LDS artists, his opera with composer Murray Boren, *The Book of Gold*, is to be premiered next fall at Brigham Young University in honor of Joseph Smith's 200th birthday. Glen is a member of the Union Square First Ward.

**TAYLOR PETREY** Taylor Petrey came to New York City in 1994 as an undergraduate at Pace University on a debate scholarship. He and his wife Stacey met in the Manhattan Eighth Ward. Taylor and Stacey left New York for Taylor to pursue graduate studies at Harvard.

**JENNIFER REEDER** Jennifer Reeder arrived in New York City in August 2004 to begin a graduate program in history, historical editing and archival management at NYU. Previously she was a research historian/document editor with the Joseph Fielding Smith Institute for LDS History at BYU, where she specialized in Mormon women's history. Jenny attends the Manhattan Third Ward.

**JOANNE ROWLAND** Joanne Rowland has lived in New York City since 1986. She presently serves as Relief Society president in the Union Square First Ward. She is an attorney who describes her solo practice as a country law office on Fifth Avenue.

**ADAM RUSSELL** Adam Russell came to New York in 1994 to pursue an operatic career. While here, he has opened his own voice studio and has produced numerous artistic and musical events for the stake, including stake wide arts festivals in 1999 and 2000. Adam attends the Manhattan Third Ward.

**SUMER THURSTON EVANS** Shortly after graduating BYU in 1997 (BS in Physics, MS in Mathematics), Sumer and her husband Steve moved to New York City for Steve to attend law school at Columbia. Sumer has worked on Wall Street for several years and has consulted; she is now a project manager for a healthcare financial services firm. Her New York experiences include getting picked up by a famous movie producer who wanted her for his next film (yeah, right), falling between the subway car and the platform (mind the gap!) and making cinnamon rolls for the Wu-Tang Clan (a gangster rap group). With experiences like these, who wouldn't want to live here!

**SCOTT TIFFANY** Scott Tiffany is a documentary filmmaker and president of Time Frame Films. He has worked on more than 40 hours of programming for The History Channel. His interest in LDS history prompted him to direct an award-winning documentary about the ship *Brooklyn,* called "Forgotten Voyage". Scott and Mariah Proctor have two daughters. Their family lived in the Inwood First Ward from 1997 to 2003.

**SARIAH TORONTO** Sariah Toronto moved to New York in 2000 with her work in financial services. She met her future husband, Doug Rollins, in the Manhattan Third Ward; they now attend the Manhattan First Ward with daughter Chloe and Baby Boy (name TBA December 2004). Sariah is looking forward to the start of the next triathlon season.